CATSKILL CULTURE

CATSKILL CULTURE

A Mountain Rat's Memories of the

Great Jewish Resort Area

PHIL BROWN

TEMPLE UNIVERSITY PRESS

PHILADELPHIA

Temple University Press, Philadelphia 19122
Copyright © 1998 by Temple University
All rights reserved
Published 1998
Printed in the United States of America

Text design by Kate Nichols

♾ The paper used in this publication meets the requirements of the American National Standard
for Information Sciences—Permanence of Paper for Printed Library Materials ANSI Z39.48–1984

Library of Congress Cataloging-in-Publication Data
Brown, Phil.
    Catskill culture : a mountain rat's memories of the great Jewish resort area / Phil Brown.
      p. cm.
    Includes bibliographical references and index.
    ISBN 1-56639-642-5 (alk. paper)
    1. Jews—New York (State)—Catskill Mountains Region—Social life and customs. 2. Jews—
Recreation—New York (State)—Catskill Mountains Region. 3. Brown, Phil. 4. Catskill
Mountains Region—New York (State)—Social life and customs. I. Title.
F127.C3B76 1998
974.7'38004924—dc21   98-11996

To the memory of

William Brown and Sylvia Brown,
my parents—Mountain Rats par excellence,
with whom I lived in this magical world

and

Marilyn (Brown) Peyser,
my half sister—whom I searched for while
I searched for Catskill memories

Contents

Contents

Photographs appear on pages 19–22, 95–106, 157–162, 201–216, and 241–250.

Acknowledgments

M y first debt of gratitude is to my parents, William Brown and Sylvia Brown, who taught me how to "work the Mountains." For better or worse, they bore me into a family of "Mountain Rats." Their life of working in the Catskills is what gave me the impulse to write this book. I wish they could be here to read it.

Most immediately, I owe a lot to Peter Conrad, dear friend and sociologist colleague. As we lunched at the American Sociological Association in Cincinnati in 1991, sharing summer experiences, Peter drew me out about my Catskill background. His sharp ethnographer's ears perked up, and he encouraged me to write a book on this great slice of life. Ever since, he has been a constant source of support.

Ronnie Littenberg, my wife, has given emotional and intellectual support and helped me in my pursuit of my family roots in the Catskills and elsewhere. My search for my parents' hotel and for their and my own experiences of the Catskills was always linked to my search for family roots. Many of my cousins (on my father's side) have been wonderful to me as I combined the Catskill quest with familial connections, genealogy, and a family reunion.

Lynn Davidman, shortly after joining the Department of Sociology at Brown University, linked me up to the original planning committee that was trying to organize a history of the Catskills conference. Without this powerful tie to others who were trying to save the Catskill legacy, I could never have accumulated the wealth of material and contacts that made this book possible, nor could I have discovered the extent of my ties to the Catskills. Lynn's sharp reading of an early draft of the book helped me to thoroughly reorganize it. Her continual interest in this project has been a great inspiration.

Alan Barrish, who helped launch the Catskills Institute, has shared memories of his lifelong residence in the Catskills, has driven with me over endless roads to explore hotels and bungalow colonies, and has introduced me to many people up there. Shalom Goldman, another Catskills Institute founder, who has co-organized the annual History of the Catskills conferences with me, has been a marvelous source of energy in keeping alive the Catskills through his lectures, articles, and other activities. Without Shalom, the first conference would never have occurred and all the rest would not have followed. His multifaceted understanding of the importance of the Catskill legacy has been a deep source of inspiration for me. Liora Alschuler, another person who helped form the Catskills Institute, encouraged this project in many ways.

Mark Hutter, the only other sociologist to have written about the Catskills, demonstrated that the Catskills were good subject matter for sociology, and he was pleased to talk over the next sociologist's plan to write about this subject. Jerry Jacobs, a sociologist born to a hotel-owning family, generously encouraged the book from its early stages and helped focus some of the larger themes. His reading of the manuscript was extremely helpful, and our conversations helped me fashion the intersection of biography and history that C. Wright Mills championed.

Deborah Dash Moore has been an energetic enthusiast from the time she heard about this book, and our conversations about the book have contributed much to its historical framing. Jenna Weissman Joselit has been an ardent supporter who pushed me to make deeper connections about the significance of the Catskills experience.

From the time we first talked about the project, as an aside to another conversation, Michael Ames at Temple University Press has had faith in the book. He encouraged me to work on the combination of personal and scholarly sources, and to develop my personal voice as a way to integrate the two. Michael's careful reading of the first full draft of the book was integral to its final development.

Eileen Pollack, whose beautiful fiction about the Catskills has been a deep inspiration to me, has always believed in what I was trying to do with my writing about the Mountains. Her warm concern for the project and her sharp reading of the manuscript have been a gift. She has given me much confidence to write in the style that I have chosen.

The Arenson family—Ted, Cynthia, Julie, David, and Marilyn—have made Sunny Oaks Hotel in Woodridge the home of the History of the Catskills conferences, thus providing an invaluable laboratory for me and others who are writing about the Mountains.

Ben Kaplan, longtime Catskill veteran, graciously supplied his hotel list, on which my appendix, "Hotels of the Catskills," is based. The *Sullivan County Democrat* has been generous in permitting me to publish the amended list. All the members of the advisory board of the Catskills Institute have aided my work with their kind words and assistance.

David Gold, Deborah Chiel, and Avi Soifer graciously shared Catskill interviews they had conducted. Lauren Bass, Bethany Kantrowitz, Avivah Goldman, and Alice Gutter conducted interviews for me. Lauren Bass, Roberta Swanson, Berit Kosterlitz, and Valerie Moss transcribed endless hours of tapes.

Caroline Ellis and Arthur Bochner helped develop my article on the Catskills for a special issue of the *Journal of Contemporary Ethnography,* which they guest edited. The article was a significant step in organizing my thoughts about what I wanted the book to include. Caroline and Arthur strenuously pushed me to put more of my voice in the project, a most important element for me. Comments made by Alan Barrish, Archie Brodsky, Peter Conrad, Lynn Davidman, Gary Allan Fine, Shalom Goldman, Calvin Goldscheider, and Ronnie Littenberg on many drafts of that article played a big role in shaping the book.

Calvin Goldscheider, chair of Brown's Department of Sociology during the time I was writing the book, made available many departmental resources to me and eased this large shift in my research direction. At Brown, the Faculty Development Fund, the Small Grants Program, the Wriston Fund, the Undergraduate Teaching and Research Assistant Program, and the Wayland Collegium all provided financial and academic support.

The Lucius A. Littauer Foundation generously provided financial support through a grant at an early stage of my research.

The many people I interviewed for this book deserve special thanks for sharing their memories and lives. They lived the life of the Catskills, and they have given over enough of that to me so that I could tell this story.

—Cambridge, Massachusetts

CATSKILL CULTURE

Chapter 1

Returning to the Catskills

Prelude: Nighttime at the Seven Gables
Hotel, Greenfield Park—1959

"Oy, what a meal. Let's get out for a quick walk and then get to the casino so we can sit up front."

Gradually, a hundred adults leave the dining room, some to stroll or sit, others to pick up their children on the front lawn. The kids have just left their circle around the flagpole, where the counselors have lowered and folded the flag to the trumpeted taps. It was hard to get the youngsters in a circle once they had charged out of the children's dining room. How long could children sit—strung along benches for six or more on each side at long, plastic-covered tables—waiting for food? How much ketchup could they pour onto their spaghetti and still eat so little of it? How loudly could they complain about another night's dessert of cherry Jell-O? But the children know that soon their parents will come and relieve the counselors of their charges, probably taking them to the concession for candy or soda.

Even with all the excitement of parents collecting children from a day at camp, it is a fairly quiet time in the hotel's daily cycle. Still light at 8:15, dusk closes in on tired children and parents who are in between the hotel's many activities. No swimming, softball, mah-jongg, basketball, calisthenics. Just quiet before the dark brings show time and a new series of adventures.

Adirondack chairs and benches fill the lawn, punctuated by regular wrought iron and wood park benches. The casino porch has two sides completely lined with benches for sitting as well. The Main House and White House have chairs on their porches. Even the stairs of guest buildings provide places to sit and schmooze. An occasional bat brings forth the common concern that it will get into women's hair, especially if the hair is put up.

The concession opens, having shut during dinner so the proprietor can rest or—if the proprietor is ambitious—sell soda in the dining room. For the patient children, what a wealth of treats: Yoo-hoo, Dr. Pepper, tubes of chocolate licorice and pretzel rods in plastic containers, frozen Milky Ways, egg creams, little packages of Drake's Cake—plain or marble pound cake and round coffee cake.

At last, the first dime in the jukebox from one of the teenagers. Out of maybe sixty-four records, perhaps five are really up to date, and those are the ones we will hear over and over—this year the hot tune is "Zing Went the Strings of My Heart." Off-duty staff can join in too—the lifeguard, some bell-hops, counselors as they are relieved. The dining room staff is still cleaning up and setting up for breakfast. Most of them won't come down till they shower away the sweat of another hectic dinner. Lindy and slow dances predominate; the twist won't arrive until around 1960. This is the young people's time to play in the hotel's main gathering spot.

Listen, the band is unpacking their instruments. The drummer has thrown the lever on the snare and is ripping off a quick paradiddle; then he stops to adjust the bass drum closer and tighten the high-hat's wingnut. With a twist of his mouthpiece, the horn player roars out a couple of riffs, some from Broadway shows, some old Yiddish favorites. Removing his instrument from its heavy brown canvas cover, the bass player turns the pegs to bring the strings up to pitch. At the keyboard, the pianist runs fingers up and down in cascading arpeggios, spinning off little quotes from old standards in the middle. Because the singer was not there for a pre-dinner rehearsal, this is the time she quickly runs through her charts and gets her cues. But she doesn't want to give away the surprises to guests already in the casino, so it's a very informal and quick thing.

Then the band fools around for maybe ten minutes doing music that they particularly like. You might hear a short jazz tune or a parody of a traditional favorite Catskill song. It's also the time for students of music to chat with the band and learn tricks of the trade.

The wooden chairs had been moved aside for a previous activity, so they are now unfolded again and placed in straight rows over the pine boards of the floor. The MC is testing the single spotlight, which is set on a black pole; some trustworthy teenage guest will have the honor of operating it.

Some of the adults sit at the bar—a counter shared with the soda fountain but separated by a folding-countertop entrance. They're having J&B ("Jewish booze"), Seven and Seven (Seagram's 7 and 7-Up), Rheingold or Miller beer, hanging out and trading stories about the day's activities, maybe setting up a poker game for after the show.

The MC consults with the concessionaire, and the plug is pulled on the jukebox to the familiar protest of the youngsters who now have to give up rock and roll for something more adult-oriented. At nine o'clock, the band strikes up their theme, signaling the opening of the night's entertainment. After several choruses, the bandleader steps to the mike:

"Good evening, ladies and gentlemen. The Barry Scheinberg Orchestra welcomes you to the casino of the Seven Gables Hotel for a wonderful Saturday night. For the next half-hour, we're here to play for your dancing pleasure, and later we have an all-star show with Broadway entertainment. Please join us in the first dance. Here's the 'Miami Beach Rumba.' Grab a partner and let's get on with the music."

❧

That was I watching the hotel nightlife, a ten-year-old who grew up in Catskill resorts. Those memories rooted around in my head, coming out often enough when I shared stories of my youth. But until quite recently, I had never understood how powerful that legacy was for my life, or how meaningful it was for millions of others. This book is my exploration of that legacy.

I grew up in a family of "Mountain Rats," a Catskill term for those who lived and worked in "the Mountains" over many years. I spent three months each year in the Catskills, from 1949 (my birth) to 1971, and I returned through the late 1970s to visit my parents who were still working there (my father died in his coffee shop in 1972, and my mother was a chef until 1978). In 1946, my parents bought a small hotel, Brown's Hotel Royal, on White Lake, which they owned until 1952. A postcard and photos of the hotel from those years show gardens of tall cannas and the omnipresent, sharply angled, broad-slatted "Adirondack" chairs. The postcard guided me in 1993 back to the hotel's location, which my parents had always kept hidden.

One year, their chef quit at the start of the season. Unable to find a replacement, my mother, Sylvia Brown, gave herself a crash course in cooking and never left the kitchen again. After the hotel went broke several years later, she spent the rest of her working years as a chef. Only small and medium-size hotels (up to approximately three hundred guests) would hire a woman because, according to my mother, the kitchen staff in a larger hotel wouldn't take orders from a woman chef. My mother's placement in the smaller hotels set the tenor for the level of places I worked in. When I was still under age sixteen, I needed her push to get jobs usually held by older teenagers and people in their twenties; later I preferred that size hotel because I had gotten used to it.

My father, William Brown, worked variously as a maitre d', waiter, coffee shop manager, desk clerk/chauffeur (for an employment agency), and operator of small "concession" coffee shops rented from hotel owners. With me in tow, my parents plied their tools of the trade, and I took in Catskill culture from their traversal of that society. A major part of my childhood was formed in these resorts, and much of what I learned about human motives and actions—coarse and fine, crass and noble—was modeled on the behavior of people working and playing in the Mountains.

The Life and Death of Hotels: My Return to the Mountains

It's thirty-four years after that scene in the Seven Gables casino. I leave Cambridge very early on an August morning in 1993, heading for three days in the Catskills to trace my life's odyssey through the resorts where my parents and I worked and lived. My first stop is Chait's Hotel, in Accord, about halfway between Kingston and Ellenville. My mother cooked at Chait's from 1970 to 1978. In 1972 my father ran the concession, and he died of a stroke on the floor of his coffee shop. My visit there includes a walk through the fields full of purple-topped statice where I spread my father's ashes (contrary to Jewish law, he, and my mother after him, wanted cremation). I knew that ex-owners Annette and Max Finestone had built a house near the hotel, and I was pleased to hear that they were still there. As I drove up the hill from Chait's, I saw Annette on the porch of her beautiful house—built on land that she kept back from the property included in the hotel sale. Max and Annette would be the only hotel owners I knew from the old days who were still around to talk, though I did converse with the son of one proprietor from my childhood.

Chait's had become Su Casa, a pleasant hotel not unlike Chait's, with yoga, intellectual and musical events, but no heavy entertainment scene. Since that visit, Su Casa was sold to Elat Chayim, a Jewish spiritual group. Elat Chayim is an outgrowth of Rabbi Zalman Schacter-Shalomi's P'nai Or, part of the Jewish Renewal movement. Based largely on the teachings of Schacter-Shalomi and his student Rabbi Arthur Waskow, Elat Chayim is run by Rabbi Jeff Roth and Rabbi Joanna Katz. They term themselves "neo-Hasidic" in that they believe in putting joy in all worship, but regular Hasidim see them as apostates. These participants observe many rituals, though with modern, often new age touches and a commitment to gender issues, ecology, and mystical elements of other religions and traditions.

I proceed down Route 209 through Ulster County, stopping at Ellenville where I went to school for parts of several years. I had loved Saturday morning ice cream sodas at Balotin's Drug Store, a reward for enduring an allergy shot at the doctor's office. I had enjoyed taking the money I earned helping my father, and spending it on stamps at the coin and stamp dealer in town. And when I was thirteen, Ellenville was home to my girlfriend, whose uncle owned the Cherry Hill Hotel where my mother worked. Here is my first glimpse of how depressed a classic Catskill town could be. The streets are very empty, and many businesses are closed. It is not what I remembered of the busy and exciting place—"the village"—that I always looked forward to visiting.

From Ellenville, it is a short hop on Route 52 to Greenfield Park, best known for the Tamarack Lodge that many erroneously claim was immortalized by Herman Wouk's *Marjorie Morningstar*. The Seven Gables, where my parents worked for six years, is gone save for "The Bungalow" (a small four-room guest building) and the day-camp building. How did we wind up there years ago? Ann and Harry Portnoy stopped at my parents' little restaurant in Fort Pierce, Florida, in the 1950s, on their way to Miami Beach. They got into a conversation about the hotel they had bought in 1946, and my mother wound up cooking for them for six years.

As in an archeological dig, brick stairs and iron railings lead to overgrown bushes and trees, with only foundation stones left from the main guest house called (as in many places) "the Main House." The other buildings—a second guest house called "the White House"; the buildings containing the casino, kitchen, and dining rooms; and staff quarters—burned long ago and were subject to bulldozing and complete removal by the neighbor who bought the land. He lived for some time in the old day-camp house. "The Bungalow" is deserted. Nevertheless, Fred, the caretaker since 1962, incessantly mows all the area, as well as seven adjoining fields divided by old fieldstone fences, stretching for countless acres. It seems almost a kind of grave-tending, since none of the land is used. Even the pool was excavated, and this is rare—old pools sporting bushes and trees abound in the Mountains, often the only remnant of dead hotels and colonies. Throughout the Catskills are hulks of resorts, skeletal handball courts, collapsed buildings, and a few buildings that refuse to fall. Everywhere is the tale of dead resorts that once teemed with life. Rows of abandoned bungalows stand watch, though overall they fared better because these small buildings could more easily be maintained and some could be converted to condos.

I first hoisted a busbox for pay at the Cherry Hill, also in Greenfield Park. The faded hotel sign still stood at the turnoff from the highway, but in a hundred feet the road stopped at a barricade. It made me think that a landslide had just taken out the whole road and the hotel. There is another nearby hotel on Briggs Highway, the Greenwood Inn, where I once worked for a weekend, now turned into the Hasidic Camp Bnos Beltz for Girls. There are still deserted buildings standing at the Birchwood Lodge, where the Cherry Hill Road hits Briggs Highway; this was the closest walkable medium-size hotel that we would go to in search of greater adventures than the small Cherry Hill could offer.

My journey continued through Woodbourne, turning left on Route 42 where the state prison dominates the landscape. Route 42 takes you through Fallsburg and South Fallsburg, the area of the largest concentration of sizeable hotels (Raleigh, Olympic, Pines, Flagler, Windsor, Nemerson, Brickman). I had learned that the Fallsburg places where I worked, the Nemerson and Brickman's, were no longer functioning; the former was now a yeshiva and the latter was part of the ashram I would visit later in the day.

As 42 winds toward Monticello, I come to Kiamesha Lake, famous for the Concord. There, the Evan's Kiamesha Hotel, another place where my mother cooked, had long ago been torn down, though its attached bungalow colony remained as a new condominium development, with many new houses built as well. In Monticello I meet up with Alan Barrish, librarian of the Crawford Public Library and one of the organizers of the first Catskills conference. We drive together past Fallsburg sites, stopping at the Siddha Yoga ashram, which I describe in a later chapter.

The first thing for the next morning would be the search for what I expected might be the ruined foundation stones of my parents' old hotel in White Lake. In 1946, Max Waldman sold the Royal to my parents, who took out a $16,500 first mortgage and a $4,500 second mortgage and owned it as Brown's Hotel Royal. I had always heard about this place and would ask my parents questions about it. They would simply say it was not there anymore, and I never thought to look despite the fact that for many years when I worked in Swan Lake, I frequently drove past White Lake on my way to Monticello. Once, while waiting for jobs to open up for my parents, we stayed at their friends' (George and Miriam Shapiro) bungalow colony for a couple of weeks in Kauneonga Lake, a village on White Lake only several thousand feet away from where the Royal hotel was; no word was mentioned of the hotel. So I assumed that like many old places, it had burned, fallen, or been knocked down. The village of White Lake was on the north side of the lake, where Route 17-B hit Route 55. To go to Monticello, I always took a left at the village of White Lake; a right would have taken me to the hotel, had I known about it.

Why had they kept hidden the location and survival of the hotel? As I matured, I was able to see more of my parents' foibles, one of which was a desire to repress the hurts and failures of their lives. They were upset that they failed in the hotel business and then had to work hard the rest of their lives doing the same work in the pay of other owners. Over two decades, they tried several times to run restaurants, and once they had a mosaic tile store, but they fared no better at these than at Brown's Hotel Royal. I have in my possession a copy of the August 4, 1952, deed that Joseph Jacobs obtained when he bought the hotel at a mortgage foreclosure for $15,325. To return to the hotel, to tell me of it, to see it on the highway would bring up sad memories and make harder their summers in the Mountains. Perhaps they feared that I would question them more about why they were unable to make a go of the Royal, when other small hotels managed to survive.

On my field trip in 1993, I found the hotel easily, having identified it by the single postcard that my parents had. I immediately saw the quite well-appointed Bradstan Hotel, a bed and breakfast. That was it! I looked and gaped, and certainly nearly every detail that I could make out from the postcard was reproduced in the real hotel. I walked into the hotel, found one of the owners in the kitchen, a young man in his thirties, and asked what was the name of this place in the old days, to which he replied, "This was Brown's Hotel Royal." I showed him the photocopy reproduction of the postcard. He was quite amazed, as was I. Here was the hotel that I had lived in as an infant, the resort my parents owned between 1946 and 1952, before it went bankrupt and they left. Here I was, back in a place I always wanted to be.

Unlike so many places in the Catskills that had fallen into complete abandonment or had been burned, this one was transformed and redecorated into an upscale bed and breakfast, with a beautiful dining room where weddings and other affairs are catered and a bar that has a cabaret on weekends and provides a local watering spot the rest of the week. The new owners found a few old things worth keeping, such as a dresser. Most other things have been picked up elsewhere, but have been designed to create a 1940s and 1950s atmosphere: brocade curtains, rattan furniture, art deco pieces, beaded curtains in doorways. The side buildings remain, though several dilapidated bungalows were torn down. Two rooms that stood on the front porch alongside the entranceway could not be reconstructed, so they had been removed. That was where my parents and I lived, with us on one side and relatives on the other.

My uncle Max was some kind of partner, at least at one point. Many of our relatives came and stayed there as paying guests, and they also helped out building tables, repairing docks and furniture—a kind of volunteer help. Others worked regular jobs—cousin Essie was a bookkeeper, cousin Gloria worked in the office, cousin Sylvia worked in the office too, aunt May worked as a chambermaid, and cousin Gene and his wife Dolores entertained. Another cousin considered buying the adjoining property and signed an agreement with my parents to trade some of his land to my parents so that they could expand their driveway, in exchange for some of their lakefront property. I have this document, but my relatives have no knowledge of the deal ever going through.

Scott Samuelson and Edward Dudek, the current owners, have framed a postcard of the hotel in the days before it was Brown's Hotel Royal and was just the Royal, before some of the side buildings were added. After 1952, my parents were out of business. Sol Pasternack bought it in 1954 from Joseph Jacobs, who had bought the hotel at foreclosure auction, and Pasternack ran it until he sold it to the current owners. It got more ramshackle—when the current owners bought it in 1991, they found many little stoves all around the place that had been put into rooms and the remnants of bungalows. It had become an increasingly seedier boarding house, filled with poor people and SSI recipients. The current owners spent two years transforming it and winning an award from the county historical society for the best preservation reconstruction project.

It is hard to leave Brown's Royal/Bradstan, but I can't take any more of Ed's and Scott's time—I, for one, know the rigors of running a hotel, no matter how small. After a walk to the lakeside, I depart and continue around White Lake, the most exquisite of lakes in the Mountains, rounding the village of Kauneonga Lake on my way to Swan Lake. I stop at Paul's Hotel, where I worked for two years. I knew that it was Daytop Village, a drug rehab center, but was unprepared for the hostility I faced. Burly staff members wanted to know why I was visiting, gave me little information, and refused to let me take any photos. I finally got some superior to let me take photos, as long as there were no people in them.

The one bungalow colony I worked at, SGS, is further down the highway. The SGS is a broken down wreck that was later bought and renamed Cayman's Country—with a couple of bungalows standing and a few people living there. The casino and coffee shop are completely shuttered, and there is no sign of any life in the main part of the colony. The pool is overgrown, the basketball court seems to have disappeared, and junk lies all around. Through the dead town of Swan Lake, I turn left at the lake to the Stevensville and the Commodore, two hotels where I also worked. The Stevensville, once a very grand place, remains standing in part, but is fenced off and decayed. Immediately next door, the Commodore is in ruins.

I progress toward Liberty, grabbing a quick bite in a luncheonette. This was a bustling town, which I visited many times each week through the years I worked in Loch Sheldrake and Swan Lake. Now it is dreary, lacking the excitement of the staff and guests who made its main drag a major shopping area. I leave, stopping at Grossinger's just outside of Liberty. I can't get past the front gate. The new Korean/Japanese owner has yet to put the place back into operation, and no one is admitted. From there I go on to Loch Sheldrake, down Route 52 past Brown's Hotel. Charles and Lillian Brown's hotel is still running (at that time, but no longer), the place made famous by Jerry Lewis, the Browns' adopted nephew, who always played to crowds there in the Jerry Lewis Playhouse. Catskill roads were full of billboards for Brown's, with a huge head of Jerry Lewis sticking out above the sign and large letters reading "Jerry Lewis says Brown's is my favorite resort." People always asked if I was related; they still do. As a youngster, I hoped I was—because I knew Brown's was an important hotel—but I wasn't.

Hardly any small hotels could duplicate Ed and Scott's rehab feat of Brown's Royal. Most are hulks; a few are incorporated into bungalow colonies. One small-to-medium-size hotel where I worked, the Karmel in Loch Sheldrake, also survives. In the early 1970s, the Jacobs and Katzes went bankrupt, and the current owner bought it in 1976 to run a children's drama camp, the Stage Door, which numbers the children of movie stars among its campers. The old nightclub has been turned into a large theater, the main lobby into a smaller one. All over are trunks, wardrobes, and piles of costumes and set props. The kitchen puts out buffet meals where the children come and make their own tuna fish or peanut butter and jelly sandwiches. While most of the original kitchen is still there, the old stoves and refrigerators and salad counters are certainly not turning out the kind of food that they used to. Overall, the place is in wonderful shape and being well used, a unique survivor of the glory days of the Catskills. This was a pleasing way to end my discoveries of the day, and I headed back to Monticello where Alan Barrish and I would drive around some more. My visit to a yeshiva and to the large ashram of Gurumayi is described in the chapter on resort religion.

My Next Return:
A Conference on the Catskills

It is September 1, 1995, two years after that emotionally intense visit to my old haunts, and I am driving up Route 17 to the Catskills, full of anticipation. The excitement accelerates when I get to the deep turn descending into the valley at the Wurtsboro Hills. I used to love to stop at the scenic overview just as the turn began, offering a gorgeous look at the Shawangunk Valley below, but the overview has been removed. A few miles later the road rises on the far side of the valley, and I am tingling as I turn off at the Rock Hill exit. Another few miles and I will be at Sunny Oaks in Woodridge, one of the Catskills' last remaining small hotels (there aren't that many large ones left either), where I will be co-conducting a conference, "The History of the Catskills," over the Labor Day weekend. Though eager to get there, I want to savor everything on the way. I stop and take photos of the Glen Wild Synagogue. I start up the stairs of the decrepit Zucker's Glen Wild Hotel, but seeing the front lawn occupied by several orthodox women I retreat, fearful of being seen as a nonobservant camera-clad male interloper.

It is hard to believe that the conference is finally going to happen. For two years, a small group of scholars, hotel families, and local residents tried unsuccessfully to get a small grant from the National Endowment for the Humanities. I was thrilled to learn of such a group, which I found out about after their first attempt, and I eagerly joined the conference planners. After the second rejection, it seemed unlikely that the event would occur. But Shalom Goldman called me in early July, while I was vacationing on Cape Cod, and said that the Sunny Oaks Hotel owners would be delighted to host the conference. Could we possibly pull off the whole organizing of a conference just six weeks down the road? It was worth trying, and it was a wonderful experience. For the first time, we brought together a terrific assortment of people with a deep interest in keeping alive the Catskill legacy: local residents, current and former hotel owners, waiters from the past, writers, filmmakers, and scholars from disciplines in sociology, history, Judaic studies, and architecture. Organizers and attendees enjoyed themselves, learned a lot, and sparked wider public and media attention. This could not possibly stop here, so we set about to build the Catskills Institute—a group to organize future conferences, collect archival materials, publish a newsletter, develop museum exhibitions, give talks, and spread the memories of Catskill culture to all possible audiences.

And what was it that we gathered to study, memorialize, and reminisce about in a gathering in a small hotel in Woodridge? More than a geographical area, more than a complex of resorts, the Catskills was a major social institution in American Jewish life. Like many other people, I was shaped by it. What is this place, the Catskills?

What Are the Catskills?

Just under a hundred miles northwest from New York City lies a magic land, enveloped in a rich legacy and rampant mythology. Many called it the "Borscht Belt," this Jewish resort area in the Catskill Mountains that was the playground of Jews, who were mainly from metropolitan New York and of all classes and occupations, from the end of the last century to the 1970s. They went as guests to hotels, bungalow colonies, and camps, and as workers to eke out a living or work their way through college. They went to preserve cultural and religious affinities, escape the drudgery of the year's hard work, and find romance. In the Mountains, Jews of Eastern European descent could become Americanized while preserving much of their Jewishness. In the Catskill resorts, they could have a proper vacation like regular Americans, but they could do it in a very Jewish milieu. As the vacationers moved into the next generation and became more assimilated, they created less conspicuously Jewish environments, but Jewish environments nonetheless.

These hotels, colonies, and kuchalayns were not merely resorts where you stayed, but were miniature societies where people knew lots about each other and created intricate relationships in a neighborhood and family mentality that could not be found at an ordinary resort. These New York Jews created a whole resortland shaped by their urban culture. They imported their music, humor, vaudeville revue style, culinary customs, language, and worldviews. There are simply no other such creations of any resort area, much less an area so thoroughly dominated by one group. The Catskills was the ultimate version of a summer-resort–based minisociety, a collective enterprise woven with humor, food, entertainment, Yiddish culture, and a myriad of patchwork efforts that built a giant community.

Without consciously intending it, these people created an environment that would linger in memories long after the Catskills declined in the 1970s. Catskill culture was a unique experience of work and leisure of the first generations of twentieth-century American Jews. This reverberated in music, humor, and teenage coming-of-age dramas. Because Catskill culture was a major facet of the Jewish experience, it also has influenced a larger, secular, cosmopolitan culture—at least on the East Coast.

Recent popular portrayals of the Catskills in film and prose include the Grossinger's mock-up from *Dirty Dancing* (filmed in North Carolina), literary recollections of the real Grossinger's, singles weekends at The Concord in the 1980s and 1990s, and memoirs of major celebrities. (At the second History of the Catskills Conference, Eileen Pollack pointed out that the kosher salt box on the dining room table in *Dirty Dancing* is shot so that the Hebrew letters are blurred—Jews will know it's a kosher salt box, but gentiles will not have to see the Hebrew letters in clear view.) These images do convey some of the Catskill atmosphere to many who knew and to a large number of those who never knew the area. But this focus fails to do justice to the ordinary guests and staff who populated the "Jewish Alps." While the large hotels were important, the heart of what we all called "the Mountains" was a hefty number of small- and medium-sized hotels laced with bungalow colonies. Strung through Ulster and Sullivan Counties, the Catskills are not even the "real" Catskill Mountains, but merely foothills to the legendary Rip Van Winkle topography.

The familiar Catskills are gone, with only handfuls of very large hotels remaining. Smaller ones burned down or were sold to Hasidic groups, redone as yoga ashrams and Zen meditation centers, converted to drug rehab programs, or just left to fall apart. Many bungalow colonies were divided up as summer condos, transformed into Hasidic enclaves, or abandoned. Yet, surprisingly, there are a good number operating as nonreligious colonies. The town streets— once vital with crowds of guests, workers, and locals who serviced the resorts— are fairly empty, lined with many vacant storefronts, and largely populated by Hasidim and unemployed people.

Studying the Catskills

This book's origins lie in a 1991 lunch at the annual meeting of the American Sociological Association in Cincinnati, where I shared Catskill stories with a friend who suggested there was grist for an ethnography. The idea seemed intriguing, but it took a personal jolt to move ahead—my mother died two months later, leaving me an orphan. Perhaps "orphan" is an odd term for a settled family man of forty-two with children of ages six and nine, but it certainly is apt—I was cast into a new look at the world where I was no longer the child of any living parents. My search for roots was also a search for the meaning of the Catskills; that formative aspect of my upbringing is also a fascinating slice of life for many others. My intent here is to present that Jewish cultural environment and its broader social context, while exploring my own roots in it.

In some way, I already had in mind an idea of preserving the Catskills. When my mother was still alive, I toyed with the idea of getting her to write *Sylvia's Catskill Cookbook,* a collection of her wonderful recipes, which had gotten out to too few people in the years she cooked in the Mountains. I realized that this project would not work. My mother was terrible at sharing recipes, leaving out by intention or accident key ingredients and by giving directions in such terms as "a bit of," "add just enough," and "you'll know when." Curiously, she had often complained about how my father's Hungarian mother and sisters would withhold proper instructions for key dishes, such as strudel, which required endlessly walking around several floured, cloth-covered tables to pull the filo-like dough evenly and micro-thin. Maybe she was getting even with the world for those slights, and I didn't want to get involved.

But in another way, I was not ready to really accept the importance of the Catskills in my life. I remember seeing *Resorts of the Catskills,* edited by Alf Evers, Elizabeth Cromley, Betsy Blackmar and Neil Harris, in a bookstore in 1979. Though I looked it over for a few minutes, I didn't rush to the cash register with it as a prize. The Catskills raised a deep ambivalence in me—criticism of its problematic parts in my life and excitement over its personal and larger social significance. It would be a while—at my mother's death—till I could at least see that this ambivalence existed and talk openly about it. I have heard very similar ambivalence from many of the people presently studying the Catskills, as well as many people I have interviewed.

Between 1993 and 1994, I started committing to notes many memories of being in the Catskills, from birth through the first year of graduate school (1949–1971). I studied scholarly and popular writing and joined a small group of scholars and Catskill residents trying to organize a conference on the Catskills. I spoke to friends and colleagues about Catskill memories. Their questions and connections helped me tap further personal memories.

My first round of interviewing took place between 1993 and 1995. Through word-of-mouth requests and an advertisement in the Boston weekly *Jewish Advocate,* I interviewed twenty-nine guests, workers, and hotel owners. A few were in their thirties, most in their fifties and sixties, a good number in their seventies, some in their eighties, and two in their nineties. They had spent time in the Mountains in all periods, the earliest in 1910. Some still visited the Catskills. A few had only begun going to the Mountains in the 1980s, though I was mainly looking for people who had at least begun their involvement by the early 1970s, the tail end of the vibrant life of the area. A local historian gave me two additional interviews, a legal scholar gave me another, and friends and colleagues in the Catskills Institute provided videotaped interviews of nine people's Catskill reminiscences. Some members of the Catskills Institute donated previously audio- and videotaped interviews and even conducted some new ones for me.

During 1995 and 1996, I began a new round of interviews. Some people I found from word of mouth; others contacted me after seeing articles about me in Brown University's *George Street Journal* and *Brown Alumni Magazine* (where I am a professor of sociology), the weekly *Rhode Island Jewish Herald,* and the main local newspaper, the *Providence Journal.* I located additional respondents from lectures I gave, from the annual "History of the Catskills" conference that I helped establish, and from related activities of the Catskills Institute that I helped organize following the 1995 conference. This second round, conducted from 1995 to 1997, provided 94 additional interviews, for a total of 126 interviews. In addition to the interviews, I received a large number of letters, anecdotes, and memorabilia from people who read the various newspaper articles. In particular, the *Providence Journal* article—reprinted in whole or part in the *Akron Beacon-Journal, Albany Times-Union, Poughkeepsie Journal,* and *Miami Herald*—resulted in 130 responses. Articles in the *New York Times, [New York] Jewish Week,* and *Middletown Times-Herald Record* brought more responses. Some responses were "second-hand," in that people who read an article then sent it to friends or relatives who independently wrote to me. I have not logged in these written responses individually, but there are at least 50 that contain usable information. So, I have interview and memoir material from 176 people.

I have additional material from archival sources, newspaper articles, and the growing number of books written about the Catskills. All extracts and details in this book that are not cited in the "Notes" section are from audio and video interviews conducted by me, by my research assistants, and by the colleagues I mentioned; from letters prompted by newspaper articles; from written responses of persons too far away to interview; and from audiotapes, videotapes, and home movies provided by various people. Those I interviewed were very receptive to my knowledge and experience of the Catskills. Most were very pleased to hear about the project and to participate. People who had kept treasures brought out boxes of old menus, photographs, brochures, and memorabilia. They sought out my knowledge of the current state of "their" hotels and of general conditions in the Catskills.

I got to speak with these people in their homes, their offices, hospital waiting rooms, coffee houses, Catskill hotels, and my own office. One of the more novel interviews was when I went to Swansea (near Fall River, Massachusetts) on the invitation of a man who called me the week before, having remembered the *Providence Journal* article. He said fifteen members of his family were going to be at his house for an annual reunion, timed to coincide with a neighborhood clambake. The family circle usually spends several hours together before moving to the nearby park for the large community gathering. Since most of this man's relatives had been old Catskill guests (many at the same kuchalayn), it would be a novel way to get material. And it was, even containing its own resort-like entertainment—one man sat with a boom box on his lap, playing Allen Sherman's comic songs from "Hello Mother, Hello Father," while the rest sang along and cackled at the humor. Afterward, we walked over to the classic New England clambake. Our table was one of about twenty tables at the large gathering, which was a clearly non-Jewish crowd. When I asked people about songs they remembered from the Catskills, they competed to see how well they remembered the words to old Jewish favorites. As one deep tenor belted out *"Schain Vi Di Livone,"* neighbors passed us lobsters and clams steamed in seaweed.

The people I spoke to came from varied backgrounds. Their parents were cutters and needleworkers in the garment district, painting and building contractors, teachers, grocery store owners, newspaper reporters, restaurant workers, dentists, doctors, pharmacists, professors, lawyers, kosher butchers, furniture store owners, coffee and cocoa business owners, dry cleaners, optometrists, unskilled laborers, wholesale jewelry dealers, patternmakers, auto mechanics, fish store owners, and so on. The second oldest person I talked with, ninety years old in 1993, had stayed several years in the Catskills, starting in 1910 at age eight. Her family would take the train from Boston to New York, then the boat up the Hudson, and then a hotel bus picked them up. She had not been back since the 1920s, yet she responded to my ad in the newspaper. Why? Because she met her husband there and they're "still in love seventy years later." Others had not been back since the 1930s, but the experience was important enough to follow up on the ad and call me. This reaffirmed for me the place our Mountains have in so many people's hearts.

My respondents' fondness for Catskill memories enabled me to tap more into my own feelings. Through these Catskill veterans, I found shared memories, common occurrences, similar kinds of relationships. Interviews and excursions to the field then served as grist for further production of my personal narrative. My voice is that both of a voyager and a researcher, and it finds itself both separately and through the voices of others.

Just before my 1993 fieldtrip to the Catskills, I made a fieldtrip to Miami Beach. The Miami Beach trip provided further observations. Since some Catskill hotel owners bought or built beach resorts, many Mountain Rats worked the Miami Beach winter season and many guests frequented both locations. In the Catskill fieldtrip, I visited nearly all the resorts that my parents or I had worked in—thirteen sites, nine of which were abandoned or burned down, two were still operating as small hotels, one was converted to a drug rehabilitation center, and another transformed into a children's theater camp. I also visited other hotels, bungalow colonies, religious institutions, and town centers. I spoke with local librarians, local archivists, historians, and current residents. At the time of the first three "History of the Catskills" conferences in 1995, 1996, and 1997, I made further visits to sites around the Catskills. I made an additional fieldtrip to the Mountains in 1997 as well.

I admit that sometimes I can't tell how much of this search is mainly a personal journey and what part is a sociological and historical excursion into a significant portion of Jewish life. Perhaps that is part of the excitement, knowing that there is a thin boundary between these two elements. I do know that there is ample reason to explore this as a research topic—both because I understand its importance and because many people have affirmed that significance. Whether they are fellow sociologists, academics in different fields, or nonacademics, people who hear about my project have responded with great enthusiasm. The sociological tradition is full of valuable books that originated in the writers' personal involvement.

Alongside the journey through my family history, marked by the memories and recollections written here, there is another realm—my realization that

Catskill life made a deep impression on my career. Through observing the re-markable communities that were created, by grasping the differences between Catskills' appearance and reality, by watching the finagling, by experiencing the hustling, I gained a watchful eye. This contributed to making me a soci-ologist—a professional observer and interpreter of social life. Part of this so-ciological apprenticeship involved understanding impression management. To create the resort environment, Catskill owners and staff engaged in an enormous amount of impression management—as is required elsewhere (e.g., the theater, the circus)—to make the ordinary seem glamorous, to make everyday experience magical. Indeed, a woman I interviewed said that the Mountains were "like a circus." I had the good fortune to spend more than two decades watching and acting in the backstage where the glamour and magic were created—by brochures that described all pools as "Olympic-sized" and menus filled with extravagant, often French, words ("roast prime ribs of beef au jus"). While larger hotels did have major entertainers and ex-cellent facilities, smaller places claimed more than was true. They advertised their shows as "Broadway entertainment"—often this could be true only if they meant that the entertainers ate at Kaplan's Deli on Broadway in Monti-cello before the show. Many MCs introduced mediocre entertainers as "di-rect from Las Vegas," which we sarcastically rephrased as "drek [crap] from Las Vegas." Owners of many small resorts promised day camps filled with ac-tivities, which were always far less than the claim; likewise for "extensive" sports facilities, which often consisted of shuffleboard, one cracked tennis court, one handball court, and an unkempt softball diamond. At whatever level of resort, more was always pledged. Everyone worked to create images, including many of the guests who pretended to be more important than they were. One owner noted that a less-than-full hotel was deemed unattractive to guests, so if the dining room was not filled, tables would be removed to make it look filled. Similarly, staff and owners' cars would be moved to the front parking lot for visibility from the road.

Being in the Catskills also taught me about ambivalence, the contradictory feelings and experiences that people have for many elements of their lives. For many people, the Mountains provided a love-hate relationship: They were drawn back to it, yet they disliked it; they worked themselves too severely, yet were proud of being part of a community of workers. I knew about my own ambivalence toward the Mountains, and indeed that is what kept me from writ-ing this book earlier. In the course of interviewing people, I found how common ambivalence is. The existence of countervailing emotions and relation-ships, I think, makes for very interesting communities. Not surprisingly, this theme comes up throughout the book.

With the backdrop of Catskill life pumping through my system, I return nearly a half-century after my birth to a White Lake hotel family to make sense of the endless stories and the many-textured legacy of this corner of the world.

BROWN'S HOTEL ROYAL, White Lake, N. Y. — Telephone White Lake 120

The hand-colored postcard of my parents' White Lake hotel, Brown's Hotel Royal, guided me back to its "hidden" location in 1993. This style is typical of late 1940s–early 1950s postcards. It is rendered as an aerial view, though it was not taken from the air. My parents owned the hotel from 1946 to 1952. I was born in 1949, in the off-season in New York City.

My father, William Brown, on lawn of Brown's Hotel Royal in 1946, the first season my parents owned it. (*Photo from Gloria Gruder.*)

Cousin Gloria Klein at garden with cannas at Brown's Hotel Royal, 1946. (*Photo from Gloria Gruder.*)

Cousin Gloria Klein
on steps of Brown's
Hotel Royal, 1946.
*(Photo from Gloria
Gruder.)*

(Below) Aunt Bess and Uncle Nat Klein
at Brown's Hotel Royal, 1946.
(Photo from Gloria Gruder.)

(Below, r.) My father holding me on
the porch of our hotel, 1949.
(Photo by Sylvia Brown.)

Me at the Royal, 1950. *(Photo from Laura Feldman.)*

Cousins in front of the concession, Brown's Hotel Royal. *(Photo from Laura Feldman.)*

A cousin on the sliding board at Brown's Hotel Royal. *(Photo from Laura Feldman.)*

My grandparents' fiftieth wedding anniversary at an unknown Catskills hotel, 1931. My father is seated at left next to his parents Philip and Mali Brown. My half-sister, Marilyn Brown, is in front of my grandfather.
(Photo from Gloria Gruder.)

My half-sister, Marilyn Brown, at my grandparents' anniversary.
(Photo from Gloria Gruder.)

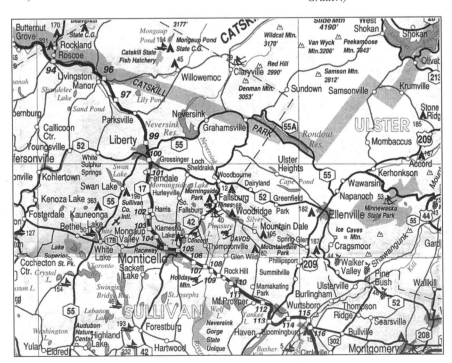

The Jewish Catskills of Sullivan and Ulster Counties.
(Reproduced with permission of JIMAPCO, Inc. Copyright 1997.)

Chapter 2

How the Jewish Catskills Started

*"It was only a farmhouse, and every year
we added a little bit."*

People have long debated what constitutes the Catskills. The original appellation referred to the area in Greene County west of the town of Catskill, an area north of the Jewish Catskills. As hotels developed in more southern areas, they sought through their promotional activities to be included in the Catskill geographical grouping. Officially, the New York State Temporary Commission to Study the Catskills, established in 1973, includes Greene, Delaware, Sullivan, Ulster, Schoharie, and Otsego Counties, as well as part of Albany County—altogether an area of nearly four million acres and 373,000 people. This is an area dozens of times larger than the "Jewish Alps," which is a 250-square-mile enclave that includes not even the whole of Sullivan and Ulster Counties.

Jewish Dreams of the Catskills

As early as the 1820s, Jews had dreams of living in the Catskills as a rural refuge. Mordecai Noah, a journalist and diplomat whose father fought in the Revolution, considered such a move. Faced with warnings of poor tilling and disputes over land claims, he opted instead for an upstate tract near Buffalo, which never got underway. The 1837 depression put an end to another attempt, this time by the Society of *Zeire Hazon* (Tender Sheep). That same year, Robert Carter leased several hundred acres in Wawarsing, Ulster County, and took five families there to create the Sholem (Peace) Colony; twelve more families joined the next year. After four years of cap making, quill production, and clothing peddling, the Sholem settlers went bankrupt and left. Their eight houses, 500 acres, and *shul* are all gone, but the Ellenville synagogue has a plaque commemorating this settlement.

Jewish farming in the Catskills developed toward the end of the nineteenth century. Archie Kinberg recounted how his parents came from Austria in 1878 and in 1893 bought a farm in Ellenville, where he was born in 1900, one of ten children. Kinberg's father, Morris, was thus one of the earliest Jewish farmers in the Catskills. Unlike most of the Jewish farmers in the Catskills, Morris Kinberg had farmed in Austria, both dairy and sugar beets. The New York Lackawanna and Western Railway ran through the Kinbergs' pasture, and the Delaware and Hudson Canal ran on the perimeter of their 160-acre farm. They had a mule station for resting and feeding the mules that drew the canal barges. Elsewhere on their property, they ran a sawmill for producing lumber. Jews were still sparse in Ulster County, and Archie Kinberg was often beat up in Ellenville. Kinberg recounts: "In the first ten years there were no Jews nearby except fifteen miles distance in a place called Mountaindale, Sullivan County. We used to drive there once a month to purchase Jewish provisions. For Pesach [Passover], Papa would take the train to New York to purchase matzohs and so forth." For Rosh Hashanah and Yom Kippur, they had to go to New York City to recruit four or five men to complete a *minyan* (in traditional practice, the ten male adults necessary for Jewish prayer services), pay their way up to the Catskills, and feed them for the holiday's duration.

Though Kinberg's very early Ellenville farm did not become a hotel as did so many other Jewish farms, it provides an account of an early Catskill flirtation with the famous borscht: "Sometime during Shvat [the Jewish calendar month including parts of January and February], we would acquire a wooden keg of about fifteen-gallon capacity from a herring dealer and we would put it into the creek to soak, also to deodorize and seal the stays. About Purim time, my dear mother would clean it well and cut about thirty or forty pounds of red beets, which we had in a cold dirt floor cellar, and set it aside for borscht for Pesach." Actually, this was very likely *russel,* a fermented borscht.

How did Jews come to be farmers, an occupation that most people do not associate with Jews? Dave Levitz and Rose Levitz are among the last remaining

Jewish farmers in the Catskills. Dave noted that "in Russia, the Jewish people couldn't own land. When they came to the U.S., the big thing was owning a piece of land." How did they get the skills? Dave Levitz continued, "They didn't farm in Russia, but it was common for them to have livestock in Russia. They knew the basics." And, in the new world of opportunity, Jewish immigrants were likely to try anything to make a go of it. Russian restrictions on owning land in the Pale did not hold for other countries. In Hungary, for example, some Jews were farmers and others were managers of large farms.

A Beautiful Place to Go

The Catskills are beautiful—that was their attraction for so many people over so many years. Massive hotels such as the Catskill Mountain House, Overlook Mountain House, Tremper House, Grand Hotel, and Hotel Kaaterskill attracted wealthy visitors to the "high Catskills." Some Jews had begun summering in those gentile Catskill hotels in the 1870s, but the massive Eastern European immigration to New York was met with nativist and anti-Semitic exclusion; the *New York Times* in 1899 termed this the "anti-Hebrew crusade."

Faced with loss of entree to gentile-owned hotels and boardinghouses, Jews did various things. Charles F. Fleischmann of Cincinnati, a U.S. senator and wealthy manufacturer of yeast and gin, bought sixty acres in Griffins Corner in eastern Ulster County in 1883 and established an elaborate resort compound that would soon become a town named Fleischmanns, catering largely to Hungarian Jews like himself. The magnate's playland included a heated pool, a trout pond guarded by a watchman in a tower, a riding academy, and a baseball stadium. Curiously, this was modeled on the "cottage park" phenomenon of the 1880s, when wealthy gentiles built self-contained cottage communities and sometimes attached inns—with names such as Tuxedo Park, Onteora Park, Twilight Park, and Sunset Park—to escape the lower-class people of all religions, especially the Jews, who were starting to visit the grand hotels. These parks were often graced by leading artists, writers, and critics of the day. Mark Twain spent the summer of 1890 at Onteora Park, failing in his attempt to write a sequel to *Tom Sawyer* and *Huckleberry Finn* (to be called *Tom Sawyer and Huckleberry Finn among the Indians*), but making a huge social success with his story-telling.

Early in the century, leading Jewish cultural figures added their mark to the Catskill origins, following the growth of the Woodstock art colony from its

1903 inception (the northeastern Ulster County town of Woodstock, still an arts center, is nowhere near Yasgur's Farm of the famous Woodstock festival; that 1960s music shrine is in Bethel, just past White Lake). The celebrated Yiddish stage actor Boris Thomashevsky (grandfather of conductor Michael Tilson Thomas) built a resort with an 800-seat outdoor theater and a 500-seat indoor one. With plays, bands, and poker games, he started the cultural and entertainment traditions that would dominate Catskill culture. Abraham Cahan, founder of the *Jewish Daily Forward,* a major Yiddish newspaper, penned a series of essays on the Mountains' virtues. In his novel, *The Rise of David Levinsky,* he described the 1910 hotel atmosphere that would be familiar half a century later—weekend husbands, grand meals, fancy dressing.

There was quite a contrast between Cahan's Rigi Kulm House and Thomashevsky's resort and the small boardinghouses. The large, elegant hotels of the 1890s to 1910s were built to emulate large gentile hotels of the time. Since it was these hotels that first refused Jews, there was a certain comeuppance to establishing large, sumptuous Jewish resorts. Archie Kinberg remembers the Grand Hotel in Highmount and the Prospect Hotel in Hunter that "catered to the more eminent class of Jewish people of the day," and also two German Jewish hotels in Fleischmanns—the Hotel Takanasie and the Hotel St. Regis. The latter was the site where in 1920 Kinberg met his wife, whose uncle owned it. The St. Regis must have been quite grand, for its $50 weekly rate was very high for those days. But neither the cottage park of Fleischmanns nor the grand hotels like the fictional Rigi Kulm were typical of the early development of the Catskills. For this we turn more to the boardinghouse and farm origins.

Simon Epstein started a Jewish boardinghouse in Saxton in 1889, but was faced with an anti-Semitic riot. Four years later, he moved his resort to Hunter, calling it the Grandview House and beginning the Jewish outpost in the Hunter and Tannersville area. There was also the beginning of a permanent Jewish population in Tannersville in that period, based on Jewish glovemakers and leatherworkers in the town that took its name from the tannery industry. By the beginning of the century, there were enough Jews to form Congregation Anshe Hashoran, the first synagogue in the Catskills since the 1837 shul of the failed Sholem settlers. Only a few of the people I interviewed, including a ninety-year-old woman, had vacationed in that northern part of Ulster County and southern part of Greene County. One man, however, started going to the Schoharie Mansion, built to resemble the White House, in Tannersville around 1921. Only one kosher hotel remained in the Tannersville-Hunter area in the early 1970s, and its owner recalled that in the 1920s there were a hundred, with seven kosher butchers working in Tannersville. By the early 1920s, auto travel (by personal car or by "hack," the Catskill version of a limousine service) made Sullivan County much more accessible, even as the greater elevations of the high Catskills made cars too dangerous. In addition, people were aware that there was less danger from tanning in the southern reaches of the Catskills. From that time on, the development of the Jewish Catskills shifted south—to southern and western Ulster County and to most of Sullivan County.

Railroad service opened the door to that shift. In 1899, the Ontario and Western Railroad's *Summer Homes* carried the first ad for a Jewish boarding home providing kosher food: John Gerson's forty-room boardinghouse in Rock Hill charged six dollars a week for adults and three dollars for children. Once the Jews broke through the anti-Semitic exclusion of the Sullivan County boardinghouses, the classic distinction among Jews was visible: In 1900, the High View Farm in Mountaindale advertised it would only take in "a good class of Hebrews," meaning better-off, Americanized German and Sephardic Jews, as opposed to the new Eastern European Jews. Such discrimination was also found in the older areas of Hunter, Tannersville, and Schoharie. The *Yiddishes Tageblatt*, the largest circulation Jewish daily in America from the turn of the century until the *Forward* overtook it around 1910, disparaged the assimilationist German Jews who sought genteel, non-Jewish accommodations. In 1897, the paper commended its readership for not being ashamed "to sit on the piazza of a summer hotel and read a paper printed in Yiddish."

As the Jewish presence in Ulster County grew, some older large resorts were sold by Christians to Jews—Lackawack House, Yama Farms Inn, Mt. Meenahga, Sha-Wan-Ga. When they bought the Swa-Wan-Ga Lodge, the Dan family even used the same brochures, replacing "No Hebrews Accommodated" with "Kosher Cuisine Featured."

Jewish overcrowding on the Lower East Side played a big role in the Catskills' growth. Life was difficult, especially in the heat of summer. Life was also unhealthy. Tuberculosis was rampant, and clean air was the best prescription. Faced with expected exclusion from the J. P. Morgan-financed Loomis sanitarium in Liberty, Jews built their own sanitarium. The Workmen's Circle, a benevolent political/cultural group with socialist and labor union roots, opened a sanitarium in 1910, built at the huge cost of a quarter million dollars and operating on an annual budget of $125,000. The Jewish labor movement viewed that facility with great pride. It was followed by other welfare societies and unions who sent members to Catskill boardinghouses. Many of these houses had already been established—in the first decade of the century, over a thousand farms had been sold to Jewish families, mostly near Ellenville, with the bulk of them used as boardinghouses. The Triangle Shirtwaist Fire of 1911 even figured in—an International Ladies' Garment Workers' Union (ILGWU) project to improve working conditions led the union to start the Unity House resort for workers to recuperate in the mountains.

Starting Small

Some of the hotel owners themselves had escaped to farms in the Catskills for health reasons, never intending to open boardinghouses. One divorced woman followed her doctor's prescription for a boardinghouse rest in 1912. The next year, she married into the owner's family and set up a fifteen-room house of her own. From another owner's child comes this history:

> My parents came to Loch Sheldrake in 1913, supposedly for their health. They bought an eight-room house in Loch Sheldrake and set-tled down with cows and horses and a few guests for seven dollars a week. They named their place the Shady Nook Country Club. From this humble beginning arose an 85–90-room hotel that accommodated ap-proximately 200 people, with some guests happy to sleep in the lobby.

Pollack's Hotel in Ferndale had a similar origin: "Like many people in Ferndale and Liberty, my family came to Ferndale because an aunt contracted TB. After a year, she was well and my parents brought the rest of her family out and started taking in boarders." From that 1919 start, a hotel developed (it held 170 adults and 40 children in 1923), operating until it was sold to Camp Gila in 1969.

Many Catskill hotels began early in the century as boardinghouses on op-erating farms, including Tamarack Lodge, Grossinger's, Esther Manor, and the Nemerson. The Kutsher brothers bought a farm in 1907, the first step in the development of Kutsher's Country Club, which still operates. A man who lived and worked in the Catskills relates a typical example of the progression of de-velopment of many hotels: "My grandfather and my uncle used to own a small Jewish hotel in the town of Woodbourne. It started out as a farm. It then be-came a boardinghouse, and then it became a kosher hotel that would hold about 200 people, most of them older, most of them forty-age and up families. And my grandfather founded the synagogue in the town of Woodbourne in the early 1900s."

The owner of the large Raleigh, who sold it before the crash of the resort industry, recounted his family's hotel history:

We had a dairy farm. We bought it from Gentile people [in 1902], and he [the seller] had a route, a milk route to Ellenville. And we had the milk route for a length of time, and then, you know, like all the other Jewish people, in the summertime we started taking in boarders. We didn't have the route anymore; we needed them [the boarders]. And it was only a farmhouse, and every year we added a little bit. In the winter we didn't have any boarders. My father had to go to New York to supplement our income.

After four years they started another enterprise:

We bought a farm on nothing [in 1906]. We had to buy a cow, a horse, oh, a little by little, and then we added on every year another room, another thing. . . . When we first came, we called it the Evergreen House because it was an eight-room house and it had four big evergreen trees in the front. That's where we got the name, the Evergreen House. As I say, little by little we worked it up. We built up until we became quite big. . . . And we called it the Ratner Hotel until 1948, I think, [but] we changed it to the Raleigh—when my parents died. We had somebody [a partner] with us; we changed it to the Raleigh.

The past owners of the Windsor, a large hotel holding 400–500 guests, also provided their background:

In 1899, my father settled in Centerville, which is now called Woodridge, New York, and he opened a hotel. He bought a farm that had about eight or nine rooms, and he made sixteen rooms out of it. And my mother did the cooking, and really the guests came up to the place because they were friends of my mother's or father's. And they would come for the entire summer. And my dad charged $4 a week for an adult and $1.50 for a child. When Prohibition came, my father bought the Lakeside Hotel, which is now the Windsor, and he built that up and we had the guests, you know, it was the normal resort hotel. It was owned by [people who] were there since 1905, and we bought the place in 1918. My father helped build the first synagogue. My grandfather participated in that, too.

Notice how narratives of early resort origins feature the importance of building a synagogue. This is one more piece of evidence that Catskill culture involved the creation of a community far broader than a collection of boardinghouses and hotels. Here is one more example. Joe Shagrin, his daughter tells, bought a farm between White Lake and Swan Lake in 1915 with money loaned from the Hebrew Immigrant Aid Society (HIAS). The society even sent a teacher to various farmers' homes to teach them Hebrew:

> Since the synagogues were so far away in Swan Lake and White Lake, ten Jewish farmers between the towns wanted to have a place of worship and to educate their children in Hebrew. One neighbor, Jake Rotterman, donated a tract of land, centrally located, and they had a synagogue built. As money-poor as these farmers were, they felt it an absolute necessity to educate their children in Hebrew. A Hebrew teacher was hired. He lived in each household for one month each year and taught us Hebrew after school. Thus the young men could be bar mitzvahed and we young girls learned how to read and write Hebrew. After a year or so of farming, my father realized that he had to supplement some income. My parents turned the farmhouse into a rooming house for the summer City dwellers. Usually a mother and children, to get away from the weather, would rent a room and cook their meals in a communal kitchen. From that, a small boardinghouse was built, consisting of twenty bedrooms, a large kitchen (one side for dairy meals, the other side for meat meals, separate dishwashing facilities, etc.) Through the year additional buildings were added to accommodate the worldlier guests who wanted private or semiprivate bathrooms. Then the swimming pool, casino—now called playhouse—day camp, handball courts, baseball fields, and entertainment were added. We hired more help, and I think we worked harder each year.

A woman born in 1910 in Luzon, now Hurleyville, told of how her father started out with a farm, turned it into a boardinghouse, and then bought up decaying hotels to fix up and sell. The largest he had was the Liberty House in Liberty, which burned in 1927. From a man born in 1915, I heard the story of his family's purchasing a farm in 1917, running a boardinghouse, and then putting up a thirty-six-room building in 1926—it became the Loch Sheldrake Inn. In Greenfield Park, the Steinhorn family's farm was established in 1910, later to be transformed into the 250-room Grand Mountain Hotel.

The Nevele Country Club, one of the few remaining grand hotels and renowned as a honeymoon spot, was a working farm until 1938. Along with Yaffe's Breeze Lawn and Charles Slutsky's Fallsview, the owners of the Nevele continued to milk their own herds into the 1930s, when pasteurization laws came into effect. Leba Sedaka, daughter of the owner of Esther Manor and wife of Neil Sedaka, whom she met when his band played there, recalled her sorrow at giving up her pet calf when the expanding hotel ended its agricultural activities.

Even when the Morningside was a large hotel holding six hundred or more guests in the late 1930s, the owners ran a farm to provide chickens, milk, produce, and fruit. Frank Goldstein remembers: "Every fall my grandmother would have 15–20 wooden barrels for making sauerkraut. We'd grow all the cabbage on the farm, and they'd come down with wagonloads of cabbages." Hotels quickly ceased their pastoral enterprise when they saw that more money was to be raised from housing visitors, even though a room for the whole summer only ran between $50 and $150.

Many farms, however, failed to make the transition to successful boarding-houses, much less to hotels. Dorothy Eagle's parents, Louis and Rose Lippman, may have underestimated the business potential but still salvaged something. As Dorothy recalls:

> When he [Louis] bought the farm [in 1919], there were roomers and he thought it was a going business. Came Labor Day everybody dispersed and went home, and he was left holding the bag. He had no money. He spent the last buck to buy the farm. Well, he had to do something about it. So he developed a barter system. He made alcohol, and I delivered it to the butcher, to the baker. They got a bag of flour in return, or bread. The butcher gave meat. So somehow [we] survived.

The Agricultural Legacy

The Jewish Agricultural Society (JAS), which started in 1900 as the Jewish Agricultural and Industrial Aid Society, constantly sought to encourage Jewish farmers to farm rather than move toward tourism. In 1904, the society counted 161 Jewish farms that took in boarders. When the organization changed its name in 1908 to the Jewish Agricultural Society, it railed against this practice. Dominated by Baron de Hirsch's philanthropic fund and the noblesse-oblige attitude of German Jews to their Eastern European co-religionists, the society feared that the public would view the farmers as parasites if they ignored 'productive' farming for tourism. Baron de Hirsch believed that farming would give self-respect and produce good health and virtue. He wanted Jewish farmers, however, to be near cities (in this case, New York), so they would have access to religion and culture. The Catskills contained the largest concentration of Jewish farmers in the United States, and the JAS started an Ellenville office in 1919 to better serve the area.

By 1908, the JAS counted 684 Jewish farms in all of New York state, 500 of them in Sullivan and Ulster Counties. That count was based merely on second mortgages that the JAS held, and hence was an undercount. In *Jewish Farmers of the Catskills,* Abraham Lavender and Clarence Steinberg describe the magnitude of Jewish farming in the region:

> A triangular area with sides of about twenty miles each, with Route 209's Wurtsboro through Ellenville and Kerhonkson on the east and Woodbourne through Woodridge (Centreville) and Mountaindale on the west, was said to have supported one thousand Jewish farm households. With easily five hundred more to the northwest, around Monticello, Liberty, Hurleyville, Loch Sheldrake, and Parksville, on the O&W main line, Sullivan and Ulster counties had three-tenths or more of all the Jewish farmer households in the United States around 1911.

By 1910, the society tallied 741 farms/boardinghouses. The new direction was clear, and in 1919 the group started a campaign to improve sanitary conditions in the boarding homes. The next year, the society spoke of helping farmers to "work out a plan of farming that will dovetail with the boarding business so that the two will be complimentary and not conflicting." By this time, about a quarter million Jews were vacationing in the Catskills. Some of the failed farmers turned to business, and the major towns of Liberty, Monticello, and South Fallsburg developed a large number of Jewish enterprises. Indeed, some towns, such as Parksville and Centreville (later Woodridge), had predominantly Jewish populations in the first decade of the century. On Columbus Day in 1928, the Jewish Agricultural Society held a fair at the Ellenville Fair Grounds and ten thousand people came—both Jews and Christians—a sign of local acceptance of the Jewish agriculturists. These fairs continued in later years in Woodridge and Mountaindale, and the foods of choice were pastrami, corned beef, and kosher hot dogs. Yiddish was spoken so widely in Woodridge that a number of gentile storekeepers spoke it with their Jewish customers.

Even while the farms still struggled to continue, the farmers spun off the requisite synagogues, Hebrew schools, and mutual aid societies. Ellenville, for example, had a Hebrew Aid Society by 1907, a synagogue in 1910, and a Workmen's Circle branch in 1911. In other towns, as well, Workmen's Circle and International Workers' Order (a communist-affiliated fraternal and educational organization) branches were important for health coverage and burial plans. There was a very strong cooperative spirit, nourished in part by socialist and communist traditions, and in part by the need to survive in a difficult environment. In 1913, Jewish farmers started the nation's first fire insurance cooperative, the Associated Cooperative Fire Insurance Company, since Jews faced various problems in getting fire insurance. Anti-Semitism was one problem; another was the higher hotel rate charged to farmers that took in boarders, as much as five to ten times higher. Business in the insurance co-op was conducted in Yiddish, including the meetings and minutes; even the policies were written in Yiddish, then translated by the office manager for legal purposes. A year later, Jewish farmers opened the Cooperative Jewish Creamery of Hurleyville. In 1934 came the very large and important Inter-County Farmers' Cooperative Association (Inter-County Co-op), often called the feed co-op. Gentiles resisted joining the feed co-op, as one longtime farmer remembered: "The saving was tremendous. Feed represents roughly 70 percent of the cost of producing eggs, for example. The nearest competitor was between 10 and 15 percent on the feed alone. On 70 percent of your costs, you could save between 10 and 15 percent. And yet they were slow to come in."

To aid in securing credit, the Cooperative Federal Credit Union was started in 1936, under sponsorship from the insurance cooperative. Taken together, this provided a Jewish institutional infrastructure that made the Catskills more attractive for Jews back in New York to consider moving to. A veteran farmer noted that the hotel owners started the credit union, even though they would not benefit from it:

They had nothing to gain from it personally because the credit union could not supply long-term money for [hotel] expansion. It could only lend me production money, and people were in dire need during the Depression. The insurance cooperative put in at least $10,000 in seed money. They come to recruit a guy like me as a member. I'm one of the original members. What'd they come to recruit me for? I didn't have the $25 to become a member with. Just so they could help, because they knew me well enough to know I was trying to build a little chicken farm, I had a couple of hundred chickens, I was an educated guy. . . . If they lent a guy $100 or $200 in 1936 or 1937 or 1938, it was a tremendous help. The banks had stopped [lending].

Tzedakkah (Jewish charity) followed closely upon Jewish settlement, as wealthy Jewish benefactors set up programs to provide vacations for Jews unable to afford such luxury. The Jewish Working Girls Vacation Society, founded in 1893, sent 150 girls each summer on a two-week vacation to its Margaretville house, to provide a "gentle refining influence." For boys, the Educational Alliance set up a summer camp in Cold Spring, in Duchess County across the Hudson, but for some people close enough in proximity to the Catskills to be talked about in the same breath. As its 1902 Annual Report noted, its boys would be "far removed from the temptations and pettiness of city life." Acculturation was part of the package: "Here, the immigrant boys felt themselves the equals of their American born brethren; and here also, all the differences in speech and manners was obliterated, to be supplanted by a healthful and generous spirit of comradeship." Another form of tzedakkah was the support of philanthropic groups that came through the Catskill hotels to raise money for Hebrew Schools, health charities, and the Jewish National Fund.

Despite the precarious nature of farming, many Jews came. Lavender and Steinberg explain it as such: "This lure was complex; it resulted from a combination of the newcomer's unrealistic appraisal of the potential profitability of the situation, the zeal for an alternative to sweatshops, and the example of other Jews who had already become established and successful." The Depression was a benefit to the Catskills in one way. Many Jews came to "the country" due to urban unemployment—1930 was second only to 1920 in the numbers of Jews seeking farms.

One man grew up on a chicken farm with five thousand hens, which was a medium-size operation. While the farm provided a good living in the 1940s, it declined in the 1950s and ultimately went bankrupt due to failure to pay back a loan. His family supplemented their income by renting two bungalows ($350–400 a season), and even divided their house into a small and large apartment so they could rent out the larger unit in the summer while they moved to cramped quarters. They also took in tourists for five dollars a night, as advertised by a sign outside the house that said "Young's Lodge: Tourists, Fresh Eggs, and Broilers." Most of these roomers were friends and families of bungalow colony people who were visiting some of Glen Wild's multitudinous colonies. In that tightly knit local economy, everyone was interdependent. The son grew vegetables to sell at a roadside table. The family sold Mortman's Bakery eggs by the gallon. They opened those eggs that had minute cracks, making them unsalable at retail; so they gained, and it saved the bakery the labor of cracking the enormous number of eggs needed for daily use. The chicken farm even offered an early version of a prepaid health plan through, as the son says, "an arrangement my father had with Dr. Fernhoff in Woodridge, where we provided three dozen medium eggs every week for Dr. Fernhoff and his family, and in return he provided medical care for our family."

For one example of getting a farming start during the Depression, we can look at three brothers-in-law who in 1937 bought a farm in Ulster Heights, near Ellenville. On their fifty-eight acres—named Maple Crest on the Lake—was a main house for the three families, a boardinghouse for renting to four other families, a barn for ten cows, and some chicken coops. They built two additional bungalow units and another chicken coop and worked the farm of eight milking cows and two hundred egg-laying chickens. The partners hired a man to farm and teach farming, though he soon left to start his own farm. Up until the time they sold the place in 1945, horsepower did all the plowing. Three children of two of the families recalled some comic episodes in a written memoir they prepared for me:

> A number of people who didn't live on the premises had permission to go down to the lake on the Maple Crest dirt road leading that way. The road went right past the chicken house. This proved very tempting for a few of the ladies one summer, who were helping themselves to eggs every day, and scaring the chickens to death to boot. In those days Little Leslie had a bantam rooster who behaved like a watchdog. In spite of only weighing a pound and a half, he would fly into the faces of strangers. We placed this bird in the hen house. This was followed by wild screaming ladies and the worst dirty looks imaginable. But the thefts stopped instantly. . . .
>
> Following Labor Day, many of the places were deserted. On one of the properties near Maple Crest, there was a small apple orchard. Naturally, the apples were left unattended to rot. The cows populating Maple Crest at that time must have smelled the rotting apples, and broke the fence to get to them. It must be remarked that rotting apples actually have a fermentation process going on, with significant alcohol production (hard cider!). That evening we had one very drunken herd of cows to get home, falling down drunk!

The Inter-County Co-op helped farmers get through the Depression with credit and education programs. Farmers learned a lot about carpentry, electricity, and plumbing, so they could then apply this to resort-building. A typical poultry farm might bring in eight thousand dollars a year in 1940 (before expenses), when unionized wages in New York averaged seventy-five dollars per week, or four thousand dollars per year. In 1953, all the Jewish farmers in the Catskills had gross annual production of at least ten thousand dollars, whereas only 14 percent of all other American farmers did so. Despite surpassing the average American farm income, Catskill farming was precarious. Agribusiness and large, automated poultry farming provided very stiff competition. By 1960, there was only half the number of farms as 1940. But this is jumping ahead too far from our early century origins—let's return to the beginnings.

Turning into Resorts

Full boardinghouses began to replace farms early in the century. Converting farms to boardinghouses could be difficult—one farmer had to install a mile of his own utility poles to bring electricity. The hard work of those days prefigured the rigors of hotel operating later on, as reported in an investigation by the Jewish Colonization Association:

> Getting up at three o'clock in the morning, going to bed at eleven o'clock at night, the whole family worked like convicts to take care of ten, fifteen, or twenty boarders, thirty sometimes, that are crowded two and three in one room (these boarders are generally of small means). The family sleeps where they can, in the kitchen, the stable, and out-of-doors. The boarders grumble and criticize all the more they pay less and it has to be born in silence.

And they did not pay too much. Pleasant Valley Farm, later to be Hotel Brickman, charged only seven dollars a week before World War I, and the family decision to raise it to nine dollars took a major meeting of all the involved relatives.

Some garment workers even managed to save enough money to go into the hotel business: Nat Lebowitz recalled, "In 1912 my father got tired of working in the sweatshops of the Lower East Side, so he and his young wife decided to go off on their own and they decided to come up to Sullivan County to start a resort hotel." They bought the Ridge Mountain House in Parksville, and then in 1916 they sold it and bought the Pine View Lodge, which had been built quite recently in Fallsburg: "It was a very modern hotel. It had running water in the rooms. That was a big thing in those years." In the 1950s, they moved old guest buildings to the rear of the property, for use as staff quarters, and built new houses, expanding the hotel to 216 rooms that could hold 450 guests and 50–70 children. The Pine View ran until 1982 when the adjoining state prison in Woodbourne took it by eminent domain to add a minimum security facility.

Nat Lebowitz offered an interesting piece of history about the building of hotels in the early part of the century: "In those years, they didn't have lumber yards, so the way hotels were built—sawmill operators would find a location where there were lots of trees, and in our case there must have been thousands of pine trees in our area. And the sawmill operator set up his shop and built two hotels—the Pine View and a neighboring hotel [the Regal] at the same time from the trees that they cut down."

In so many cases, people didn't know what they were getting into. Simple dreams and desires became transformed as small enterprises grew. Often, the transformation seemed a very positive development. Murray Posner recalled the origins of Brickman's:

> This was the Pleasant Valley farmhouse that my grandparents acquired back in 1910. My grandparents didn't come here to be hotel owners or resort operators. My grandfather was a farmer in the old country, and when he came to America the city was not for him. The children bought him a farm. Those years, you know, the farms, they weren't profitable. My father used to go to New York. He'd get a job and he'd send up his salary; it was forty dollars a week. He'd send it up to my grandfather to keep the farm going.

The more the place developed, the more they took pride in the growing resort. Recorded on videotape, Murray Posner provides a twenty-four-minute tour of Brickman's, riding on an electric cart used for maintenance, similar to a golf cart. He points to specific trees and shrubs he personally planted, noting that they were taken from nearby woods on their property—cheaper and also more acclimated to the specific conditions than nursery purchases would be. Posner regales us with tales of laying stone pathways, tromping through chicken-manure-covered fields, and all the time talking of the great "pride of owner-ship" he had in the place.

For others, it was not all so positive. Reuben Wallenrod's 1957 novel, *Dusk in the Catskills,* provides a glimpse into the incremental expansion of many hotels and the attendant disenchantment:

> When he had come here about thirty years ago [1916], he had not thought of a noisy hotel but of a quiet farmer's life between the mountains. He had tried for a while to be a real farmer, but then he saw that even the farmers of this part of the Catskills were selling their land to hotel keepers. When he and Lillian left New York, their friends had banqueted them and praised them for their decision to become farmers, but little by little the farm became a boardinghouse and then a hotel. At first they accepted only their own friends as boarders, and their house became a kind of gathering place for actors, would-be actors, writers, and aspirants to the arts, and then it became a real Catskill hotel. In addition to the old farm house, which had become now "the old house," he had built "the main building," the casino, and now he was over his head in mortgages and debts, owing money to neighbors and friends, and even "the old house" was not his any longer.

The familiarity and comradeship gave way to a more bureaucratic structure:

> In the days when he was young and the hotel was small, only friends and acquaintances would come. He knew everybody and all knew him. On busy weekends Toozin and Newman and others would roll up their sleeves and give a hand, joking and singing. On Friday nights Lillian would stand in the kitchen and dish out gefilte fish, earmarking each plate: "This is for Toozin, he likes the head. Give this, please, to Weiser. . . . Don't let Molly have any fish. She is not allowed to." And after the meal they would gather in the children's dining room, while the large room was being cleaned up, and one guest would read aloud some story of Peretz or Sholom Aleichem, or a guest writer would read something of his own. Now he, Leo Halper, had actually become a servant to the guests.

Besides bureaucracy and disenchantment, there was guilt—how could Jews enjoy themselves while their fellow Jews suffered and perished in the Holocaust? Again, Reuben Wallenrod's novel is informative:

You said you were free and you enjoyed the wide spaces. But there, there in the little village you were born and in other villages like it, in this same year, men and women were tortured, old respected men insulted, old men and children were hiding, hungry and cold in the woods and in the snow of the field; mothers bereaved of their children were running dazed, seeking them with bewilderment and madness in their eyes. Armed, well-fed, and well-dressed murderers were laughing and mocking, and respectable men honored for two generations were made to crawl on their knees—and you, Leo Halper, the owner of Brookville Hotel, how did all these things affect your freedom, your eating, your everyday life? Had it any bearing upon your desires or fears? Had it at all lessened this great beauty of the Indian Summer in the Catskills which spread from horizon to horizon?

This was a powerful ambivalence, indeed. Again, Wallenrod:

All these two or three hundred people, men and women dancing in one of the casinos in the Catskill mountains, these two or three hundred lives are nothing but little narrow circles, dancing their own dance, desiring only their own little desires, living their little lives. The heart knows that there is another great, wide, threatening world outside you, but you are afraid to stop your dancing and think of that world. Such knowledge may well break up the charm of the circle, it may well break up your very being, all of you.

Getting the Mountains in Your Blood

Wallenrod's Leo Halper was one of countless people who gravitated to the Catskills, lived a life of adapting to changes in the resort environment, and got hooked. Aaron Raskin's family moved to Ellenville in the early 1930s for his older brother to have a healthy environment to recover from a severe burn accident. His father, a tailor, had little sense of how to run a farm, and like many others their place turned to taking in boarders. They ran an eight-room *kuchalayn* (cook-for-yourself boardinghouse), Raskin's Orchard Farm House, named for the twenty acres of land full of apples, cherries, and plums. As a youngster, Aaron drove the horse and buggy to buy bread and other food that his family sold to the boarders. He also milked their six cows, and tended to the chickens. They bought five hundred chicks every spring, raising them in a brooder house heated by coal, until they were ready for slaughter to feed the guests. At that point, the family drove a mile and a half to Ellenville where they paid the *shochet* (Jewish ritual slaughterer) five cents each to kill the chickens in the kosher manner.

Within a few years, they built a twenty-room house and converted the kuchalayn to a small hotel that held at most fifty guests. Whereas the kuchalayn charged forty dollars a season for the room and kitchen privileges, the new hotel rates were fourteen dollars per week with three meals included. The guests, virtually all from the Lower East Side, were quite regular; some of them returned every year until the hotel closed around 1951. To make sure they returned, Mrs. Raskin went to New York City in May and visited last year's guests in their apartments to take deposits. Maintaining such a hotel was hard work: Mrs. Raskin cooked, the daughters waited tables, the sons did maintenance work, driving, agricultural chores, and more. Still, Aaron held a full-time outside job, driving a laundry truck for eleven years, delivering clean laundry to many local hotels, including some my parents worked at. Later, he would work on road crews, repairing Ulster County highways. Like many other small proprietors, Aaron Raskin's father worked winters in New York's garment district, where he was proud to be a labor activist with David Dubinsky and the ILGWU.

It was always hand-to-mouth, but when asked why they stayed, Aaron said they had no idea of what else to do. Like Aaron Raskin's family, multitudes of others had no idea of what else to do, except stay—the Mountains got into their blood and became a way of life. They had become transformed into Mountain Rats.

Everyone worked hard in the Mountains. Local residents remember how the coming of spring transformed a quiet, rural atmosphere into an intense, bustling environment, where many locals made the bulk of their year's income in the short season. A forty-nine-year-old man who grew up there recalled: "Most of the store owners, particularly the people selling foodstuffs, would really start to work at six o'clock in the morning, and those stores would often remain open till eleven o'clock at night, seven days a week. It really bred people with a tremendous work ethic. Your parents worked liked that. Your neighbors worked liked that. Your friends worked like that. You worked like that."

The Golden Age: Two Glorious Decades

The end of World War II ushered in a golden age in the Catskills, extending through the 1960s (though some maintain that the best years were before the war). At the war's end, American Jews were no more a primarily immigrant community, but a more modern, largely American-born one. Traditions of Jewish culture coming from Eastern Europe were cut off by the destruction of most of European Jews in the Holocaust. Jews were more integrated in the economy and society and wanted a lifestyle to mirror that achievement, a lifestyle that would include grander vacations.

For obvious reasons, most hotels did not expand during the Depression, and during World War II lumber and other supplies were not widely available. So, much was left in an older state, awaiting a fresh burst of energy. The postwar financial boom and social exuberance allowed for hotel expansion and widespread car ownership, as well as allowing more people to afford vacations. Better roads, even before the new Route 17 highway, made it easier to get to the Catskills. Before the George Washington Bridge was built (in 1931), the trip to the country was long and uncomfortable in the 1920s, as detailed by a waiter/musician:

> We would go from New York City over to the Weehawken side of New Jersey where trains went from there up to the Catskill Mountains, and that in itself was quite something to go through 'cause trains of those days were not the very best in the world. A very common thing was a train went up along the Hudson River and reached a point where it would start going inland off the Hudson River and start climbing uphill off a flat grade. There very often would be troubles with the railroad and the train couldn't go any further. Now I am referring to periods when there was intense heat; air conditioning was virtually unknown at that [time]. And it was not uncommon for passengers of the train. And most, the bulk of the passengers were going to the resort areas of the Catskills, and it was, as I say, it was rather common for the train to break down, and people would have to get off the train

and sit along the roadbeds on the side, on the grass, waiting for many hours for the train to be repaired and corrected so the trip could continue.

By car, the trip was not easy either. The old Route 17 had two lanes, passing through many small towns. At the Wurtsboro hill, the entrance into the Jewish Catskills, many cars routinely overheated from the stress of the climb. Anyone remembering auto trips to the Mountains prior to the late 1950s instantly recalls that travail. Some local youngsters even made money hauling water to people whose radiators spouted steam.

In 1957, the Route 17 Quickway was completed, making the Catskills only ninety minutes away from New York City. The Ontario and Western Railroad ceased operation the same year as the Quickway opened, bringing to a close the long tradition of rail trips to the Mountains. But the Quickway led to a new boom in hotels, with expansion of pools, nightclubs, sports facilities, phone wiring, and deluxe accommodations. Then, in 1958, Monticello Raceway was built by a consortium that included many top hotel owners. At its height in the 1960s, fifteen thousand people attended the harness races on crowded nights. The federal Small Business Administration supported many pool and nightclub additions, but often without the requisite room expansion that would make smaller hotels better able to utilize those amenities. Hotels often started winter operations to get cash flow over the whole year and to not have to totally pay off suppliers after the season—this caused many hotels to go bankrupt because of the added cost of winterizing: burying pipes in the ground, insulating buildings, buying stronger furnaces, and building ice skating rinks. Once small- and medium-size hotels expanded, they had to add management staff—steward, convention manager, superintendent of service—whereas before they used primarily or only family labor. This addition to salaries, combined with higher costs for bigger name entertainment, drove expenses too high for family businesses.

In 1952, the hotel association census counted 509 hotels and boardinghouses in Sullivan County; an equal number of bungalow colonies dotted the Mountains. This figure of approximately 500 hotels is widely quoted, but as the appended "Hotels of the Catskills" list (at the end of this book) shows, there were at least 926 hotels in Sullivan and Ulster Counties, not even including those in the northern Ulster County and southern Greene County area.

By the early 1950s, the hotel industry was the third largest employer of Sullivan County's 15,500 workers, behind agriculture and construction. Plus, the endless building and renovating of the resort industry supported many in construction. As contractor Jerome Nosenchuck points out, "Right after the war there was a big push; everyone had to have a pool. Over a fifteen-year period we put in 100 to 150. There were hundreds and hundreds put in throughout the county. It became a thing. Pools were what people demanded. I never heard of a hotel without a pool."

This was a supernova period—the Catskills grew large and bright, before exploding. In the postwar years, the Catskill fame, its fabled entertainment, and its amazing group of resort facilities became well known to a wider group of people. Around one million people a year vacationed in the Mountains each summer. A shopkeeper who ran a clothing and linen store in Monticello recalls staying open till midnight on weekends, waiting for movies to let out. The delis were important hot spots of village life; Kaplan's in Monticello, Singer's in Liberty, and Frank and Bob's in South Fallsburg might be open till three or four in the morning on weekends.

From 1957–1967, Ben Kaplan was the executive director of the Sullivan County Hotel Association (Ellenville was included, even though it was in Ulster County). He recalls how the hotels organized a large party in a New York City armory during the winter, with hotels putting ads in a specially published journal, grouped by town. In this era, New York City's newspapers sported endless pages of ads for Catskill hotels.

This was also the time when Catskill resort owners expanded into Miami Beach. Ben Novack of the Laurels built the mammoth Fountainbleu, the epitome of a glitzy Miami Beach modern hotel. The family that ran the White Roe owned the Plymouth and leased the Adams; and the Kutshers owned the Beacon and the Haddon Hall, the latter a well-photographed tropical-deco hotel where my parents ran a restaurant in 1958. The Grossinger family built the Grossinger Beach Hotel in 1940, only to have it requisitioned by the Air Force shortly after it opened, since Miami Beach was a major military installation in World War II. In 1945, they sold it and bought the Pancoast, a previously restricted-to-gentiles hotel; soon after buying the Pancoast, they sold it to a group of investors who were putting up the new Seville Hotel. Dave Levinson of the Tamarack built the Algiers in 1951, and at various times also owned or managed the Marlin, Sorrento, and Edgewater. The Gibbers' owners ran the Cadet, the Olympic ran the Avalon, the Evans had the Seagull and the Governor, the Stevensville operated the Ritz Plaza and Lucerne, and the orthodox Pioneer ran the King David. Charles Yavers left his family hotel, the Loch Sheldrake Inn, in 1950 to open the Nautilus Hotel in Miami Beach. George and

Sarah Blum ran Blum's Hotel in Youngsville in the summer and operated the Lord Balfour in Miami Beach in the winter. As their daughter, Roberta, recounts, "They decided they would like to reside in Miami Beach permanently, so they put their Catskill Mountain hotel up for sale through an ad in the New York Times and were answered by a family so enthusiastically interested in the eighty-eight acres for operating a dude ranch that they exchanged their hotel in Miami Beach [The Viking Hotel] for the Catskill Mountain one, sight unseen."

A crucial element of this 1950s and 1960s period is that these Jews were playing and relaxing to escape fresh, piercing memories of the Holocaust. The escape to the Mountains was in part an escape from the horror of having many of their family and friends killed by the Nazis. A bellhop who spent much time at a resort with many survivors recounted that "for the post–World War II refugees, the survivors from the camps, it was almost like heaven. It was freedom from everything." The resurgence of religiosity or at least Jewish self-awareness led Jews to seek their Jewish cultural roots in the Catskill Yiddishkeit, even though they sought the modernity of affluence and vacation life at the same time; the miracle of the Catskills was that it could provide both.

Even as the golden age brought growing numbers to the Catskills, the seeds of decline were already there. By the mid-1960s, enough hotels were in trouble that the future of the Catskills seemed fragile. But the story of the Catskills' decline can wait until after I tell about the rich life of the area.

Chapter 3

Kuchalayns and Bungalow
Colonies

"It was like an exodus in the summertime. Everybody went."

Whereas Catskill hotels were famous for their food, kuchalayns and bungalow colonies were not—simply because no one was serving you there. You cooked for yourself, and in circumstances that constrained against culinary excess. In the golden age of the 1950s and 1960s, kuchalayns were mainly gone but bungalow colonies were plentiful. Their clientele was younger than the hotel clientele, since many older people were reluctant to do all the work of daily life and preferred being served in a hotel. Sports were also important at many colonies because of the younger clientele, in contrast to the situation at many small hotels.

Kuchalayns

Descending from the early boardinghouses, the kuchalayn lodged people in a large house where renters cooked for themselves in a common kitchen. "Kuch alayn" is Yiddish for "cook alone," and it is variously transliterated as cochalein, kocheleyn, and kuchalein. Some early bungalow colonies were combinations of separate bungalows and a central house with a common kitchen—a kuchalayn. Indeed, the term kuchalayn was frequently used to refer to bungalow colonies.

I had always known about the kuchalayn tradition, though I had not known many people who patronized these places. Interviewing people, I was surprised to find out how many had vacationed this way. In the 1930s, people were paying as little as fifty dollars a summer to live in a kuchalayn. Some owners gave a five-dollar discount if you put down a deposit for the next year before the summer ended. Kuchalayns became more popular during the Depression. Even if poor, city people still wanted a vacation, and a polio epidemic provided extra incentive to leave the city. The kuchalayn worked out better for farming families to run, since the wife could work more on the farm and could sell more farm goods if she didn't have to be cooking and serving for boarders. By the 1940s, costs might be seventy or eighty dollars for a ten-week season. One seventy-four-year-old man, in speaking of his first visit in 1931, said that his family couldn't even afford a kuchalayn, but instead found a farmhouse that was cheaper. There were also *kucheleffls,* where each room had its own stove, though these were far less common.

Eugene Calden was moved to write an essay on his kuchalayn experiences, which he graciously presented to me at the first History of the Catskills conference in 1995. It provides a wonderful glimpse into this communal resort experience. Starting in 1929, he spent summers at his aunt and uncle's kuchalayn at Anawana Lake in Monticello. His aunt and uncle rented houses and leased them in turn to roomers. Then they bought one, calling it Berejansky's Green Apple House. Calden slept with his aunt, uncle, and three cousins in the hayloft above the barn, since they rented all the rooms. The two-floor house had fourteen rooms, with a toilet per floor. At night there were no lights so you had to use a flashlight to get to the bathroom. The proprietors used an outhouse.

Obtaining food was often a project:

Every Friday morning we went with Aunt Minna to buy fresh chickens. The husbands were coming in the evening and most of the women would have a roasted chicken ready for dinner. Aunt Minna drove her vintage Model T Ford to a live chicken farm, where we watched each chicken's throat being cut in the traditional ritual manner by the authorized slaughterer. The creatures were thrown unceremoniously on the grass, where they continued jumping around aimlessly, until succumbing to their fatal wounds. When all the chickens finally stopped dancing, Itchy and I put them in bags and dumped them into the car. We drove back and unloaded them on a table in the grocery. The women rushed in and started squeezing chickens, in order to get the fattest ones. Having made their selections, with their hair up in curlers, the women congregated into chatty groups and started to pluck the feathers.

In the kitchen, there was an icebox for every two families. A dozen gas burners lined a wall, with cupboards below them. "Once in a while someone would look into a neighbor's pot and make critical comments, sometimes with a look or sneer, wounding fragile culinary pride that could result in feuds that would last through the summer."

Just as the hotel owner watched every penny, so too was the kuchalayn proprietor staying on top of everything:

Aunt Minna, with arms folded, somewhat like a prison tower guard, scanned the room. Woe to the woman she spied leaving gas on without cooking something. She would yell, "You're wasting gas; I rent the rooms cheap enough. You'll put me out of business. This isn't Park Avenue." If she stopped there, Aunt Minna was in a good mood. The short wall, with the only window in the room, supported two large sinks, where Aunt Minna went into another tirade if you were caught wasting water. [The water was pumped by an old electric motor that turned a wheel with a leather pulley belt, which continually broke down.]

Each family had its own round table, except for a few unlucky ones that had to share, for there wasn't enough space for any more tables. This invariably led to arguments and negotiations for a reduction in the rent. Aunt Minna, always tactful, informed the complainer, "Nowhere does it say that you have a table alone. I could rent your room fifty times. So if you're not happy you can leave and I'll give you back your money. And don't think I didn't see you throw a cigarette on the lawn. I don't have to pick up after you," she would add for good measure.

Recreation was minimal. For swimming, Calden recalled, the owner drove people to the Neversink River, a mile away, making two trips. I heard from other kuchalayn residents, bungalow dwellers, and hotel guests that they, too, went to that wonderful river as a primary form of recreation. Entertainment was homegrown where Eugene Calden stayed, as at so many other small places. On Saturday night, the dining room tables were moved aside and the chairs put in a semicircle. The owner, Uncle Max, played a mandolin and led the singing with his two sisters, singing in Russian, Polish, and Yiddish. Then Max played dancing music. Following that, a guest told stories. Occasionally there was a mock wedding, skits, and joke telling.

Another early kuchalayn dweller recalled the simple entertainment: "I remember swimming in part of the Neversink, putting my ears to the rails to listen if any train was coming, going into a grotto in the mountain nearby for a cup of cold mineral water." Since proprietors might well promise more than they could deliver, guests were left to their own devices: "I had already become a dog-paddle swimmer and was sorely disappointed to find that the advertised swimming facility was a large mudhole inhabited by catfish. No matter, I and the other boys fashioned a raft and poled our way across and back." This dweller adds, "There were two events which fascinated me: The coming of the *schochet* to slaughter the chickens. [He let] them run around until they bled to death and then hurled [them] into a metal drum. The other was the mock marriage with a man dressed as the bride and a woman as the groom—the ring was made of a raw potato."

Recollections of mock marriages set an early date for an entertainment ritual that was curiously common in Catskill resorts, a burlesque form with switched sex roles and rabbis speaking Yiddish gibberish. Peter Davis's documentary *The Rise and Fall of the Borscht Belt* shows a 1980s revival of the tradition by old Catskill hands now living in summer homes near the site of Laurels on Sackett Lake. For some observers, the gross nature of this event was an unfair smear on the Catskills. Why was the mock wedding so popular? It enabled people to stage an event that reminded them of Lower East Side Jewish vaudeville houses, without having to possess either music or comic skills, and without having to hire any entertainers. As well, the mock marriage was an ethnic self-criticism of the tradition of arranged marriages; in the new world, without the customary arranged marriage, the very institution of marriage could be mocked. Likewise, the rabbi, otherwise a venerated center of the community, could also be the butt of humor and sarcasm. This mockery enabled Jews to keep in mind their ambivalence toward tradition—they sought to break out of tradition to be more American, yet they also felt comfortable in the old, established ways.

A fifty-seven-year-old woman, daughter of a cutter in the garment industry, spoke of going to Kaminsky's twenty-room kuchalayn from the late 1940s through 1955, when she graduated high school:

Well, that place originally was a working farm, and the woman who owned it—her husband passed away and she had all daughters and they all wanted to go to the city, so she had nobody to run the farm. So then she decided to make a kuchalayn out of the place, and she got rid of all the animals and that stuff. She just made it a summer resort place. What they used to do was they used to go shopping for everybody. She used to go around and [ask] everybody [if they] wanted anything in town, and she used to pick up the orders for everybody. Go to the butcher, go to the fruit and vegetable store and whatever, and do all [the] shopping. A couple days per week she used to do that. Pick up milk, bread, the whole bit.

Guests, especially children, often participated in the kuchalayn workday. After all, the farm was a unique experience to urban Jews. As one woman described: "Joe Rakusin ran the farm, and I was his 'nokhshlepper'—taking the three cows out to pasture and feeding them in the barn. On occasion, I would go with him into town via horse and buggy to buy provisions and fill the orders of the mothers."

"Everyone was in close quarters," this woman continued. "They look what each one is cooking to give an idea of what they should make that night." But when asked whether the kuchalayn took away privacy, she responded, "I think nobody ever gave it any thought, it was just natural. That is the way it was supposed to be." After all, "it's like a second family, a second home, because every year the same people were there." Indeed, many of these people were coming from three-generation extended-family living arrangements on the Lower East Side (even if they had recently moved to Brooklyn or the Bronx, areas of second settlement, the memories of the Lower East Side were close at hand and constant family gatherings kept that tradition alive). The kuchalayn was not such a stretch. When she had children, this tenant of Kaminsky's didn't go back to the Catskills because the kuchalayns were gone and "nothing else appealed." She commented, "I think my kids missed out on something by not going to those kuchalayns."

In the Catskills, hierarchy was always present—with the kuchalayn at the bottom. As one kuchalayn dweller recounted:

Then there was a bungalow colony, Jacques or something like that. That was for the richer ones. I used to hear, every so often, when somebody mentioned that they are going to a bungalow colony, "Oh they're rich." Or if someone who went for years at the kuchalayn, and all of a sudden, that someone is not coming there, they are going to the bungalow colony: "Oh, oh they've gone up in the world."

When I queried, "Then the hotels were a whole other step?" she exclaimed, "That was the rich, rich! You came from Scarsdale or something!"

Bungalow Colonies

Bungalow colonies were groups of small cottages, frequently arranged in a semicircle or oval, with various features depending on their size and level of quality. Individual bungalows might have as little as one bedroom and a living room/kitchen combination; others might be more substantial. Colonies with a dozen or more bungalows were likely to have a social hall or casino, but only larger colonies provided much in the way of outside entertainment. Handball courts, basketball courts, softball diamonds, and (later) pools provided recreation. Commonly there was a store run by the owner, where people bought food and household items. Starting in the 1950s, day camps became prevalent.

Why did Jews in the Catskills develop the bungalow colony style of resort? It is, after all, unique to Jewish vacationers, at least in its origins. The bungalow colony is an odd mix of vacation and community living styles. There are two direct sources related to vacationing. One is the ramshackle expansion of boarding houses and outbuildings, an inexpensive way to expand small business. It did not take too much construction skill to put up these small buildings, especially for farmers used to fashioning large chicken coops. Even if plumbers and electricians needed to be called in for some of the work, these modest dwellings were an easy way to go. The other source is the copying of the gentile and, later, German Jewish cottage parks, which were wealthy houses grouped together but without the degree of sharing and contact found in the bungalows.

Besides these two vacationing styles, the bungalow colonies reflect a community living style that has roots in the Eastern European *shtetl*. Shtetl relationships were maintained in New York City in the neighborhood groupings where people lived, in their synagogues that were often named after the members' town of origin, and the *landsmanschaftn* societies that provided friendship and economic communitarianism for people originating from the same shtetl. From this background, it made sense to live in a bungalow colony largely populated by neighbors, friends, and relatives, where people could share varying degrees of responsibility for shopping, child care, and entertainment. So the bungalow colony has characteristics of a transplanted shtetl, though much modified.

As with the boarding house and then the hotel business, people often started up their enterprises without much background. As one veteran recalled, "My dad, David, purchased our bungalow colony in 1941, swapping his diner and armed with just New York City smarts. He never held a hammer, sawed a piece of wood, re-primed a failed pump, or moved a refrigerator in his life." Their colony survived until 1961, when they sold it to a black church group.

Some colonies were still making the transition in the 1930s from the kuchalayn period and so offered both facilities. Where a kuchalayn in the 1930s might cost fifty dollars, a bungalow in the same place would go for ninety dollars. Even in the late 1940s, some places, such as Camp White Lake, combined a kuchalayn with a bungalow colony. A season's bungalow there went for around $250, five times the weekly salary of the man whose son remembered this place.

Irwin Richman writes of his family's colony in Woodbourne that developed from a kuchalayn when they built two duplex bungalows in 1940. In Richman's kuchalayn phase: "Rent for the season (July 4th to Labor Day) was $90, and Grandma (who ran the business) collected $3 per week from each tenant for 'gas and electric.' Gas was via propane tank. In a day when a tank of propane cost $5 and electricity was very cheap and electrical appliances few (irons and an occasional broiler), 'gas and electric' was a lucrative profit center."

Once the Richmans built their bungalows, they rented them for $125 a season, plus utilities, but by 1943 they were up to $250 a season, and then $400 by 1945. Kuchalayn rooms remained available in the main house, rising to $125 and then to $300 during World War II. This provided a good income:

> With taxes on the property around $100 per year and services minimal, the return was very satisfactory. . . . By 1945, the rental income was $2,700 (plus gas and electric) and the total cost of house, grounds, and bungalows, including furnishings, had been approximately $6,500. With expenses running about $500 a season (taxes, insurance, utilities, repairs), the return on principal was outstanding—and we had our "free" summers in the mountains.

But like all Mountain businesses, it was not worry free:

> When tenants arrived, they were expected to pay in full upon arrival. There was anguish if they waited a day or two or suggested a payment schedule—what would happen if they backed out? When payment was made by check, the check would be deposited as quickly as possible.

"The season" was serious business. You either made the money in the eight weeks, or you lost it.

Some colony operators set up payment schedules calling for preseason installments in January, March, and May. Large colonies held "reunions" at New York City restaurants during the winter in order to collect deposits.

For some farmers, bungalows were an investment for the future, when they would be too old to farm. Bungalows were easy and inexpensive to build, and farmers usually had enough skills to do it. Even when farming operations ceased, bungalow colony owners were often called "farmers" by their renters. In 1945, a boom was on:

> When the war ended, the demand on the mountains was overwhelming. You could rent anything! Not only did more people have more money than before the war and more cars, but as veterans returned home, they returned to an incredible housing shortage. Many had to double up with their in-laws. The summer could provide an escape. The "farmers" rallied for the buck. Even chicken coops (not ours) became bungalows.

So great was the post–World War II housing shortage in New York City that one bungalow colony owner even bought fifteen retired New York City trolleys, but the owner couldn't get permission from transportation officials to move them on the highway.

An interesting variant is the bungalow colony that was essentially a family compound rather than a commercial establishment. I heard from one person how a mini-colony started from simply a search for summer places for eight families of relatives:

> In 1944, after spending several years in different kuchalayns, my father, Max Rennert, and his brothers went looking for a place to permanently bring their families to from New York City during the summer months. They purchased the house, barn, and 100 acres of land from a farmer up a dirt road off Route 52, between the Brentwood Bungalows and Brown's Hotel.

In preparing the place for habitation, a workman's carelessness during the winter caused a fire that destroyed the house.

Since they knew they had to get away that summer, they decided to build some temporary bungalows for the family and friends who were buying into this venture. They went up to Liberty and managed to get some workmen and materials and finished two bungalows with four apartments in each (a walk-in kitchen, small bath, and one bedroom to the back). They also built a pump house for the water pump and a service house for the water heater and washing machine as well as the propane gas attachments. They started putting in phone lines later. Those temporary buildings lasted from 1945 until we sold the place in the late 1980s.

They never rented to others, but just kept for family and friends' use the place they named "Ren-Ka-Scher," after several family names. These noncommercial colonies were somewhat common and often were composed of roomier houses than typical bungalows. They were rarely called colonies; for some reason, people tended to call them "country clubs," such as the Jay-Mar Country Club and S.I.G.'s Country Club, named for Sarah and Isidore Goldberg. (A good number of hotels also called themselves country clubs.)

Another such family place was the Wachtel Colony in White Lake. Six brothers, a sister, and three cousins bought their five acres in 1930 for around $500, after they had been coming several years just to vacation. In the words of a forty-two-year-old woman who still vacations there every summer, "We're still die-hard Catskill goers," and "I would say that I am one of the more impassioned people. There is something in all of us—all of the cousins—you just mention it. There is something healing about going back there." Proudly noting that "my kids are, I think, the thirty-fifth or thirty-sixth kids in the fifth generation," she tells the history: "These ten purchased the land together, and then the land was partitioned into ten partitions. There were nine houses built in a semicircle on the lakefront, and then there was one extra little house on the road behind it. It stands that way now as it was in 1934." As she puts it, "We call it a schlock family compound."

The relatives set strict rules that the houses were not to be rented out. Some houses have barely been occupied over the last two decades and are falling apart. Yet there are some weekends when every house is occupied, with relatives coming from Ohio, California, and Philadelphia. When an owner dies, the house remains in the family and sales must be to blood relatives. These colony relatives had a semiformal system of running the place:

There were committees made. They would have these meetings, which they still do once or twice a summer. It happened more often when I was younger. A rep from each house would drag a chair down to what we call the campus—the common green right in front of the houses. They'd sit in a circle. There are these old books. All the family personalities would come out when these meetings would happen. There was always the one that lost his temper and the one trying to calm everyone down. People would get very impassioned about whose garbage pail was being used. Generally [we were] a wonderful loving family. But you live together for a summer and personalities come out. There would be people in charge of keeping the grounds nice. There were all kinds of rules made by a rep from each house. You can't hang towels on porches that face the lake because it doesn't look nice. There are no dogs allowed. Very clear rules about not selling. It's okay to have friends come up.

They even had a somewhat organized summer camp with flag raising and the pledge of allegiance for the twenty to thirty children that stayed there in the earlier years, up to the 1960s, when the colony was filled all summer:

There was a flag captain. It changed every week. I think there was a captain and an assistant. They were in charge at night of taking the flag down, and if it ever rained. For one of the jobs, somebody would walk to the village and get the mail and bring it to each house. Another job was milk order. There was a dairy that would deliver. One person was in charge of going to each person's house and finding [out] what they needed, then posting it on the water house. At the end of the summer, there was a big flag-raising ceremony. Uncle Mac would give out a bit of money to the kids for doing their jobs, and Charms [candy].

This woman reflects on the closeness of the family connections. "There was a very group feeling. There were other people watching. Everybody was everybody's kid. My daughter said to me the other day, 'When you're at White Lake, you have so many parents.' It still feels that way to them."

This colony's family group made a video to document their generations on White Lake. Interestingly, she notes, "The one thing I learned from doing that documentary thing, I always assumed that the grandmothers and grandfathers bought this place so that the family could stay connected over the generations. No. They bought this thing so that they could have some quiet on the weekends." Nevertheless, the colony did preserve family ties. Many come up for collective Chanukah celebrations and Passover Seders. To commemorate this legacy, "We made these White Lake Wachtel Colony T-shirts five years ago. We had one cousin who was an artist design them. I was in charge of calling all the cousins and taking the orders. July 4th weekend we handed them out. We have pictures of a hundred people wearing these bright blue T-shirts."

Like hotels, colonies often started small and kept growing each year. An ex-hotel owner recalled the Gold and Rados bungalow colony: "They built themselves up nicely. And you know they started with nothing. They'd build one bungalow at a time. They didn't do like the big hotels, all of a sudden splurge, and with a swimming pool and with all those things. Little by little, every year they'd build another bungalow, or two bungalows, and they have a beautiful place." Pools were a big expense, and for some owners the money came in a curious fashion. In the 1950s, New York City achieved a major boost in water supply from the completion of the Neversink Dam, thus making the river too warm and too shallow to swim in. Bungalow colony owners with riparian rights received amounts up to $15,000 for this loss, and many built swimming pools to replace the lost swimming spots.

Some colony owners benefited from the constant return of large cliques of people, often meaning that they never had a vacancy to advertise. But such groups might break up or decide to change locations after many years, and the proprietor would then have to scramble for people to fill up the place.

In many cases, the renter's choice of a bungalow over a hotel was economic, but not always; it might be a matter of cultural connections and personality style. One woman told me, "I knew some families went for a week or so to a hotel. But that was kind of foreign to us. We didn't go to hotels." When asked if that was because of the family's modest means, she replied:

No. We were probably not of modest means, but I think it was because of my family background, because my family were immigrants. You are what you are, and you bring your background to whatever you do. The hotel was just a foreign thing to do. It was not an expectation. You couldn't go to a hotel for a whole summer. It was more important to go there for the whole summer. My mother was the immigrant type that loved to cook. She also loved to go to this place where she could pick blueberries. These were things from the old country that she could relate to. There was a place called the Majestic Hotel. We had the Majestic Hotel in Hurleyville and there would be lovely blueberry bushes

CHAPTER 3

and she would go with these big tremendous pots and a smock to put on her head to keep from the sun. She would go with friends, but they would each go their separate way because they shouldn't steal each other's good bushes. They would come back with these huge pots of blueberries. My mother would bake these wonderful blueberry pies, or cakes. They were more like cakes because they didn't have a crust. I don't think my mother ever went to a hotel in her whole life.

In his book *Borscht Belt Bungalows,* Irwin Richman makes a strong point that the colony-hotel distinction was not primarily economic. He notes that wealthy customers rented at his family's place because they were "my grandfather's landsmen [fellow residents from the old country] and longtime buddies." From working in other colonies, he observed that it was common for doctors and lawyers, as well as teachers, to stay in bungalow colonies.

Some chose the colonies for the greater friendships that were possible: "Looking back, I seemed to have enjoyed the years spent in a bungalow colony for the camaraderie more than I did at the hotel. At the hotel, I would meet you and you'd be here for a week or two and then you're gone. I was up there for the whole summer. It was different. I found it a lot nicer in the bungalow colonies."

A forty-four-year-old man, whose parents started vacationing in the Mountains in 1951 and still go there, spoke of other reasons for going to a bungalow colony:

I think for two reasons, one was the flexibility of not having to have three meals a day and be locked into being at the hotel. We ate out, I remember, quite a bit, and my mother cooks and she liked to do that, and it gave me more flexibility. But I'm sure that [it was] the fact that it would have been much more expensive for three weeks in a hotel. There were summers where we would have gone away for a month like maybe July or August.

A woman in her fifties recounted the ease of her bungalow experiences at Daitch's Paradise Inn in South Fallsburg in the 1950s and early 1960s:

It was easy. The husbands were gone. You just had your kids. The bungalows were little and, you know, nothing really to clean up. If they got messy, you just cleaned it up. . . . When the kids were young, . . . the kids had freedom. They could run around the bungalow colony, so I had freedom. You know, we played mah-jongg, the women. We went shopping a little. We would play mah-jongg at night because the kids would go to sleep in the bungalow. The bungalow colonies were not fenced in, but like an enclosure, and we would play in somebody's bungalow and run over every once in a while and listen. Or the kids knew where to get up and find us, or some of the older kids would all be hanging around outside, so they would listen and come tell us if one of the kids cried. We cooked; it was nice. We cooked and we had things going on with all the women. It was great. It was visiting and freedom that we didn't have in the city.

Safety was another kind of freedom. Recalling seven summers in the 1960s, a woman spoke of how free her children were: "We came from the city, and [they were] at a young age; they weren't allowed to go out by themselves in the evening. My grandchildren certainly in this day and age don't go out by themselves. Up there they are allowed to roam the colony till 10 P.M."

Bungalow colonies fostered a cooperative system. Families took turns watching the children. One colony dweller remembered, "We used to make birthday parties with the children and invite all the kids. Sometimes we had thirty children at the birthday party. It was very exciting because everyone participated, like one big family." Another man said, "It was a time of great communality, almost a kind of utopia. Everybody was sort of equal." At Richman's colony, women took turns to have a "girls' night out"—half the mothers watched the others' children while the other half walked to town to the movies.

The same cooperative mentality helped renters create their own entertainment. In the 1940s, small colonies such as Richman's didn't provide paid entertainers, so people kicked in a quarter a person to a party fund, supplemented by five dollars from the owner, and bought hot dogs, soda, and marshmallows. Richman describes how those parties grew: "In 1952 we had added another 'improvement,' an outdoor speaker for our phonograph, so people could have music on the lawn. Now with the patio, dancing became a regular event at the Saturday night parties, and parties became more regular."

But it was not the utopia mentioned above, if that meant egalitarianism. Bungalow colonies could have clear hierarchies. A longtime renter remembered that even at the bungalow colonies there was a hierarchy of class:

The bungalows were situated in a semicircle on a hill. The structures at the top of the hill were nicer and they became more dilapidated on the decline. A couple at the end were practically uninhabitable and the kids said they were haunted. Because we were poor and stayed only one week, we always occupied a bungalow at the low end. It was humiliating for me, an emotional state that is punctuated by the olfactory memory of stale, rancid rooms and furniture, especially the kitchen.

Like the kuchalayn, a bungalow colony often had its own store to sell food and supplies to renters. Since few people had cars before the 1950s, this was often the main source of necessities. But these stores were typically less well-stocked and more expensive than local stores. One colony owner's child remembered the frustration of competition: "My father also resented it when the tenants went to Monticello to do their grocery shopping rather than doing it at our store on the premises." Weekend husbands were another source of frustration as they often packed shopping bags full of food to bring from New York City. Loyalty was another factor: When my parents arrived in the Catskills one year without jobs in hand, we had no place to live, so we rented a shabby bungalow for two preseason weeks from a George and Miriam Shapiro, who had a colony in Kauneonga Lake. I remember helping out in the store there, and my parents' feeling compelled to buy from George, despite the high prices.

Not all bungalow colonies had concessions, but even those that did could not carry all the necessities. So peddlers arrived:

The butcher used to come. Somebody on the colony worked at a butcher's, so every Friday he'd come early. . . . We'd all make orders with him. So the food was coming in, and big, big bags of chicken feet we used to put in chicken soup, you know. It was wonderful. It was a wonderful time. I look back on it with great joy. There were constantly cars and peddlers pulling up in the bungalow colony. One guy would pull up his entire wagon—he had a station wagon—it was piled without breathing space. He had sheets, and pillowcases, and we'd stand and bargain for sheets. Then a guy would come up who used to yell, "The *shmatte* man is here!" with bathing suits and blouses. . . . You had the knish man every night [who] would come by, and you'd buy knishes or the Takee cups, with the little cup that you could eat the Chinese food. . . . The merry-go-round man would come by in a big truck with a merry-go-round. . . . There was just constantly something going on all the time. And the kids would go on the merry-go-round and pay a nickel, or whatever they charged for it. It was just constant, constant. That loudspeaker didn't stop announcing, "The *shmatte* man, the bathing suit. . . ." "You vant bathing suits, go to the parking lot; you vant this, go here. . . ." It was constant.

I must admit that I shared the attitudes of hotel staff and guests in looking down on bungalow dwellers. Perhaps my own attempts at upward mobility from a working-class, occasional small business family made me think less of people who weren't staying in better accommodations. What male hotel staff did appreciate about bungalow colonies was that they provided an alternative source of girls to meet. In the same way that colony dwellers came to hotels looking to crash shows, bungalow girls came looking for boys—just as the male hotel staff were more appealing to young female guests than the teenage male guests, they were more attractive to bungalow girls than their boy neighbors.

Evolution

As an institution, the kuchalayn was doomed. There was, curiously, a brief revival of kuchalayns after World War II, when the severe housing shortage put many married couples back in their parents' houses, leaving them to relish the time away in the summer, no matter how plain it might be. But ultimately, one writer notes, "the suburban housewife who presided over a modern kitchen would have no part of the primitive facilities of a kuchalayn. The families living in modern split-level houses of suburbia were not attracted to bungalows, which were crude wooden shacks." This writer's prediction was accurate for the kuchalayns, though bungalow colonies managed to stay around for quite a while. In the 1950s and 1960s, some bungalow colonies even expanded, the larger ones adding day camps, improving pools, and to a slight degree bolstering entertainment. In the 1950s, Cutler's Cottages in South Fallsburg was one of the largest colonies, with 150 bungalows, some of them specially fixed up for wealthier customers who returned yearly. Cutler's day camp even had children bused in from Ellenville. Since they didn't require services for guests, the colonies were unfazed by the hotels' problems in attracting staff, providing expensive entertainers, building and maintaining indoor pools and other costly facilities, and keeping up large sagging buildings. There were some necessary costs for expansion, such as minimal entertainment and improved sports fields and courts, but these were very small compared to what hotels faced for their modernizing needs.

By the mid-1960s, small colonies rented small units for around $275 a season, large units for $450. But larger colonies with many amenities got $600 to $800 for a one-bedroom bungalow and $1,000 to $1,200 for two-bedroom ones. Day camp was an extra $65 to $125 per child, and even entertainment was charged, ranging from $35 to $150 a couple.

This was also an era of change in renters' age structure. As Richman describes:

> How did our tenants change? I remember the buzz that went through the colony when we rented to the Karotkins—a couple in their late sixties—in the mid 1950s. While some of our tenants had been with us a long time and were near this age, the Kay's, as everyone called them, were the first people without young children to rent at Richman's. Behind their backs they were called the "Old People." Within the next few years, most of our crowd was old people. By the mid-1960s, we didn't have any resident children. . . . Because we lacked a pool, only our older tenants stayed with us. Most of them were European born, and as they aged, the religious practices of their youth became more important and, with most of the men in retirement, they had more time on their hands. Cards and TV couldn't fill it all. In the 1960s, our religious tenants organized evening prayers in our garage.

Some hotels like the Irvington, Evan's Kiamesha, and Grand Mountain had their own colonies attached, where the rental price included the hotel's sports facilities and entertainment. Other hotels had special arrangements where colony residents could pay a seasonal fee to use neighboring hotel amenities, as with the Sunshine Colony and Tamarack Lodge. The Esther Manor bought up nearby colonies, partly to protect its surroundings, and they sold not only entertainment use but dining room privileges as well.

In the 1990s, more bungalow colonies than hotels remain. Fires were less common in bungalow colonies, and if they occurred they did not destroy a whole huge building, as might happen with the main part of a hotel. Nor was there much incentive to demolish abandoned bungalow colonies, as occurred with hotels. The less-expensive maintenance allowed some colonies to continue in operation. Other colonies became condos, offering cheap summer homes. There are a fair number of well-kept colonies catering to a nonreligious clientele, but the number of colonies catering to religious clientele is greater. Hasidim and other ultraorthodox Jews found colonies easy to adapt as summer lodgings and religious institutions. When you speak of bungalow colonies at present, this is the population that most people immediately think of. Throughout Sullivan and Ulster Counties, these groups dominate the colonies, many of which are quite dilapidated. Occupied units often share the grounds with crumbled ones. Ironically, then, the lower end of the resort spectrum remains more visible at present, and many abandoned colonies stand silent witness to the glorious past.

Chapter 4

Hotel Life

"For the first time, you had a luxury vacation offered to a working-class population."

Why were so many people—including my parents—willing to make a go at the hotel business? In part, it was not too expensive to get into the business—at least at the low end. Frank Goldstein's father bought six hundred acres in Hurleyville in 1905 for $8–9,000 to build the Morningside, one of the largest and most elegant hotels of the 1920s to 1940s. He was a plumbing contractor who had lost money in New York City real estate, so he moved to the Catskills. Because he was a plumber he could easily put bathrooms into the hotel, at a time when many others had outhouses: "Most farmhouses and most of the hotels had outhouses. Because of my father's ability, he put baths and toilets in the hotel. So, we became a fashionable hotel." Other proprietors adapted their skills to the hotel business as well. One of the Granite's owners was a carpenter who was able to build many of the hotel buildings himself. The Aladdin's owner was a civil engineer, so he built an outdoor pool, maintained much of the equipment, and in later years built an indoor pool.

The Flagler, in South Fallsburg, was also elaborate at an early time. Unlike many other resorts, it did not begin as a farm, but as a gentile hotel built in 1872. Asias Fleischer and Philip Morganstern acquired it in 1908, turning it into a kosher hotel. As early as 1920 it housed over 250 guests, and its hot and cold running water and telephones in each room were a rarity for that era. The Flagler's 1,500-seat theater was the largest in Sullivan County at that time. The Brickmans bought Pleasant Valley Farm in 1910 for $4,000; it included ninety-eight acres, a thirteen-room farmhouse, a barn, supplies, and livestock. The $400 down payment came from the Jewish Agricultural Society and was paid off at $50 a year.

In the economic boom of the post–World War I era, Murray Posner of the Brickman's remembers, "Everybody was putting up these stucco buildings." One hotel veteran recalled how in 1926 the Granite Orchard House (later the Granite) was bought by his father, two grandfathers, an uncle, and one outsider. Combined, they put down $2,500 and were left with a $3,000 mortgage, payable annually at $250, including interest. Another hotel child recounted that her grandfather actually bought a hotel for his wife as an anniversary present. From another person came this memory: "My father bought a hotel because he loved the idea that he could play pinochle and the business would keep going at the same time."

On October 15, 1929, less than two weeks before the great stock market crash, Hyman Jacobs bought the Cozy Nook, a farm nestled on a hill overlooking Route 52 between Liberty and Loch Sheldrake. The property consisted of a guesthouse, with about twenty rooms, and a large barn. He invested $1,000—the proceeds from the sale of his tailor store in the Ridgewood section of Queens. He "borrowed" $500 each from his son Harry and his son-in-law Herman Tischler. He changed the name to the Jacob Inn, which later became the Delmar Hotel. The hotel remained in the family until 1986, operated most of that time by Hyman's son, Max Jacobs, and his son's wife, Claire.

As I mentioned in a previous chapter, resorts were often started for health reasons. Another such example was the Excelsior: "My family got to the Catskills because my mother had TB. . . . My grandparents had a cousin who already ran a small hotel in Liberty, so [in the 1920s] they bought the adjacent farm of eighty-four acres that had a large wood-frame house with a lovely porch and moved in with the idea of starting their own hotel like that of their cousins, the Fleischmanns, and caring for my mother."

Even during the Depression, some people entered the hotel business. Anne Chester, her husband, his brother, and his brother's wife owned a summer home in Woodbourne, and their New York real estate business was hit hard in the Depression, so they started a resort, Chester's Zunbarg (Yiddish for Sun Hill).

Carrie Komito still runs the Aladdin Hotel that her parents bought sixty-five years ago in 1932, after being guests there for ten years, "before my mother got us into this mess." They entered the hotel business in a curious way:

> In 1932, the people that owned this place before us were neighbors with my parents in the city. They had a butcher shop; my parents had a paper store. When they moved here, they put up the main building. The man had eleven children. Instead of turning in the money, they were spending it. He was an easy parent. Business was good so he put up the second building. He was getting $18 a week. With the new building, he charged $30. He was being foreclosed. We were guests here. Every time my mother came out of the dining room, they way-laid her and asked her to help out, until one day she went with them and bought off the second mortgage.

The end of World War II brought another major building boom. Comedian Mac Robbins put this in perspective in terms of places he worked: "After the war I worked as a tummler at the Lorraine, then the next year at the Anderson, then at the Rose Glow, later the Delano out on Liberty Road. They were owned by a milliner, a furrier, and a barber who [each] had a few bucks after the war and bought a hotel up here. A lot of people were doing that then."

For $70,000, Charles and Lillian Brown bought the Black Apple in 1944 from the Appel family, who had run it since they built the Black Apple Inn in the early 1920s. For another $100,000 in renovations, Brown's began its famed career as one of the largest hotels, and it only closed in the 1990s. With their money, the Appel family bought two Miami Beach resorts, the Ritz on 14th Street and Collins Avenue, and the McAlpin a block south of that. Like other Catskill operators, they had prior experience with Miami Beach, running the Seabreeze on 5th Street two decades earlier.

Harry and Ann Portnoy had saved money from operating a grocery store in Jackson Heights in Queens, New York, during World War II. They were very excited to buy the Seven Gables Hotel in 1946 for $32,000. This small place held 100–110 guests, with twenty-five rooms in the White House, thirty in the Main House, and four in the Bungalow (hotels often had such small buildings, though they were larger than bungalow colony units and were only filled with hotel rooms, not self-cooking units). The owners felt like they were climbing the social ladder. They never made much money, coming home with a few thousand at the end of the season. Because they lived there six months a year, living and food cost them nothing for half the year. But they felt it was a prestigious thing to own a hotel, and that counted a lot. My parents also joined that post–World War II hotel boom, buying their hotel in 1946.

Hotel ownership was often a hand-to-mouth operation. As a second-generation owner of a hundred-room hotel remembers: "We were so poor, there was no profit. It was just a matter of having a place to live and have food on the table. We lived on grains and beans. We lived on credit. We paid it off in the summertime." Many male owners retained city jobs for the security. Some proprietors took on extra work, as with the owner who worked as a school bus driver, which required providing his own station wagon. He bid very low in able to win the contract and hence be able to buy a new wagon, which he also needed for the hotel. One owner of a rooming house/colony combination painted many hotels and colonies in the neighboring area during the off-season; as his son remembers: "He was famous for his sponge and stencil work on the walls, which he often painted while singing Yiddish songs." Another hotel owner ran a full-time painting contractor business while still operating the hotel with his three brothers and their wives. Sometimes the profits were not enough to support owners through the year. Proprietors of small- and medium-size hotels and bungalow colonies, along with their children, often worked in larger hotels in the off-season. That often included Passover, since very small hotels lacked heating facilities to open that early.

Hotels with a full range of facilities and entertainment did not spring up overnight. Early hotels had few amenities, and owners only developed them when they worried that competitors were taking away their guests. Many staff members worked multiple jobs, whereas in the "mature" years of the Catskills, from World War II to the early 1970s, it was mostly only the small "shlock houses" that maintained the practice of multiple jobs. In most places my parents or I worked, there was a social director—often called the social macher—who organized calisthenics, arranged and announced special trips or activities, emceed shows and other nighttime entertainment, and sometimes sang or joked on stage. But there were special staff for most other tasks—lifeguards, bellhops, camp directors, camp counselors, chauffeurs, waiters, busboys, chambermaids, kitchen help, maintenance staff.

One area where multiple jobs remained important was in hotel basketball teams, which played an informal intramural league. Large resorts, such as Young's Gap, Kutsher's, Brickman's, Klein's Hillside, and the Ambassador, hired college players for the dining room. Criteria for the job included basketball rather than dining room skills, and players such as Bob Cousy and Wilt Chamberlain were among the recruits. Betting pools resulted in point shaving, and racketeers recruited players in the Catskills for regular college season game fixing.

Expansion moved slowly for most hotels, which lacked the ready capital of the large entrepreneurs. Some early hotels even had guests sharing rooms with strangers. Private rooms came later and were often smaller than the average motel room, even though a family of four might sleep there. Bathrooms were shared in most of the smaller hotels, with a smaller number of higher-priced rooms containing baths and, less commonly, telephones. For many of the smaller resorts, things stayed this way even until the last years of the 1970s.

Catskill hotels were built in a continuous process over many decades. Even many of the large hotels had started as farms and kuchalayns. This was a very unique style of growing by accretion, always adding to buildings. Many hotels used the "Sullivan Country mission" style, a unique style that some believe is derivative of Californian mission architecture, but which bears strong similarity to Polish synagogue architecture of the eighteenth and nineteenth centuries. In fact, Monticello's Landfield Avenue shul, built in 1912, and the Mountaindale shul, built in 1914, have a mission style that precedes any mission architecture in hotels. You can see this mission style in the most curious places: On the main street of Mountaindale, there is a small bungalow next to the shul that has the rounded mission top added on, even though it is completely out of place on such a small building; a small store or storage building on Route 42 in South Fallsburg similarly features that pattern. Others emulated Grossinger's half-Tudor and stucco architecture. Hardly any small- and smaller medium-size hotels employed architects; they used easy designs instead. This led in some resorts (including some larger ones that *did* use architects) to strings of buildings connected by corridors, with weird connections between wings and many small series of steps up and then down where old buildings were connected.

In the 1950s and 1960s, medium and large hotels typically put modern fronts onto those older styles, giving a semblance of continuity between buildings and freshening up old facades. Medium-size hotels might construct one or more modern buildings of twenty to thirty fancier rooms with private baths. Smaller hotels might add separate buildings, especially "bungalows," that had from four to ten rooms. Almost every small hotel had the "Main House," containing the office, main lobby, kitchen, and dining room. If owners put up a second large building, it was often called the "Annex" or the "White House." Is there any clearer way to signal the desire to be American than to call your building the "White House"? But other fanciful names were also employed. At

Stier's Hotel, the outbuildings were named after trees—the Redwood, the Pine, and the Spruce. At the Delmar, the buildings were named after French resorts—the Biaritz, the Capri, the Deauville, the Lido, and the Riviera. At Brown's, aristocratic names prevailed: Regency, Princess, and Empress. In some small places, the casino was a separate building, occasionally attached by a porch to another building. No matter what size the hotel, it most likely had more buildings than seemed rational.

Brochures and postcards commonly advertised the resorts as being far more elegant than they were. Don Prowler, showing slides of his tremendous collection of hotel postcards, pointed out that postcards frequently were seemingly aerial views, but in reality were just rendered by the artist. Many nonaerial shots were likewise rendered. In some cases, optimistic owners had postcards printed showing buildings that they *planned* to build, but never did. Prowler views this as the proprietors' way of saying, "This is our vision of ourselves." Brochures showed tennis and basketball courts as they might have been three decades ago, when at present they were in fact quite disheveled. These promotional materials were often used many years after they were printed, so that hotels without day camps might still advertise not only day camps but also "full teen programs."

Hotel Owners

Family Operations

Catskill hotels were family operations. Sometimes one family owned the whole business, but frequently a hotel would be owned by two or more related families to maximize capital and provide most of the management without hiring outsiders. Ownership was often as quirky as you could imagine. The three Charlow brothers who co-owned the Irvington Hotel, which held about two hundred guests, gradually built fifty bungalows on separately controlled parts of the huge property, each retaining ownership of the units they built. The particular kind of owner partnerships that were necessary to run these small- to medium-size hotels were part of an old world/new immigrant culture. They were hard to recreate in later years, and thus new partnerships were unlikely to emerge to keep the hotels alive—even if the other components of the Catskills' decline had not been so powerful.

This form of partner ownership meant lots of bosses running around, keeping tabs on staff—and on each other. A common division of labor would be one as kitchen steward, one as office manager, one as financial manager, another in charge of the physical plant. In one smaller medium-size hotel with three part-ners, one woman served as maitre d'. Even though they had some degree of specialization, any boss could tell any worker what to do, and never hesitated to do so. Sometimes more than one owner tried to run the kitchen, and sparks flew. The office, too, was a source of control. One owner commented on the power of the cashier in running the inner office:

> You have to control the books. You have to control the bills, and also, by virtue of the fact that you are now controlling the departures, you also, in a sense, control other departments, like the kitchen. The kitchen [chef] has to know how many meals to prepare for. The maitre d' in the dining room has to know what vacancies there are at different tables. The housekeeper has to know what beds to strip and what beds to make. And the front office has to know also what vacancies are cre-ated by the departures.

In a good number of hotels, the women handled the bulk of daily operating. Sometimes this was because the men retained jobs in the city to make enough money, to keep seniority in the garment trades, or because they couldn't stand the routine exasperation of running a resort. Some owners ran businesses on the side, even during the season, in order to ensure sufficient income. Other times, men were present but stayed in the background because they were too volatile and could not offer the familial friendliness that was expected of a Catskill proprietor. Men could often not resist taking on a male role, though: One owner's husband worked at his business in the city and was relatively un-involved with the hotel, yet he was the one who attended the Hotelmen's As-sociation meetings. Women were less likely than their husbands to be building careers or nonhotel businesses, so they had a greater propensity to run hotels. A good number of owner's children speak of the very women-centered com-munity of hotel management. Sunny Oaks in Woodridge, where we hold the History of the Catskills conferences, is now in its fourth generation of opera-tion in a matrilineal line. One owner's daughter said she grew up thinking men and women could do the same work, since that's what she observed in the ho-tel business, seeing women as owners and decision-makers.

There was one curious variant of hotel operation: Some hotel operators merely rented hotels from owners and ran them for a season or two. In the late 1920s, a doctor referred William Fink, a skirt operator in the garment industry, to a particular farmhouse in Woodridge for his health. Over sixty years later, his daughter recalls his experience:

> He stayed ten days and was hooked on the lovely climate and setting. That summer, when the garment center closed for a few weeks, he took his family there. He rented a horse and buggy, and with my uncle as his partner, he sold ice cream all summer, while my mom and her children vacationed. Then, in 1929, he saw an ad in the *Forward* advertising the Apple Grove Hotel for rent. The two partners ran that hotel, and did likewise in a host of others—the Lake Shore Chateau and the Sackett Lake Lodge in Sackett Lake; Goldberg's, the Capital, and the Park Manor in Loch Sheldrake; the Grand Mountain in Glen Wild; the Ferndale Mansion in Ferndale; the Arcadia in Hurleyville; the Anderson in Monticello; and the Evans Kiamesha and the Rosemont Lodge in Kiamesha Lake. Loyal customers would follow them from one hotel to the next.

In a similar variant, hotel operators joined existing owners as partners for one or a few years. These operators had a sizeable following of guests whom they could bring to the hotel, and they didn't have to put up a lot of money for the temporary partnership:

> The first hotel that I remember we had was the Sunset Villa in Woodbourne. There we went to Greenfield Park to the Windsor Lake and Camp. We were there three years. From there we went to the Warnock House in Loch Sheldrake. From there my father became partners with Ben Lestitsky, who built the Capitol Hotel and Camp in Loch Sheldrake. We were there for ten years. After the Capitol, we spent three years at the Normandie Hotel with Hammerman and Deutsch. After that we went to the Levbourn hotel in Woodbourne with Mrs. Camille who owned the hotel. After that we went to the New Leroy in Loch Sheldrake, and after that I didn't go to the mountains anymore.

Hotel owners had to come up with a variety of devices to satisfy guests. The classic tummlers were always poised to engage in wild antics to entertain people who were on the verge of leaving after several days of rain. When the kitchen was running late in preparations for the meal, owners could simply hold off on opening the dining room doors for ten or fifteen minutes. But what happened if the kitchen got bogged down once the meal began? A family member tells this delightful story:

> At the Granite, the orchestra played in the dining room. A march shepherded the guests in when the doors opened, and background music entertained them through the meal. "It was usually on [the very crowded] Sundays that the orchestra was called upon when the kitchen fell behind. The orchestra would play the "Star Spangled Banner," usually between the soup and main dish courses, and the guests would stand in respect. As soon as they sat down, the band would play the "Hatikvah" [the Israeli national anthem], and again the guests would stand. This would give the kitchen about five or more minutes to catch up. Of course, after many years, the guests became wise and realized what was happening whenever the orchestra played the "Star Spangled Banner."

Precarious Finances

Bosses lived with the constant threat of drunken laborers disappearing, or waiters talking back to them and bad-mouthing them to the guests. Waiters usually came in as late as possible to set up for breakfast, because they were partying late the night before. When I worked as a waiter, instead of sitting down to eat staff breakfast, we filled a tall glass with coffee and drank it while setting up. One owner found this untenable and frequently yelled at me, "Philly, what are you, on drugs or something, drinking coffee like that?" Waiters could deflate a bossy owner or difficult chef by telling guests to not order a dish that was especially costly and difficult to prepare, thus leaving the kitchen with a surplus of the fancier item. I remember many occasions when we would convince guests that the best thing that night was boiled chicken, a tasteless dish of which the kitchen always had a mere handful of servings.

These were small businesses with a high degree of anxiety. Green Acres owner Cissie Blumberg saw that anxiety enter her dream life: "During all my years 'behind the front desk,' I had two recurring nightmares. In one, I saw streams of cars driving up to the hotel's entrance on the first of July—but nothing was ready and the place was dismantled and disheveled. In the other, we were spruced up, shined and primed to receive our guests—and no one came!" A longtime observer notes that "you've got to be pretty slick to survive in a business where you must rake in enough from Decoration Day through Labor

Day to keep you the other 280 days." Owners seemed convinced that every plate that was dropped, every second portion ordered, each extra entertainer hired was the straw that would force bankruptcy. As a result, many were tight-wads, always nervous, frequently screaming. I knew an owner who saved nails to straighten with a hammer for reuse. A waiter recalled that "one Sunday a guy dropped a whole tray of steaks. They [the kitchen staff] picked up the steaks, brushed them off, and put them on clean plates and served them." As a maitre d' of a large hotel remembered, the owners sat in the dining room near the kitchen door to keep tally of how many main dishes the waiters carried out. Another maitre d' recalled the owners doing the same from the kitchen side, clip-board in hand. A man who drove laundry trucks to the hotels recalls that most owners would give him a meal, though one miser "would look in your teeth to see if you ate."

In Eileen Pollack's novel *Paradise, New York,* based on her resort upbring-ing, the daughter is immediately captive to the dictates of resort economics when she takes over the hotel:

> I did nothing that summer that anyone else in business wouldn't do. I scrimped. I cut corners. I placed the Eden's survival above all other things. I argued with Jerry to use cheaper beef cuts. I didn't hire a handyman. I even stopped putting chlorine in the pool (dead or alive a germ was invisible, and what would it hurt if someone should swallow a mouthful of pee?). I had no time for weighing this claim, that defense, niceties of feelings, oughts and ought nots. Was it good for the Eden? No, no, and no.

Owners would, in fact, do many things that seemed improper, such as writing cards to people whose spouses had recently died. For Pollack's fic-tional narrator, "So many guests died every year that my mother had mimeo-graphed our family's regrets. When she sent condolences to the dead guest's survivors, she slipped in a reminder to make reservations for the upcoming year. Sometimes this worked, but usually the spouse faded too quickly to send back the form." Some things were less improper, but nonetheless seemed a bit sneaky. According to the son of a small hotel owner: "My dad would have his sister, who lived in Brooklyn, write away to other hotels and get their rates as a way of keeping track of what the competition was charging, to help us make decisions on setting rates for the hotel." Elmer Rosenberg, Cissie

Blumberg's husband at Green Acres, once handed out brochures to competitors at the Hotelmen's Association saying, "Save me postage. Here's the rate."

Routine costs were high. A limited number of food wholesalers made the cost of a hotel's primary expense higher than it might otherwise be. Jerry Jacobs, whose parents ran the Delmar Hotel, noted that "many expenses were based on a full year even though the hotel was only open in the summer. So we had to pay liability insurance, fire insurance, and taxes for twelve months, and had to make enough to cover those fixed costs based on just two months of business."

Routine operating costs were not the only problem. Many owners financed too much expansion in the hope of competing in a declining market. Indoor pools and elegant nightclubs were frequent examples. Once built, pools were often underutilized by the aging clientele; and nightclubs were just fancier places to watch the show, but not places to drink. One hotel owner sadly recalls sinking $25,000 into a pool in 1960, dropping insurance coverage at the broker's suggestion, and having the hotel burn down the next winter, leading to them going out of business and owing a lot of money.

One interesting element of hotel hustling was the "due bill." In the Depression, hotel owners were short of money to pay the entertainers, so they gave them a form of scrip called a due bill. The entertainers would sell the due bill for cash to someone in New York who wanted a vacation at a discount, which the hotel then honored. Guests paying with due bills didn't get the best rooms, however. Due bills were also used to pay off people who supplied the hotel with paint, food, and other items, and these businesspeople later used the due bills to take a vacation or sold them at discounted prices. This financial device was very helpful to many hotels in the 1930s.

Expansion or modernization was often done even when it seemed obviously a poor choice. Henrietta Lichtenbaum notes that her grandfather, George Barrack, owner of the Excelsior, "entertained ideas of becoming another Grossinger's," but:

> he expanded at the wrong time—1929 to be exact. It was then that two stucco buildings were added to the hotel. One housed the casino, another the middle house—a building with a porch and eight rooms. After the expansion, our capacity was eighty guests, including children. . . . We were keenly aware of our competition—hence the casino, the clay tennis court, the handball court, and serious thought of a swimming pool. Toward the end, the expense of constructing a pool was a

big factor in selling the business. Most of the guests wanted to be in a hotel that had everything. Though very few people actually used the tennis court, it was a status symbol for the hotel. In the 1950s, competing without a tennis court was unthinkable.

In the 1940s and 1950s, the casino often represented a major expansion; by the 1960s, owners would likely go beyond the casino to a full-fledged night-club. In his novel, *Summer on a Mountain of Spices,* Harvey Jacobs recounts owner Al Berman's desire to build a center of entertainment: "The Willow Spring Hotel boasted its palace of pleasure, the font of Al Berman's passion, years before even Henderson's [the larger competition, next door] had a social hall." Overflow crowds sometimes had to sleep in tents, but Berman preferred the casino to additional rooms:

> He wanted a casino with a stage, a dance floor, and stand to sell refreshments, not [guest] rooms. The Willow Spring would have a resident band of music, a social director, regular entertainment. . . . Carpenters from Monticello went to work in the spring following Al Berman's blueprint. A long flight of wooden steps was built leading to a long porch held by white columns. The interior of the building was left hollow to the roof beams. A smooth wood floor, waxed and mellow, led to the stage. Two dressing rooms, stage right, stage left, were added, and under the stage a storage room accessible by trapdoor was a final inspiration. The concession was placed to the left of the stairs with its front serving the porch, its side serving the inside of the casino through a large window. The result was a Catskill masterpiece, a local wonder. The casino itself was a handsome structure. The idea of so much empty air with walls around it, not a church or synagogue, was totally unique. Naturally on the busy weekends the dressing rooms held paying guests and the dance floor hosted rows of army cots for bachelors, so all was not lost. . . . "We had a casino practically before Jennie Grossinger," Al Berman said many times over twenty-two years. And it was true.

Hotel owners were in a rut of always having to expand. Anne Chester wrote that:

> If business is good, there are constant improvements, additions both in accommodations, facilities, and staff. Then if sizeable accommodations

are added, the kitchen, dining room, living rooms, play areas, theater, etc., become too small—athletic facilities have to be enlarged as well—and so it goes. And if business is not rewarding—then one must think of what additional [services] to offer.

The drive to improve and compete made it hard to see clearly, but easy to deny one's personal needs. Jerry Jacobs recalled:

My parents were much more willing to invest in the hotel than to spend on themselves. I remember my mother ordered stainless steel counter-tops for all of the working parts of the kitchen, at a cost of three or four thousand dollars. At that point it wasn't clear how much longer they were going to run the hotel. My brother Howard and I said, "Gosh, why don't you go on a vacation and spend the money on yourselves?" It always seemed like the Delmar came first.

Children grew up knowing that the hotel did in fact come first. Yet, at the Irvington in South Fallsburgh the three sets of parents who owned the place would actually stop the main line to give any of the eight children what they wanted to eat:

It could be the middle of dinner, hundreds of people waiting for their dinner, the waiters screaming, yelling, sweating, and the fans running, one of the tykes would run in and come up and say, "Uncle Irving, I'd like some dinner," and he'd stop everything; the whole production line would stop, and [he'd say,] "What would you like?" and the chefs would be muttering under their breath.

For this family grouping, hotel life seemed great for the children:

We had the run of the place. It was like a huge playground. We had the run of the kitchen. You wanted something in the middle of the after-noon [while] sitting at the pool and everybody said, "Gee, it's hot," [and] we'd just stroll in to the kitchen, get the keys to the fridge, open it up, and there it was, a vast cornucopia at your fingertips.

Instead of expanding and improving, some hotels tried marketing tech-niques. One year that I worked at Paul's, the owners tried to boost business by advertising 'one child free with each adult.' For the guests with more than two children, this meant that grandparents came along, too, with a child in tow. The owners balked at this, but the guests threatened to leave. Thus, the place was completely packed and chaotic. The children's dining room was simply too small to accommodate the explosion of youngsters, so the overflow was placed in a little room used for card playing. Even that got filled up, and several children ate in old-fashioned phone booths, which had little shelves.

Owners tried other ingenious methods to maximize attraction while minimizing cost. Many hotels, such as Sha-Wan-Ga Lodge, hired dining room staff who had some artistic capacities that would enable them to perform in Talent Night every week. Even in the late 1970s, Chait's Hotel in Accord hired classical musicians to work the dining room, salad room, and other jobs. Then, instead of bringing in entertainers, the owners presented nighttime classical concerts in the lobby.

Overall, a proprietor had to know how to hustle the guests, while still satisfying them. From one owner's daughter comes this story:

This family came back three years in a row. Well, their room was #78. They were due to arrive on a Sunday. The people who were occupying the room refused to leave. They were going to stay another week. What to do? In those days, the door numbers were nailed on. They were made of metal. When the occupants went to the pool, my dad switched the numbers. He put 78 where 77 was. It was directly opposite. When the #78 guests checked in, the bellhop showed them into 77, which was now numbered 78. The woman, Mrs. Marcus, said to her husband, "Why does this room look different?" Her husband said, "After a whole winter you forgot. Look at the number. It's the same room." And so it got by and my dad was so proud of himself. They never knew the difference.

Another hotelkeeper's daughter offered her family's method of having a black bellhop who understood Yiddish show rooms to prospective guests:

[The bellhop] had this little system with my mother where she would be trying to get [guests] to take this room, and he would bring them upstairs to see the room [while the owner stayed in the office], and then they [the guests] would talk to each other in Yiddish, you know, "It's too small." "Look at this, it's too old," or "Boy, this is a real bargain for this price." And he [the bellhop] would convey this back to my mother.

Dorothy Eagle, owner of the Pine View Country Club in Loch Sheldrake, remembered the challenge of talking people into renting rooms with a shared bath. "I had to sell rooms," she pointed out, but people resisted the idea of a bath on the floor. So she said to them:

When you close the door, you're private. No one's going to bother you. So they'd say, "You son of a . . ." Then I'd say, "Let's go down and have a drink." And I'd treat them to a drink and have my busboy bring us something to snack on. And they'd say, "[You're] the most terrific hostess."

The Whole Family Worked

Running a hotel was hard work and involved the whole family. Blum's Hotel in Youngsville, on eighty-eight acres, was quite typical of a small hotel. It was descended from a farm, bought in 1944 because the owner's son expressed a desire to live on a farm. It was then transformed into a kuchalayn, and in a couple more years into a hotel, with the owners adding new rooms and bungalows each season. Sarah Blum cooked, helped by her son, Melvin. Her husband, George, did all the food shopping and picked up guests at the bus station. Irving, the other son, ran the dining room with its four stations for 150 guests, all elderly. Irving's wife, Roberta, managed the office, where she "made reservations by phone and letter, answered all correspondence, kept the books, escorted the guests to their rooms upon arrival, wrote letters for elderly people, checked on the help, handled complaints."

Pre–World War II hotels had additional kinds of labor-intensive tasks:

The stove was wood-burning and had to be lit at 5:00 A.M. [It] had to be stoked with the wood brought into the kitchen from the woodpile out back. Perhaps what was missed most was an automatic thermostat in the oven. The baker's hand was the thermostat. . . . The icebox had to be loaded with blocks of ice retrieved from the ice house, an unpainted large building in the orchard behind the main house. There, ice had been packed between layers of straw in the dead of winter. It was cut from our lake, about a mile or so from the house, or from Kramer's lake a few miles away.

Children were rarely too young to work. The daughter of a White Lake hotelier wrote to me: "My first 'employment' was at the front desk, selling the daily newspapers (I'm not sure how old I was, but I might not have been old enough to read yet)." At a small Loch Sheldrake establishment, "the smallest children would count the napkins that went out with the laundry and got the laundry ready for the pick-up, [then] checked the laundry when it came back." Herbert Megel started running the Granite Hotel's concession in 1932, at age eight, since his father didn't want to be bothered by the guests who wanted the office to carry cigarettes, sundries, soda, and candy. Because his parents owned the hotel, Megel never even served a token apprentice year as a busboy before becoming a waiter at age thirteen, serving thirty people during the week and sixty on weekends. At age ten, Robin Charlow sorted and delivered mail by bicycle twice a day to the hotel's fifty bungalows. And Jerry Jacobs traces the history of his different responsibilities in the late 1950s and early 1960s:

> At age eight or nine, I was put in charge of the swimming pool. I'd use a wide brush attached to a long metal pole to sweep the algae off the bottom of the pool. I was also in charge of the mats. We had wooden chaise lounges, and we would rent out cushions to make them more comfortable: fifty cents per day, three dollars per week. I would put them out in the morning on sunny days and collect them around dinnertime. I made a game out of seeing how many mats I could carry on my head at the same time. I remember sometimes being afraid when I had to turn off the pool lights. The floodlights around the pool were kept on until the show was over. I had to go back to the underside of the pool and walk across two wooden planks to reach the switch to turn them off. It was dark and a little bit scary. From age eleven to twelve, I added the candy store to my responsibilities. Running a candy store was an interesting job for an eleven-year-old. I had to figure out what to order. I would go to a wholesale candy store (Briker Brothers) to order cases of potato chips, pretzels, and other snacks, and they would let me pick out a candy bar for myself for being such a good customer. I felt grownup, in charge of my own business. When I was thirteen, I worked in the pantry (as a saladman); at fourteen, I was a busboy. At

fifteen, I started my stint as a waiter, which continued until I graduated college. I tried to make the work more fun by getting my friends from high school hired to work with me in the dining room. Once I was in graduate school, I decided enough was enough.

That was exactly how I felt—the summer following my one-year M.A. degree (in 1991) was the first summer of my life I was not in the Mountains. Perhaps I left New York for Cambridge, Massachusetts, to distance myself from the grind of being pressed to work there every summer.

You could understand why "enough was enough"—since the dining room staff would leave on the Monday of Labor Day weekend, Jerry and his older brother, Howard, often missed the first day or two of school in order to serve the guests who still remained. Even the saladman would leave, and the brothers would have to prepare all the salad dishes as well as serve them. Jacobs also remembers the way hotel life could interfere with his own religious observances:

> My family never really sat down and had a Passover dinner until after my parents sold the hotel and retired. So in a funny way I was in the middle of this sea, but couldn't drink the water. We were surrounded by Jewish traditions but were too busy working to really participate. One thing I'll always remember about Passover is that, being the youngest in the congregation, I always got to ask the Four Questions. This was my role every year from age five until age twenty-two. I would go into the dining room and recite them into the microphone in front of at least 150 people, and then I'd go into the kitchen to help prepare the rest of the meal, so I never stayed to have the Four Questions answered.

Eileen Pollack's novel of hotel life also portrays typical family work in the preseason kitchen:

> This was the custom: the day before opening we made five hundred blintzes—potato, cheese, cherry, blueberry, and prune. Nana was in charge of Operation Blintz, but her talents were limited to destruction—cracking eggs, beating them. She hated to depend on her son-in-law, but she needed his skill in the art of creation. He would stand by the stove with a tiny curved ladle—quick dip in the bowl, a question mark of batter in the heavy iron pan, a shake of the handle, one, two, three, *flick*, and

a wafer of dough would float to the counter. As a child my task had been to spoon a gob of filling in the center of each crepe. With his long heavy fingers, my father would fold the skin around the filling, fold, fold, fold, *tuck*, then he would flip the blintz and pat it as tenderly as if it were a just diapered infant.

I found it not at all strange that a very similar preseason blintz story was told to me by the son of a small hotel owner hardly a mile away. From another owner came stories of hand-making noodles in the children's dining room before the season.

Another off-season task I heard about from many early owners was that of visiting guests in New York City to make sure they returned:

The customers were recruited each year with letters and personal visits during early spring. I remember mailing the letters, not knowing the Bronx from Brooklyn or the lower East Side from Harlem, but we drew customers from these areas and my grandmother, Rose Barrack, who could not read or write English would travel the subways with an address in hand. By inquiring of subway passengers and passersby, she would somehow find her way around New York City to the homes of patrons. This apparently was expected of hotelkeepers and keeping up with the competition was necessary to a hotel's survival.

Hotels sometimes conducted winter reunions in the city to keep in touch with guests. The Pine View Lodge hosted a winter day-camp reunion at a West Side hotel. Not only was this kind of event a way to keep owners and guests connected, but it also served to continue friendships among guests, and they would make decisions about returning based on the networks of people that would be going back the next summer. For a number of years, many hotels rented a Manhattan armory to have a daylong event where each hotel had a table with brochures to entice customers.

At the Delmar, in Loch Sheldrake, Jerry Jacobs remembers the travails of making a resort work:

During the season, running a hotel was extremely demanding. My mother would get up at 6:00 in the morning to cook in the kitchen. She would take a short break in the afternoon, but she was usually

CHAPTER 4

wasn't done in the kitchen until 8:30 or 9:00 o'clock at night. My
dad would also get up at 6:00 in the morning. He would go to the
bakery, get newspapers for the guests, and run a dozen other errands
while being in charge of the front office and supervising the staff. He
would be up until the end of the show in the casino, usually 10:30 or
11:00 at night, and would check to make sure the tearoom was running smoothly. It was a long day, and of course it was a seven-day-a-
week operation. As my parents got older, it became harder to run
things. For many years, my mother, Claire, did all the baking, the supervising, the short-order cooking, and all of the crisis management
work in the kitchen. Around the time she was fifty-five, the cook, who
had worked for us for many years, slipped, hurt his back, and went
out on disability. He was never replaced. My mother added all the
cooking to her other jobs. Eventually, it just got to be too much for
them.

These were family hotels, and that meant the family could not get very far
away from them. One owner's child from the Shady Nook Country Club in
Loch Sheldrake relates: "We were six children. We all worked at the hotel, even
as adults. I was the baby, and from [age] eleven to thirteen was the bellhop."
A White Lake veteran recalled the 1940s and beyond:

Every summer from the time we were married, and of course before
that, we would know that we were expected, and did go up to Shagrin's
to work at the hotel for at least ten weeks, from June 15 to after the
High Holidays. Our children were born, and they were brought up at
the hotel every summer. As they grew up, as early as twelve and thirteen years, they, too, had specific jobs—bellhop, busboy, waiter, and
even running the concession in the playhouse.

In some small hotels, so many of the staff were relatives that it would be hard
to make them eat separately, so all of the staff ate with the owners in the
kitchen.

Having grown up in the Delmar Hotel, Jerry Jacobs recalls that "another
challenge was that there were no barriers between you and the guests. There
wasn't a staff person at the front desk who could say, 'This is the rate and I'm
not authorized to offer discounts.' Guests typically talked directly with the
owner. Everybody always wanted to cut a deal."

One hotel owner felt his son needed a trial of work outside of the family business; as that son, Jack Landman, recounts:

I started working in the Catskills when I was sixteen years old, back in the early 1930s. At that time, my father had bought a hotel, the West Shore Country Club on Kauneonga Lake. He wouldn't hire me because I was too young and he wanted me to get work experience elsewhere. My first job was as a busboy at the Hotel Glass across the street from the Flagler in Fallsburg. I worked there for one weekend. Most of the staff quit. It was Decoration Day weekend. We were not treated too well. I was used to it since my father didn't treat staff members any better. I understood the conditions. They were normal to me. To others they were abnormal. After the last meal, the older boys in college felt that they were treated so poorly that they could say, "we quit." They left the dining room in [a] shambles of used dishes and unreturned bus boxes. Two of us—both [from] families affiliated with the hotel industry (his parents were in the catering business)—felt that we could not expose ourselves to the criticism inherent in leaving a job unfinished. The two of us cleaned up the entire dining room. As a result, Mr. Glass called my father to tell him what a fine young man I was. My father's response was typical: "If you're such a fine young man, why work for someone else? You'll work here from now on." That's how I became a busboy at West Shore.

In the off-season, hotels continued to rule proprietors' families: "The hotel had a weekly menu, and somehow our family stayed on the same weekly menu all winter. We would have brisket of beef Monday night, corned beef and cabbage Tuesday night, meatloaf Wednesday night, liver and onions Thursday, and of course roast chicken and matzoh ball soup Friday night. The hotel dominated our lives." At another hotel, the end of the season culminated in an assembly-line operation where the hotel owners butchered whole cows, separating parts into busboxes prior to being wrapped for freezing, to serve them through the off-season.

The off-season also included a tremendous amount of labor. Rooms were often renovated then, especially by the 1960s when guests' distaste for shared baths led many proprietors to transform rooms with private bath accommodations. Curtains were taken down and cleaned, or new ones sewed. Cracks in pools had to be repaired, and wooden chaise lounges fixed. Endless electrical and plumbing work was done. New buildings might be put up. New wallpaper was hung. A hundred venetian blinds were cleaned and many restrung. Chairs were rewebbed. Prior to the season, while snow still covered the ground in March and April, the Irvington's owners used to drive from their home in town to sit in the hotel, waiting for prospective bungalow renters to come browsing. One son remarked, "My parents really were busy with closing the hotel down till at least November. They were busy with preparations for Passover from February on. So the hotel was a year-round job in a way that I think a lot of people wouldn't necessarily appreciate."

Despite the economic pressures, many owners prided themselves on gracious service, abundant food, and many special extras. At her parents' Maple Court Hotel, Alice Gutter remembered, "What other hotel had a special aunt whose sole duty at breakfast time was to preside over ten electrical outlets for ten percolators so that each table was supplied with still-perking coffee?" Her mother's insistence on top quality ingredients contributed to keeping down the family's income.

The famous Grossinger's hominess comes through in this recollection:

One Friday while checking in at Grossinger's, pandemonium at the check-in counter prevailed. All was confused, busy, mixed up, and impossible. Each clerk was too preoccupied to pay any attention to me. Finally I located an elderly woman stationed behind the counter, who appeared to embody the stance of calmness, orderliness, and concern. Within moments, she calmed me down, checked me in, answered all my questions, and made me feel welcome. I was sufficiently impressed so as to attempt to get her name from another clerk in order to compliment her to superiors. I asked another clerk the name of my benefactress. It was Jenny Grossinger.

I interviewed a fair number of children of hotel families, many of whom dwelled on the warmth and familial feeling of their enterprises. "Guests were often almost like family," one said. Another owner's child remarked that his parents "liked the spirit of the place, the fact that there were lots of people who came year after year who would tell them how clean it was, how nice it was, how home-like it was." Jerry Jacobs, despite his share of complaints about the rigors of hotel life, still could say: "At the hotel there was a special feeling that you are part of a team, that you're all working toward one goal, everybody has to help out. We felt that when the family was all working together we could overcome any challenge." From a hotelkeeper's daughter came the belief that "without doubt, it contributed to making me a strong and independent person, with a strong work ethic and the ability to interact with others." From another owner's daughter came this:

> I have noticed throughout my life, and I have noticed this about every hotel kid that I know: They have an unbelievable work ethic. And every employer I've ever worked for, every employer my brother and sisters have worked for, . . . every place we go, every place we've worked, people are amazed at what terrific workers we are no matter what the job is, whether we know it before we get there or don't. We just grew up with an unbelievable work ethic, and I know that came from the hotel business.

And a Monticello veteran recalls, "From the time I was ten or so, I did all the paperwork for my parents [at their bungalow colony]—correspondence, leases. The work I did for them was a factor in my subsequently becoming an attorney." Another person did all the electrical work for the extensive entertainment at his family's hotel, leading him to a career in engineering.

Still, hotel owners' children saw how hard the life was. Eileen Pollack's fictional hotel owners' children studied hard because "they feared they would otherwise spend the rest of their lives serving herring and soup to ill-tempered guests." Pollack's narrator laments, "This was the bed our parents had slept in from May through October for the past thirty-four years, except for those nights when the Eden was so full they rented out their bungalow and slept in the lobby." The daughter in the novel remained attached to the hotel, but her brother resisted to the extent of cultivating mainly WASP friends: "If his mother and father wanted to work twenty hours a day, seven days a week, that was their choice. They had no right to sacrifice their son's youth to an idol whose welfare they placed above their own child's."

I heard many tales of people giving up their own rooms. Herbert Megel recalls what happened when his parents rented their own room on a busy weekend. The parents slept in the car, and Herbert walked two miles down the road to the kuchalayn that his grandparents operated for its owner. But another dislocation proved quite favorable: Herbert met his wife one crowded season when she rented a cot in the kitchen of the hotel owner's private residence.

For some, the resentment was even greater. One man hated being the bosses' son because, as he says, "I was part of the establishment but I wanted to be one of the kids." Another man spoke of being an "indentured servant" at his parents' bungalow colony: "The debate with my brother has always been, Did the Catskills make [our father] a hard, loveless man, or was he born that way? What we don't argue over is that he become more distant the longer he lived there, more like an overseer than a father, squeezing as much work from us as possible, robbing us of our childhood."

Given this, would owners' children follow in their parents' paths? One man and his two brothers worked for years at the family hotel where his mother cooked and his father ran the office. He was clear about his mother's feelings: "My mother didn't want any one of us to go into the hotel business. It was a miserable business." My own parents told me on countless occasions to make sure I never got myself into the hotel or restaurant business, having given their lives over to it. Another owner's child, who knew many other hotel brats, felt that most people wanted their children to go to college and become professionals.

But if some parents wanted to keep their children out of the business, many others had different experiences. At the Excelsior, the owner's child recalls that "neither son wanted to continue working the hotel after the war [World War II]. Their wives were not suited to the life of a hotel *balabouste* [homemaker]. This greatly upset Rose Barrack, who thought the hotel had finally achieved viability as a business. . . . George always said, 'Hard work never hurt anybody.' They were long-lived examples of that truism." The owners of a medium-size hotel, which closed in the 1980s, tried to get their sons to work there. One, a local lawyer, worked there at night. Another, after getting his doctorate, was asked to work at the hotel now that he was finished with his education. It was as if he had satisfied some peculiar urge and was now ready to get back into the real world of the Mountains. Another hotel child received a doctorate in biology; he had a hard time finding a job in the mid 1950s. He explains, "In the back of my mind, I was probably waiting for the call to help manage the hotel." But he didn't get that call. Another hotel child did get the call:

I started running the hotel in 1960. I really wasn't a cosmopolitan person. I didn't care for the hotel. I didn't see any dollars there. I went into the millwork business. I went into the military. Then the lumber business. I wasn't successful. My father separated from my mother, and my mother was running the hotel. She was depending on me more and more. She called me. As time went on, I thought I can't do any worse at the hotel. That's when I got into the hotel.

One owner was more realistic about her daughter's reluctance to even consider taking over the business: "Why would she like this place. She has no time and she's not interested. She spent her childhood here; that was enough."

Whatever their experiences were in their parents' hotels, hotel children typically did not take over the family business, at least not after the 1960s. The Jewish resort owners may not have succeeded in becoming rich hoteliers, but they did succeed in becoming Americanized enough to offer their offspring a choice. Jerry Jacobs comments:

> Although many of my friends' families owned resorts, I can't recall anyone who planned to take over their family's business. We all went to college, often very selective schools, and didn't look back. For example, Stanley Lipkowitz (Lipkowitz's Bungalow in Ferndale) went to Cornell en route to becoming a doctor; Eileen Pollack went to Yale and became a writer; Marc Stier (Stier's Hotel in Ferndale) and I both got Ph.D.'s at Harvard and became academics. When choosing between the prestige of the Ivy League and careers in law, medicine, and other elite professions on the one hand, and taking over the small and often precarious family business on the other, there really was no contest.

Similarly, one owner's daughter recounted:

> No one wanted to live there anymore. Everyone wanted to move away. It was interesting because most of the hotel owners that I knew wanted their children to do better than they did. Their parents were the immigrants. They wanted their kids to do better. Owning a hotel was better—you had done better than your parents. But then it was the next generation and their view of doing a lot better was to go to college and be a professional. That's what we were taught. My view was that I was supposed to go off and make it in the larger world. We were expected to go to college. So that was the big achievement. Once everyone went off, nobody wanted to come back.

So the success of the hotel owners, in moving a step up from their parents, was at the same time a harbinger of a poor future. The American dream had become more attainable once that generation's children found themselves in the 1960s, where college was more widespread and anti-Semitic exclusion had largely disappeared.

Despite the hardships, the ambivalence we encounter in Catskill veterans comes through in owner's children as well. One recalled wanting to be like the other waiters, but having to maintain his loyalty: "I wanted to torture the salad-man but I didn't want to see the food wasted." Pollack's novel features a daughter trying to revive the hotel run by her parents but still legally owned by her grandmother. Another owner's son got married at the family hotel, despite his desire to get away: "I had my wedding at the hotel, but I was a little uncertain of how my friends from college would react. It was not quite as polished and refined as I would have liked things to be. But everyone enjoyed the wedding, and one of my college friends even told me how impressed he was with the hotel."

My parents no longer had a hotel after I was a toddler, but it was completely expected that my mother would cater my bar mitzvah at our home, and likewise my wedding seventeen years later. The glorious spread of food was exactly like it would have been in a Catskill hotel. And why should I be surprised that two-thirds of the photos in my bar mitzvah album are of the food?

Life at the Hotel

Hotel life was a mini-society played out for public consumption. One way in which this open community was maintained was by the steady blare of the loud-speaker. It was a constant accompaniment to the day's routine—announcing meals, calling people to activities, fetching people for phone calls, locating missing children, and summoning staff to tasks needing immediate attention (especially the handymen who were busy fixing archaic plumbing, leaking roofs, and sprung mattresses). With its electric power, the loudspeaker was an emblem of the proprietors' control of their domain, often exercised playfully. As Jerry Jacobs told it, "My dad would always enjoy making funny announcements. Maybe it was his chance to try his hand as an entertainer. He would announce 'Good morning ladies and gentlemen of the Delmar Hotel. The sun is shining, the herring are jumping, and breakfast is now being served; the main dining room is now open.' He would add his commentary on the weather, the day's political events, whether the smoked whitefish to be served for lunch had enjoyed their last moments in this world."

Owners could humorously compare their hotels to the grandest resorts, as did Morris Katz at his Cherry Hill Hotel in Greenfield Park: "Dinner is now being served at the Concord Hotel . . . and at the Cherry Hill." "Katzie's" humor also extended to paging nonexistent guests whose fabricated names were sexual puns: "Mrs. Rass, telephone call. Sonia Rass, telephone call." Staff members were called all the time. At the Evan's Kiamesha, just down the road from the Concord, I remember how "Paging Snapper, the teenage counselor. Snapper, please pick up the phone" got abbreviated into "Snapper teenage!" The loudspeaker was a plaything for children, who begged to be allowed to make announcements for the day camp, especially if there was an activity the parents were supposed to attend. Owners' children were particularly privileged to make announcements of all sorts, while slipping in digs about other children.

Often enough, in the small and crowded office, the microphone switch was left on inadvertently, and you could hear all sorts of background conversation in the office, including owners arguing with each other, yelling at the staff, and badmouthing difficult guests. It might take five minutes before another owner or an office staffer noticed this and came running in to switch it off. Because hotels and bungalow colonies were often right next to each other, you often heard the neighboring resort's loudspeaker and couldn't tell whose it really was, until you finally ascertained that there was no such person at your hotel.

Some small hotels were so declassé that they didn't announce meals with the loudspeaker. Instead, they rang a tremendously loud siren for several blasts. You could hear the symphony of these sirens bouncing off valley walls within minutes of each other. During my six years as a young child at the Seven Gables, I loved to hit the siren at lunchtime and would hang around waiting for the privilege. By some quirk of design afterthought, the switch was in the women's bathroom in the kitchen area, so I always had to knock to make sure it was empty.

The pool was the major social center during the day. In between breakfast and lunch, and lunch and dinner, a large proportion of the guests was there, even if they didn't swim. Cards and mah-jongg were played there. Bingo games and other contests were held. Shuffleboard courts were often adjacent. Bands played Latin music. Day campers had certain times that they could use the pool, so that it would not be too crowded and raucous for the adults. I remember endless days of lying on the side of the Seven Gables pool. The four-inch pipe at the deep end delivered a constant flow of cold water from the well. This water was so good that we cupped our hands and drank from the pipe before the water hit the pool. Because of that deep, cold well, when they first filled the pool in June, it took a week or two for the ambient temperature to make the water swimmable. I loved the water, being used to nearly year-round swimming in Florida, and that was one reason why I begged my parents to not send me to day camp—I wanted to be at the pool all day. As a veteran hotel kid, I felt I could take care of myself without supervision and without getting into trouble, and I simply did not want counselors telling me all day that it was time to make lanyards, time to make plaster of Paris casts, time to play kickball. Mostly, my parents disagreed, and I went to day camp. The only time in my life I was glad that my father had a concession was the one year at the Seven Gables when I could avoid day camp in order to work behind the counter, a big, grown-up, eleven-year-old.

It seemed a long walk through the woods to the camp house at the Seven Gables. Seeing the ruins of the hotel today, it is astonishing how close together everything was. But there were so many trees that you could have all sorts of adventures while still within earshot of the hotel. There was a small stream for catching frogs, and stands of sumac trees that we assiduously avoided just in case they were poison sumac. The best thing was getting off the grounds on camp trips—swimming in Ulster Lake, bowling in Ellenville, taking a bus to the Catskill Game Farm, even walking a few hundred yards down Route 52 to Kass's Corner to get pizza, or hiking up a nearby road past the "haunted house." Day camp made the hotel more palatable for parents, since they didn't have to be with their children for large portions of the day. In the 1960s, hotels started providing care even for infants—anything to keep the guests coming up. The Brickman's Murray Posner heartily boasted, "People ask what age we'll take children at. I tell them, 'If the kid breathes we'll take it.'"

Weekend husbands were a hallmark of the Catskills. Men received only one- or two-week vacations in most jobs, and people in business for themselves were reluctant to take much time off. So wives and children often spent a month or even the whole summer in the Catskills, with husbands coming up for weekends and perhaps one or two weeks, or even just for a couple of extra days tacked on to holiday weekends like July 4th and Labor Day. When the Ontario and Western Railroad provided the main transportation, the Friday evening "husband train" (often called the "bull train") was a major event and was sometimes greeted with bands in the 1920s.

Some women claimed they were happy to have the time away, but it clearly made them work harder taking care of the children. For some, in hotels, it provided time for romance with men on the staff. People I spoke with often recalled the Friday return as special: "I remember the Friday nights, all the cars pulling into the parking lot, all the fathers coming in for the weekend." Another remarked that: "My father used to come out on weekends like all of the fathers there. They all came out Friday night, and all during the week the mothers used to always say, 'Wait till I tell your father what you did, he's going to kill you.'"

The men did not always arrive in time for the regular seven o'clock dinner, thus inconveniencing the staff: "Of course, as waiters, we always resented the fact that the husbands would come up late on Friday night, and they would be late for dinner, and we would have to be serving all these extra dinners after everybody else was done."

Just as the owners sought to maximize their profits in the short, treacherous season, so too did others hustle. Everyone was trying to figure out how to get something special or to make an extra buck. One baker recounted how he made a deal with the bellhop, whose additional responsibilities included cleaning the bakery and handling the newspapers; the baker gave the bellhop a cake, and the bellhop gave the baker free papers every day. Social directors convinced guests to go horseback riding, for which the farmer kicked back a third of the charge. Comic and tummler Mac Robbins recalled that "The tummlers used to have to take the people into town—a dozen or so at a time—if they wanted [something from] a luncheonette, a soda fountain, a deli. The owners used to give us not exactly a kickback but a little something—a free lunch, a pair of tickets—to encourage us to bring our guests to their store." To get a birthday cake for a family member you had to pass money to both the baker and the maitre d'. If a guest wanted a fancy dish, such as sturgeon, rather than ask the waiter he had to tip the maitre d' to bring it. A waiter alone could not get it—I know, because I tried to get sturgeon from the saladman when I was a waiter at Brickman's; he refused and referred me to the maitre d'. I guess it's safe after thirty years to say that it wasn't for a guest, it was for me.

Political Culture in the Mountains

In the Catskills, comics often made jokes about college activists, and the guests seemed to share negative opinions about those antiwar groups, such as Students for a Democratic Society (SDS). The hotels openly opposed unionization of their staff and certainly didn't treat the lowest levels of the workers very well. Guests were very concerned with upward mobility, a logical desire given their Eastern European background.

Altogether, that made the Mountains seem conservative to me. By age sixteen, a junior in high school, I was very involved in civil rights and antiwar activities at home in North Miami Beach, and by college I was a full-time activist. But I always felt like I had to keep my mouth shut about this during the Catskill summers. The few conversations I ever had about politics there always made me look like a far-left outsider. Thus, I was completely shocked at the age of seventeen to be introduced to the wonderful political ballads of Phil Ochs by a dining room colleague who brought a portable stereo to the Karmel Hotel's staff quarters. (Ochs was one of the best known political folk singers in the 1960s.) Yet, overall, I experienced the Catskills as an encapsulated world that the activist 1960s had not yet captured. Certainly my radical friends were not even considering working summers in a place like the Catskills.

By the early 1970s, my mother was working at Chait's Hotel in Accord, where political discussion was common, and she very much liked that atmosphere. I then realized that there was a leftist tradition in the Mountains, and my current process of revisiting the Catskills' legacy has shown that radicalism was an important, even though small, part of Catskill culture. As early as the first two decades of the century, Workmen's Circle chapters were significant components in the life of Jewish farmers and other residents, bringing a combination of socialism, union organizing, Yiddish culture, and benevolent association. In the 1930s, when some Jews believed in the Soviet Union's plans for a Birobidjan homeland for the Jews, camps in the Catskills were organizing training centers for that effort. My mother toyed with the idea of going to Birobidjan, but my father talked her out of it.

The fervor of the 1930s was so strong that politics made its way even into hotels that were not expressly radical. A waiter who worked at the Huntington Lakeside told me how political entertainment might crop up in the 1930s: One of his guests was the famous Yiddish actor Mikhl Rosenberg, who organized a costume ball where he dressed the waiter up as Trotsky, and they lampooned the Moscow show trials of 1936. One man who worked a variety of jobs for seventy years recalls his own activism:

In 1934, we had a young Jewish group that studied Marxism. We had classes; we had a dramatic class. The girls and boys from Monticello [were] a very nice bunch. We had dances. And came May Day, we had a May Day demonstration. We had a speaker on the corner with an American flag. There was almost a riot there. The police department came out, the fire department came out, [and] the American Legion. Some guy threw a tomato. They thought the speaker picked up the flag to ward it off, but he didn't. They hit the flag [with the tomato] and it bounced off and hit him in the face. Well, there was a trial in the fall, and our lawyers made monkeys out of them and threw it out of court.

Three years later when this man was attempting to organize waiters at the Flagler, he found it hard to sign up union members because a floating work force typically didn't return the next year to the same hotel—"I had my head cracked a couple of times."

In her memoir of hotel ownership and local life, Cissie Blumberg notes that the town of Woodridge donated an ambulance to the Spanish Loyalists in the 1930s. She and her husband raised money for the Progressive Party's 1948 campaign to elect Henry Wallace as President, and they organized "Farmers for Wallace" and "Women for Wallace." In the antiwar 1960s, they ran up against roadblocks in organizing a meeting featuring Dr. Benjamin Spock when officials wouldn't provide a public building to hold the meeting. I heard from others that Green Acres made a point of hiring blacklisted entertainers such as Zero Mostel. A son of chicken farmers told me about how his parents were active in the American Labor Party (ALP). His father ran for state assembly in 1950, and his mother spoke and leafleted, sometimes with his help—"They were part of an identifiable left-wing group in the community." The ALP fought against the cold war mentality, racism, and anti-Semitism, and it ran candidates for local and state elections, supported the 1948 Wallace campaign, and raised support and money for the Rosenbergs. (Julius and Ethel Rosenberg were executed as "atom spies." Widely understood as a frame-up of political activists, the Rosenberg case was a touchstone of McCarthyist repression on the one hand and progressive politics on the other.) The son adds, "One of the most memorable and important activities that I remember was organizing the black laundry workers at the Sullivan County Steam Laundry" to help them win improvements in their working conditions. One retired farmer, still living on the same farm his father started in 1904, remembers a red-baiting attempt by the local Liberal Party to defeat him when he ran for the board of the fire insurance cooperative.

When people think about leftist resorts, three names typically come to mind: Maud's Summer Ray, Chester's Zunbarg, and Arrowhead Lodge. At Maud's Summer Ray in the years before World War II, most guests were leftists. Their numbers included socialists, communists, and Trotskyists, though the communists predominated, at least as measured by the sales of newspapers: the Communist Party's Yiddish *Freiheit* (Freedom) was the top seller, as a veteran guest of Maud's told me. Chester's Zunbarg had leftist entertainers such as Pete Seeger, the Weavers, Woodie Guthrie, Paul Robeson, Leon Bibb, Ossie

Davis, and Rubie Dee. Moreover, W. E. B. DuBois even lectured in the Catskills.

Henry Foner speaks of working in the band at the Arrowhead Lodge, which was affiliated with the leftist Jefferson School, an adult noncredit school in New York City. Indeed, the Jefferson School handled all of the Arrowhead's reservations and supplied political lecturers twice a week. This was very helpful all around: "For the hotel it was great because they were filled throughout the summer. For the Jefferson School it was good because they were getting a percentage of the take. For us it was good because a new crowd was coming up each week so we didn't have to worry about repeating material." At this time, the Rapp-Coudert Commission, a New York State forerunner of the McCarthy committee, forced the firing of about fifty teachers from city colleges and public schools. Foner remembers that:

Leonard Lyons, who was a columnist in the [New York] *Post,* wrote a piece in which he said, "Some of the teachers suspended from City College are forming an orchestra and they are calling it 'Suspended Swing.'" So we called our orchestra "Suspended Swing." We printed cards and that's how we were known—The Foner Brothers and Their Suspended Swing Orchestra.

As Foner recalls, they had a busy schedule:

While we were up there in '47, my brother, Moe [Foner], was the education director for the Department Store Union, and he got the notion, based on "Pins and Needles" [a very successful musical comedy created by the ILGWU], that it was time to do another musical comedy for the unions. So Norman Franklin and I were commissioned to write "Thursdays 'Til Nine." So we used that summer—since we were writing material, we were able to try it out during the summer—and we wrote a full-scale musical comedy. The performers were all workers of the Department Store Union. Irving Berlin came to the opening.

Like any Catskill hotel, Arrowhead had weekly campfires, but in this case they sang union songs and Spanish Civil War songs. Though the resort was quite leftist, it still could attract talent that was not expressly political. Foner continues:

I had been teaching at Tilden High School with Sam Levinson, so we convinced the owner of Arrowhead that she should hire Sam Levinson as the MC [in 1941]. It was a very successful summer, and as a result, Sam became well known, and from that year on he began to go up to the country and to take a bungalow and go out to perform at the hotels throughout the Catskills.

Another radical hotel lasted a shorter time. The Fur Worker's Resort, later called White Lake Lodge, started in 1949. As the education director of the Furrier's Union, Henry Foner therefore worked at that hotel, too:

It was [union president Ben] Gold's ambition to have a resort that the fur workers would be able to come to when they were on vacation. The best-laid plans of mice and men . . . the busiest season for fur workers is the summer, and why it didn't occur to him I don't know, but workers' vacations were in the wintertime. So it became a resort for the progressive movement. Howard Fast came up regularly and would lecture.

The hotel probably lost money each season. In 1955, the Furrier's Union merged with the Meat Cutters and they decided to stop operating the resort. It was bought and became a Jewish camp, Camp Hi-Li.

But this radicalism was atypical. Harvey Jacobs's novel, *Summer on a Mountain of Spices,* offers a dramatic portrayal of the loneliness of Catskill political activists in the late 1940s and 1950s, including a trip across the Hudson to Peekskill to the famous 1949 Paul Robeson concert, where the singer and his audience were stoned—while state and local police looked on with encouragement before arresting them. Paul Robeson was a frequent visitor at the Fur Worker's Resort, and many people staying there went to Peekskill to support the concert and protect Robeson. Radical politics was a minority perspective, even in the turbulent 1960s; resorts just couldn't provide a fertile location for this, being too busy providing entertainment that was geared to take people's minds off such troubles. Indeed, Mountain comics frequently used social activists and hippies as a convenient butt for humor.

Zionism had an easier time in the Catskills. There were always many Zionist camps, including training grounds for Jews going to Israel. Fund-raising by selling Israel Bonds was quite common. I remember accompanying a friend to a labor Zionist camp to visit his brother; it was shocking to see paying campers actually living in more primitive conditions than the hotel staff quarters that I was used to.

American Jews in the first few decades of the century were very often connected to leftist politics. But this often innate radicalism diminished as they became more Americanized, and as they moved away from working-class occupations and unions. These trends, plus the fierce anticommunism beginning in the mid-1940s, meant that the post–World War II Catskills was not a likely place to find leftism. This was yet one more way in which the Catskills formed a tracing pad for the transitions of Jews in America.

Raleigh Hotel
South Fallsburg, N.Y.

Dinner Menu
GOOD EVENING

TONIGHT
2 SHOWS

After Dinner
Lobby Lounge
Enjoy The Songs
and Entertainment
of the
FERRARI
BROTHERS

GALA
VARIETY
SHOW

1st Show
With The
Delightful Team

JOANNE
WHEATLY
and
HAL
KANNER

New Copa Comedy
Star
RALPH
POPE

dick
curry, m.c.

SWINGING
LATE SHOW
With The Dynamic
LINDA
HOPKINS

DON EDWARDS Orch
BILL DIABLO Band
The FERRARI BROS.
The SILVER CABOOSE
in The Nuru Buru

****

APPETIZERS
Chilled Honeydew Melon
Iced Tomato Juice   Cold Grapefruit Juice
Chopped Egg Salad

SALAD
Pickled Beet Salad
Assorted Table Sours

SOUPS
Chicken Gumbo New Orleans
Consomme with Alphabets
Bouillon, En Tasse

DINNER
Broiled Choice Liver Steak, Saute Onions
Corned Brisket of Beef, New Cabbage
Southern Fried Chicken, a la Maryland
Potted Swiss Steak, Jardaniere
Boiled Beef Flanken, Beet Horseradish
Roast Philadelphia Caponette, Pan Gravy
Steamed Yearling Pullet, Cressonier
Garden Vegetable Dinner, Baked Idaho

VEGETABLES
Mashed Parsley Potatoes   Whole Baby Carrots

DESSERTS
California Fruit Cake   Linzer Tart
Black & White Layer Cake   Sugar Bow Ties
Clover Leaf Honey Cake   Orange Sponge Cake
Rainbow Sherbet   Fruit Jello

BEVERAGES
Orange Pekoe Tea   Cafe Noir

(Parve Oleo Margarine Served on Request)
(Parve Mocha Mix Served with Coffee)

Mr. Alan Babbitt, Maitre D'

Thursday, July 31, 1969

★ OPEN ALL YEAR ★

Dinner menu from the Raleigh, 1969.

Chaits

Menu

* *

LUNCH

Saturday, September 5, 1970

Chilled Sacramento Tomato Juice

Roman Chick Pea Soup
or
Chilled Borsht — Boiled Potato

Choice of:

Broiled Eastern Sea Bass Steaks — Cucumber Sauce

Hawaiian Luau (Sweet & Pungent Duck
              (Chicken Livers & Chestnuts
              (Polynesian Rice
              (Fresh Pineapple Coconut

Garden Vegetable Plate with Stuffed Tomato

Fluffy Onion Omelette

Kashe Varnishkes   Buttered Spinach

Cold Entrees:

Tuna or Salmon Steak Salad Platter
Imported Sardine and Hardboiled Egg Salad, garni
Bowl of Sour Cream with Boysenberries, Bananas, Sliced
                  Fresh Fruit or Cottage Cheese.

Desserts:

Russian Coffee Cake   Wild Cherry Jello
Chocolate Pudding   Tapioca Pudding
Rainbow Sherbet
Chocolate, Vanilla or Butter Pecan Ice Cream

Coffee   Sanka   Tea   Milk

2:30 p.m. — ARTS & CRAFTS with STEVE KLEINMAN

3:30 p.m. — FOLK & SQUARE DANCING with KARL FINGER

6:30 p.m. — COCKTAILS and HORS D'OEUVRES in the Lounge

9:30 p.m. — DON SHERMAN — Comedian

My mother's lunch menu at Chait's Hotel in Accord, 1970.
(From Annette & Max Finestone.)

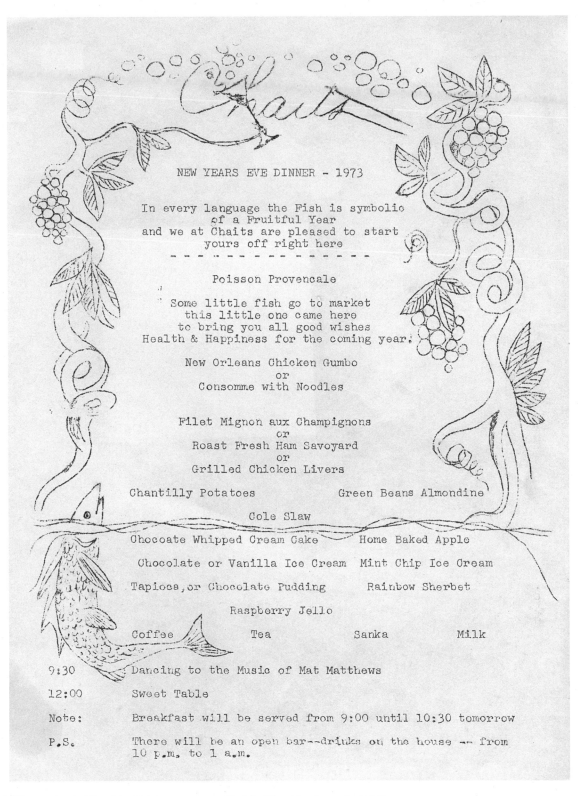

NEW YEARS EVE DINNER - 1973

In every language the Fish is symbolic
of a Fruitful Year
and we at Chaits are pleased to start
yours off right here

- - - - - - - - - - - - - - - -

Poisson Provencale

Some little fish go to market
this little one came here
to bring you all good wishes
Health & Happiness for the coming year.

New Orleans Chicken Gumbo
or
Consomme with Noodles

Filet Mignon aux Champignons
or
Roast Fresh Ham Savoyard
or
Grilled Chicken Livers

Chantilly Potatoes   Green Beans Almondine

Cole Slaw

Chocoate Whipped Cream Cake   Home Baked Apple

Chocolate or Vanilla Ice Cream Mint Chip Ice Cream

Tapioca,or Chocolate Pudding   Rainbow Sherbet

Raspberry Jello

Coffee   Tea   Sanka   Milk

9:30   Dancing to the Music of Mat Matthews

12:00   Sweet Table

Note: Breakfast will be served from 9:00 until 10:30 tomorrow

P.S.   There will be an open bar--drinks on the house -- from
        10 p.m. to 1 a.m.

My mother's New Year's Eve menu at Chait's Hotel in Accord, 1973.
(From Annette & Max Finestone.)

√2 Ribs
2 Pork Loins
1 Liver
√ Italian Sausage
√ 30 lb Chop Meat
√ 3 Pastramis
√ 1 box of Chix
1 Beef Shoulder
Fresh Brisket

Bones saved
for Kitchen

Weiners

Chain Store
Spirals
Rigatoni
Capers

1/2 Chinese
lettuce
1 escarole
carrot
scallion

Frances
Special K
gr. Split peas

Hamburger Rolls
5 dz.

Produce

Mushrooms √
Dill
Parsley
Parsnips
Celery
Green Peppers
Squash (Green
Yellow)
Tomatoes

Sorry I'm a week late !!

Fredericks
egg roll leaves
1 Box Ducks
French Cut Beans 12
Spinach 6
Asparagus
Broccoli 6
Potato Chip
Small Pizzas
Beef Patties
Green Peas 6
Lo Mein Noodles
O. J.   2 jars
Choc. pudding   citrus
Vanilla "   Mayo.
Sauer Kraut
? Beets   whole
Tomatoes   sliced

Green Split Peas
Kidney Beans # 10
Tomato Sauce
Bow Ties
Alphabets
Choc Pudding
Vanilla "
Irish Potatoes Whole
Chinese Noodles
Baked Beans
Taffy
Boysenberne

My mother provided a weekly food order every Sunday night at Chait's, and she wrote poems to her bosses on the back of each order, conveying her affection, anger, frustrations, and observations on hotel life: "The time has come the cheffie says/To talk of many things/Like poorly organized ordering/Unlit steam tables and related things/Like how we 3 survived a year/With nary a ruffling/I think

The Time has come the cleffie says
To talk of many things
Like poorly organized ordering
Unlit straw tables and related things
Like how we 3 survived a year
With nary a ruffeling
I think we're really a dandy trio
With not a stress or strain
And hardly a forte or even con brio
That wouldn't wash down the drain
Nor a gummy sink nor a tattered rug
Can ruffle our peaceful calm
So here's to another wonderful year
~~_____~~ on the Finestones ~~farm~~

2½   apple strudel
5   blu ~~pie~~   Wed nite
5   apple
4   flicksut   — Tues.
14   Parfaits —
1   Frozt B_____ — Wed lunch

we're really a dandy trio/With not a stress or strain/And hardly a forte or even con brio/That wouldn't wash down the drain/Nor a gummy sink nor a tattered rug/Can ruffle our peaceful calm/So here's to another wonderful year/Down on the Finestones' farm." *(From Annette & Max Finestone.)*

THE CONCORD

KIAMESHA LAKE, NEW YORK

Menu

Good Afternoon

CHOICE OF JUICE
CHILLED TOMATO JUICE COCKTAIL
HEARTS DELIGHT PRUNE JUICE
CAPE COD CRANBERRY COCKTAIL

SOUP
MANHATTAN FISH CHOWDER
CREAM OF SUN-RIPENED TOMATOES
COLD SHAV

ROAST
HALIBUT, SCALLOP STYLE, TARTARE SAUCE
PLAIN OR OMELETTE CONFITURE
FRESH MUSHROOM PIE JARDINIERE
SPAGHETTI ITALIENNE
CHEESE BLINTZES, SOUR CREAM
COMBINATION VEGETABLE DINNER
CAULIFLOWER POLONAISE   BAKED IDAHO POTATO

COLD SERVICE
FILLET OF MATZES HERRING IN WINE SAUCE

DESSERT
ASSORTED DANISH PASTRY

BEVERAGE
COFFEE   TEA   MILK   POSTUM   BUTTERMILK

Friday, September 7, 1945

Lunch menu from the Concord Hotel in Kiamesha Lake, 1945, with a menu and price estimate on the reverse for a Hadassah affair.

Hadassah Installation Dinner & Dance

150   15.00

Celery en Branche *Relish* Radishes   Sweet Gherkins
Colossal Ripe Olives   Jumbo Queen Olives
Fruit
Chilled Persian Melon

Soup
Fresh Garden Vegetable Soup

Entree
Calves Sweetbreads Financiere en Pate

Roast Quarter *Roast* Parker Farm Broiler Au Cresson
Apple and Raisin Dressing

Fresh Stringbeans   .   Potato Duchesse

Salad
Princess Salad   Newport Dressing

Dessert
Water Ice   .   Petit Fours

Beverage
Orange Pekoe Tea   Demi-Tasse
Iced Tea
Monticello Chapter of Hadassah

The Morningside
ON MORNINGSIDE LAKE
Hurleyville   New York

Menu

PRUNE JUICE

CHOPPED EGG SALAD-GARNITURE

CREAM CHEESE & CRACKERS

SOUP:
        CREAM OF CORN
        COLD BORSCHT

CHOICE OF:
        BOILED WHITE FISH
        VEGETABLE PLATE
        JELLY OMELETTE

DESSERT:
        RICE PUDDING

CHOCOLATE LAYER CAKE

COFFEE   TEA   MILK

WEDNESDAY LUNCHEON
OCTOBER 2, 1946.

Lunch menu from the Morningside Hotel in Hurleyville, 1946, with a mock-up for a brochure on the reverse. Included in the text: "Tropical countries may be glamorous

Week-End Special

at

The MORNINGSIDE

on Morningside Lake

Hurleyville. N.Y.   Phone Hurleyville 200

To acquaint the vacationing public with the MORNING
side we offer special rates for week-ends.
All outdoor sports on premises.
music & entertainment.

During cold weather ice skating sleigh riding
Tobogganing & skiing.

Tropical countries may be glamorous but
add little to your health. Robust sports, invigorating mountain air & stimulating winter
activities coupled with excellent food abun-
dantly served will add years to your life.

Be practical, and enjoy your winter vacation
as nature intended. This outdoor life will
supply you with a new store of vim vigor
& vitality

The morningside
your Host
Arthur Patt

Table of Rates

Friday Supper to and including Sunday dinner
and round trip bus ticket free.

① "Plaza" building rooms & running water 22⁵⁰   ③ "Lake-West" building rooms & shower $24⁵⁰

② "Plaza" building room & bath 24⁵⁰   ④ "Ritz" building de Luxe rooms with bath are these 27⁵⁰

These rates include room & board & transportation for two full days.

These rates do not include Thanksgiving week-end
xmas & N-Year holidays. Lincoln's Birthday. Washington's Birthday
or Easter week.

Prices subject to change | Reservations accepted at this depot

---

but add little to your health. Robust sports, invigorating mountain air, and stimulating winter activities coupled with excellent food elegantly served will add years to your life."

IN THE SULLIVAN COUNTY CATSKILLS

Fannie Shaffer's

VEGETARIAN Hotel

Natural Foods

Phone: (914) 434 - 4455

P.O. BOX 457
WOODRIDGE, NEW YORK 12789

VITAMINS A to E • FOOD CLASSES

A&D

Butter	Cheese
Egg Yolk	Milk
Mushrooms	

A

Apricots	Kale
Carrots	Parsley
Spring Onions	Tomatoes

Green Vegetables
Mustard & Cress

Vitamin A is gradually destroyed by cooking.

Vitamin D is not destroyed by ordinary cooking.

Function of vitamin A-D in the body:
Anti Rickets. Influence on bones and teeth.
Protects from eye disease.
Necessary for growth, nutrition and resistance to disease.

$B\&B_1$

Artichokes	Nuts
Bran	Oat Meal
Barley - Whole	Oranges
Beans - Dried	Parsnips
Buckwheat	Peanuts
Cabbage	Peas - Dried
Egg Yolk	Potatoes
Leeks	Rice
Lentils	Rye
Maize	Tomatoes
Marmite	Water-cress
	Wheat Germ
	Wheat - Whole meal
Mushrooms	Yeast

Not destroyed by cooking but by the use of Soda.

Function of vitamin B, B1 in the body:
Increases appetite. Promotes digestion and growth.
Protects against intestinal trouble and nerve diseases.

B_2

Bran	Molasses
Egg Yolk	Milk
Marmite	Tomatoes
Yeast - Dried	Wheat Germ

Vitamin B2 is not destroyed by ordinary cooking.

Function of vitamin B2 in the body:
Promotes growth in the young. Purifies. Clarity of Skin.

E

Vitamin E for muscle health.

Extra vitamin E should be taken for all muscle deterioration, and in middle and late life. It is to to be found in wheat germ, sesame seed, sunflower seeds, wheat germ oil, and all sprouting seeds and cereals. It protects the health of the heart, blood vessels, muscles, and the reproductive system.

C

Apples	Oranges
Bananas	Peaches
Beetroots	Pineapple
Blackberries	Parsley
Black Currants	Sprouts
Cabbage	Raspberries
Grapefruit	Sweet Pepper
Strawberries	
Green Vegetables - raw	
Kale	Tangerines
Lemons	Turnip Tops
Milk - Raw	Tomatoes
Mustard & Cress	
Watercress	

Vitamin C is destroyed by heat.

Function of vitamin C in the body:
Protects against disease and malnutrition. Prevents Scurvy. Protects against teeth defects.

STARCH & DEXTRINES

Carbohydrates
Predominant chemical elements: Carbon, Oxygen, Hydrogen.
Function in the body: Produces Heat and Energy. Utilises fat.

CEREALS — The inner white parts of Barley, Buckwheat, Corn, Oats, Rice, Rye and Wheat. Cornflour, Oatmeal, Soya Flour, Tapioca. Wheat and Wholemeal Bread.
VEGETABLES — Beans, Dried Peas, Green Peas, Lentils, Parsnip, Potatoes, Pumpkins, Roots and Runner Beans.
FRUITS — Bananas.
NUTS — Brazils, Chestnuts, Peanuts and Walnuts.

FATS & OILS

Predominant chemical elements: Carbon, Oxygen, Hydrogen.
Function in the body: Heat and energy for future use by storing.

FRUITS — Olives.
DAIRY PRODUCTS — Butter, Cream, Cheese and Egg Yolk.
NUTS — Almonds, Almond Cream, Barcelona nuts, Brazil nuts, Cashew Nut Butter, Coconut, Peanuts, Pine Kernels and Walnuts.
COMMERCIAL OIL — Olive Oil, Peanut Butter, Peanut Oil and Vegetable Cooking Oil.

SUGAR

Carbohydrates
Predominant chemical elements: Carbon, Oxygen, Hydrogen.
Function in the body: Heat and energy.

VEGETABLES — Beets, Carrots and Melons.
FRUITS — Apples, Bananas, Dates, Figs, Grapes, Orange Juice, Pears, Prunes, Raisins and [illegible]spberries.
DAIRY PRODUCTS — Milk.
NATURAL SUGARS — Honey and Maple Sugar.
COMMERCIAL SUGARS — Syrup and Glucose.
NUTS — Almonds and Coconuts.

PROTEINS

Predominant chemical elements: Carbon, Oxygen, Nitrogen, Phosphorus, Sulphur.
Function in the body: Heat and energy for reserve only. Building and repair of tissue and nerves.

CEREALS — The outer dark parts of — Barley, Corn, Oats, Rice, Rye, Wheat and Wheat Germ. Oatmeal, Soya Flour and Wholemeal Bread.
VEGETABLES — Beans, Lentils, Mushrooms, Peas, and Potatoes.
FRUIT — Dried Apricots, Dates and Figs.
NUTS — Almonds, Almond Cream, Barcelona nuts, Brazil nuts, Chestnuts, Coconuts, Hazelnuts, Peanuts, Pecan nuts, Pine Kernels and Walnuts.

FOODS CONTAINING THE 16 MINERAL SALTS

(1) OXYGEN FOODS

Horseradish	Potatoes
Mint	Radishes
Onions	Rhubarb
Parsley	Tomatoes

Function in the body: Intensifies and brightens Mind.

(2) CARBON FOODS

Apples	Grains
Beans	Lentils
Cereals	Grapes
Candies	Peas
Dates	Potatoes

Function in the body: Acts on Oxygen, generating body heat.

(3) HYDROGEN FOODS

Berries	Milk
Fruits	Melons
Vegetables—Non-Starchy	

Function in the body: Gives energy, cleansing acid perspiration.

(4) CALCIUM FOODS

Almonds	Limes
Apples	Milk
Apricots	Mushrooms
Asparagus	Nettles
Blackberries	Oatmeal
Bran	Olives
Brazil nuts	Onions
Cabbage	Oranges
—Savoy	
—Red and White	
Cauliflower	Parsnips
Carrots	Peanuts
Cherries	Pears
Chives	Peas
Citron	Pineapple
Cottage Cheese	Plums
Cucumber	Prunes
Currants	Pumpkins
Dandelion leaves	
	Radishes
Dill	Rhubarb
Eggs	Ryebran
Egg Yolk	Sorrell
Figs	Soya Beans
Filberts	Spinach
Gooseberries	Strawberries
Grapes	Tomatoes
Hazelnuts	Turnip Tops
Horseradish	Walnuts
Honey	Watercress
Lemons	Wheat
Lentils	Wholewheat
Lettuce	

Function in the body:
Bone makers. Fortifies against Tb. Strengthens enamel of teeth for unborn children.
Necessary where poor circulation of the blood is known.

(5) NITROGEN FOODS

Almonds	Milk
Beans	Peanuts
Cheese	Peas
Egg White	Walnuts

Function in the body:
These act as a check on C.O.H. foods.
Prevents excessive heat.

(6) PHOSPHORUS FOODS

All seeds	Mustard Seed
Barley—Whole	Olives
Beans	Peanuts
Blue-berries	Pecan nuts
Buttermilk	Prunes
Cabbage-savoy	Pumpkins
Cauliflower	Radishes
Celery	Rhubarb
Cheese	Rice Bran
Cucumber	Rye Bran
Dill	Sea Foods
Egg Plant	Sorrell
Egg Yolk	Soya Beans
Grain shells	Spinach
Kale	Truffles
Leek bulbs	Walnuts
Lettuce	Watercress
Milk	Wheat Bran
Mushrooms	Whole wheat

Many fruits have a small percentage of phosphorus.

Function in the body:
Feeds nerves and brain, giving increased mental energy. Thinking consumes phosphorus, and it also gives us the power to get "things across", so necessary to the actor, teacher, salesman and others too numerous to mention. Cooking destroys the phosphorus in foods.

(7) CHLORINE FOODS

Asparagus	Onions
Beetroots	Prunes
Butter	Radishes
Cabbage	Rhubarb
Celery	Roquefort cheese
Coconuts	Sorrell
Dill	Spinach
Egg White	Sweet Potatoes
Goats Milk	Tomatoes
Kale	Turnips
Lettuce	Whey

Other foods have a smaller percentage of chlorine.

Function in the body: Reduces fat and eliminates waste.

(8) SULPHUR FOODS

Almonds	Kale
Asparagus	Kohlrabi
Brussel Sprouts	Lettuce
Cabbage	Mustard
Carrots	Okra
Cauliflower	Onions
Cherries - dark	Parsnips
Coconut	Potatoes
Cucumber	Prunes
Egg Yolk	Radishes
Figs	Sorrell
Garlic	Spinach
Greens	Strawberries
Gooseberries	Turnips
Horseradish	Watercress

Function in the body:
Assists the body to throw off impurities through the skin.
Sulphur is a blood purifier. Plenty of these foods should be eaten in the early spring to assist the body in throwing off toxins collected through the winter, through eating extra starch foods, less exercise and possibly more sitting over fires.

(9) FLUORINE FOODS

Barley	Leeks
Beetroots	Oatmeal
Brown rice	Red Cabbage
Brussel Sprouts	
	Roquefort Cheese
Cabbage	Rye
Cauliflower	Sauerkraut
Egg Yolk - raw	Spinach
Garlic	Watercress
Goats milk	Whole wheat

Function in the body:
For the enamel of the teeth, and the glossy surface of bone. Helps the eyes.

(10) MAGNESIUM FOODS

Almonds	Okra
Beechnuts	Onions
Bran	Oranges
Cabbage	Pecan nuts
Celery	Prunes
Chestnuts	Rice
Chick peas	Rice Bran
Coconuts	Rye
Dandelion	Sorrell
Dill	Spinach
Egg Plant	Tomatoes
Grapefruit	Turnips
Kale	Walnuts
Kohlrabi	Watercress
Lettuce	Whole Oats
Oats	Whole Wheat

Function in the body:
Makes blood alkaline. Balances over taut muscles. Laxatives, sleep promoters and hardens teeth. Vitalisers of brain and nerve tissue.

FOODS CONTAINING THE 16 MINERAL SALTS

(11) POTASSIUM FOODS

Artichokes	Dried Olives
Asparagus	Grapefruit
Beetroots	Kale
Bitter Herbs	Kohlrabi
Brussel Sprouts	Parsley
Cabbage	Peppermint
Carrots	Potatoes
Cauliflower	Radishes
Chicory	Rhubarb
Cress	Sorrell
Cucumber	Tomatoes
Dandelion	Wintergreen

Nearly all vegetables and legumes are well supplied with potassium, but fruits, cereals and nuts show a deficiency generally.

Function in the body:
Stimulates oxidation of tissues. Aids in metabolism.
Stimulates Nerves.
Concerned in generation of vital elasticity.

(12) SODIUM FOODS

Almonds	Leeks
Apples	Lemons
Apricots	Lentils
Artichokes	Lettuce
Asparagus	Mushrooms
Barley	Nettles
Beans	Oats
Beechnuts	Okra
Beetroots	Olives
Cabbage - Savoy	Oranges
Carrots	
Cauliflower	Peanuts
Celery	Pears
Cheese	Peas
Chives	Pecan nuts
Coconuts	Prunes
Cucumber	Pumpkins
Currants	Radishes
Dandelion	Raisins
Dates	Red Cabbage
Dill	
Dried Figs	Sorrell
Eggs	Spinach
Egg Yolk	Strawberries
Filberts	Tomatoes
Gooseberries	Turnips
Grapes	Water Melon
Horseradish	Whey
Kohlrabi	Whole Wheat

Function in the body:
Increases osmosis and holds calcium in solution.
Helps to form saliva, bile and pancreatic juice.
Gives calmness and stability—needed by the people who live on their nerves.

(13) IRON FOODS

All Greens	Lettuce
Almonds	Milk
Apples-Red	Mushrooms
Artichokes	Nettles
Asparagus	Nuts
Barley	Oats
Bartlett Pears	Oranges
Beans	Parsnips
Beetroots	Peanuts
Beet Tops	Pears
Blackberries	Peas
Brazil nuts	Pineapple
Cabbage-Savoy	
Carrot tops	Plums
Cauliflower	Prunes
Celery	Pumpkins
Cheese	Radishes
Cherries	Raisins
Chives	Red Cabbage
Coconuts	Rice - whole
Cucumber	Rye
Dandelion leaves	Rye Bran
Dates	Sorrell
Dill	Spinach
Egg Yolk	Strawberries
Figs	Tomatoes
Filberts	Turnips
Gooseberries	Turnip tops
Grapes	Walnuts
Horseradish	Wheat Bran
Leeks	Whey
Lentils	Whole Wheat

Function in the body:
Carries Oxygen. Increases resistance against disease.
Increases personal magnetism, gives vitality to the body, endurance to the mind, strengthens the will, gives courage and that essence which in character makes us see a job through.

(14) SILICON FOODS

Artichokes	Leeks
Asparagus	Milk - raw
Barley	Oats
Beetroots - Red and White	
Cabbage	Parsnips
Cauliflower	Potato Skin
Celery	Pumpkins
Cucumber	Radishes
Dandelion	Rhubarb
Dill	Rice
Fruit Skins	Spinach
Grain - outer shells	Strawberries
	Sunflower Seeds
Horseradish	Tomatoes
Kohlrabi	Turnips
Lamb's Lettuce	
Nearly all vegetables	

most cereals and all fruits contain silicon.

Function in the body:
Increases brain activity. Clears Skin. Anti-septics. Strengthens Hair. Raises the resistance to ulcers, Tb. and Growths. Increases grit and self confidence.

(15) MANGANESE FOODS

Almonds	Parsley
	Peppermint leaf
Chestnuts	Pignolias
Egg Yolk - raw	Pumpkins
Endives	Squash
Nasturtium flowers	
Okra	Walnuts
Olives	Watercress
Wintergreen	

Function in the body:
Anti-septic. Increase metabolism. Carries Oxygen.

(16) IODINE FOODS

Artichokes	Irish Moss
Asparagus	Kelp
Beetroots	Leeks
Berries - dark	Lettuce
Cabbage	Melons
Carrots	Mushrooms
Celery	Onions
Cucumber	Pineapple
Dry White beans	Potatoes
Dulse	Radishes
Egg Yolk	Spinach
Endives	Strawberries
Fruits - dark	Tomatoes
Garlic	
Grapes	
Green Kidney Beans	
Green Peas	Turnips
Vegetables - dark	

Function in the body:
Stimulates and balances glandular excretions.

CALORIES

A calorie is the amount of heat required to raise one kilogramme of water one degree centigrade.

1 gramme Protein = 4 calories
1 gramme Carbohydrates = 4 calories
1 gramme Fat = 9 calories

There are 28.3495 grammes to the ounce.

For easy calculation this may be calculated at 30 grammes to the ounce.

Nutrition information sheet from the Vegetarian Hotel in Woodridge, a health rarity in the Catskills. *(From Verb Konviser.)*

-BREAKFAST-

Fruits

Orange Juice	Baked Apple	Figs Preserved
Melons (in season)	Orange, Half	Prunes, Stewed
Grapefruit Juice	Sliced Orange	Pineapple Juice
Tomato Juice	Prune Juice	Sauerkraut Juice
	Grapefruit, Half	

Appetizers

Pickled Salmon   Sardines   Smoked Salmon

Herring (as you like it) Pickled, Plain, Matjes

Baked or Fried Herring with Potato

Cereals

Oatmeal	Cream of Wheat	Wheatena
Corn Flakes	40% Bran Flakes	Pep
Rice Crispies	Whole Wheat Biscuit	Wheaties
Puffed Rice	Crackles	Grape Nuts
All Bran	Huskies	Corn Kix

Eggs and Omelettes

Boiled any Style, Scrambled, Fried, Poached, Tomato

Jelly, Plain, Parsley, Onion, Lox Omelettes

Breads, Cakes and Preserves

Assorted Breakfast Rolls	French Toast
Griddle Cakes with Maple Syrup	Cinnamon Toast Dry or Buttered
Coffee Cake	Fruit Preserves

Beverages

Coffee   Tea   Milk   Postum   Cocoa   Chocolate

Meal Hours : Breakfast, 8:00   ✦   Luncheon, 1:00   ✦   Dinner, 7:00

✦ Extra Charge for Room Service ✦

Where Every Vacation Desire is Fulfilled

Breakfast menu in green and purple from the Stevensville Hotel in Swan Lake, where I once waited tables and where my father once ran the coffee shop.

GOOD AFTERNOON!

ICED DOLES PINEAPPLE JUICE

CHILLED APPLE CHAMPAGNE   FROSTED OREGON PRUNE JUICE

BISQUE OF TOMATO SOUP
RED BEET BORSCHT, BOILED POTATO
COLD SCHAV, ROMANOFF

CHOICE OF:

    BAKED FILET OF SEA TROUT, HOTELIERE
    GOLDEN BROWN MUSHROOM LOAF, SAUCE DUXELLES
    GEFILTE FISH BALLS, MOTHER'S STYLE, CASSEROLE
    CANTONESE STYLE VEGETABLE CHOW MEIN, GARNI
    FLUFFY PLAIN OR JELLY OMELETTE, GARNITURE
    GARDEN FRESH VEGETABLE LUNCHEON, BAKED POTATO
    CHOPPED EGGS AND SPINACH SALAD, LETTUCE AND TOMATO
    MINCED ALBACORE WHITE MEAT TUNA FISH SALAD
    ROYAL CHINOOK SALMON SALAD, LETTUCE AND TOMATO
    INDIVIDUAL GREEK SALAD BOWL, HERRING TIDBITS
    CALIFORNIA FRUIT SALAD PLATE, COTTAGE CHEESE
    HEAVY SOUR CREAM WITH: STRAWBERRIES
                                      BLUEBERRIES
                                      SLICED BANANA
                                      GEORGIA PEACHES
    ANNA POTATOES   COTTAGE CHEESE
    WHOLE KERNEL CORN   DICED VEGETABLES

CHOICE OF:

    BANANA CREAM TART   OLD FASHIONED JELLY ROLL
    DANISH BUTTER HORN   VANILLA FUDGE WAFERS
    CHOCOLATE PUDDING   FRUIT FLAVORED JELLO

COFFEE   MILK   BUTTERMILK   CHOCOLATE MILK   SANKA   TEA

MR. KERMIT BUCKTER, MAITRE D' * TUESDAY LUNCH, JULY 29, 1980

Salt Free and Sugar Free Diets Available
* * * * * * * * *

Brown's Hotel (the very large and famous Brown's in Loch Sheldrake, not ours) lunch menu, 1980.

Chapter 5

Entertainment

"At Cohen's [bungalow colony] it was a barn.
We used the upstairs as a casino,
and the downstairs they used to roller skate!"

M uch is written about the fabulous entertainment in the large Catskill resorts, and a good deal of the glamour of Catskill memories involves the career launchings of famous singers and comics. That is certainly a part of the legacy. Sid Caesar started at the Avon Lodge in Woodridge, just down the road from Sunny Oaks, site of the History of the Catskills conferences. Freddie Roman, too, worked in the neighborhood as a staff entertainer. He readily recalled it when he spoke in 1996 at the second History of the Catskills conference, reminiscing about the life of comics in the Mountains:

In 1957, my first job in show business was three quarters of a mile down this road. I worked at a place called the Biltmore Hotel. It was just across the road from Avon Lodge. And I was the social director and master of ceremonies. I was twenty years old. I got thirty-five dollars a week. But my deal was that Saturday nights I could go out and do an act at other hotels, which was a terrific deal except that I didn't really have an act at the time. I stole four minutes from Larry Best, four minutes from Larry Alpert, six minutes from Myron Cohen, and that was my act, it really was. So, being the entrepreneurial businessman that I am, I drove along this road and I stopped at Sunny Oaks and said,

"Hello, I'm the comedian and star of the Biltmore Hotel, but I'm allowed to be off on Saturday nights and I thought maybe you could use some entertainment. I would like thirty dollars for the evening." And they said, "We were thinking more of fifteen," and I compromised at twenty.

Although that was Freddie Roman's first summer as an MC, he did get a start five years before, while working in his uncle and grandfather's Crystal Springs Hotel in Youngsville. At fourteen he ran the concession:

I was fascinated being in the casino with the entertainers that came in. I would watch the rehearsal, and I loved that part of the business. So next summer, at age fifteen, I asked him [his uncle] if I could not only do the concession but if I could also MC the shows. So that was really my first time ever on the stage. I would get up and I would do one joke and introduce the act. And everyone said, "Isn't that cute, a fat little kid in a pink dinner jacket. And he's the owner's nephew, he's adorable, and he sold me ice cream this afternoon. He's so busy, this young man." And that was my introduction to show business, really.

Red Buttons, Alan King, Leslie Uggams, Billy Eckstine, Totie Fields, Jackie Mason, Buddy Hackett, Billy Crystal, Milton Berle, Eddie Fisher, Robert Merrill, Neil Sedaka, Joey Bishop, Myron Cohen, Don Rickles, and countless other comics and singers got their start in the Catskills. But in smaller hotels, performers were not necessarily so great. Indeed, on talent night in the Seven Gables, guests and staff frequently did imitations of acts they found wanting. I once got the nerve up to do this, and they let me perform. My act was mimicking a comic who had appeared the week before, doing a take-off on a pasta commercial. In my attempt at verisimilitude, I goofed on the comic's take-off by casting noodles from a box. When I finished the act, the MC made me sweep up the noodles, which affronted me, since I felt that I was the act at that moment, and the act shouldn't have to clean up from his own performance.

Except for the few grand ones, the earliest resorts had no formal entertainment. Murray Posner reflected on the simplicity of entertainment in the 1910s at the boardinghouse that would become Brickman's: "The boarders came here and they rocked in hammocks and my grandfather took them on hayrides and that's how they entertained them. At night they sat on the rocking chairs and had community sings and they entertained themselves." In the 1920s, recalled an eighty-two-year-old man, it required little to amuse the guests:

> A favorite way of spending time was to walk the two miles to Hurleyville in the morning after breakfast and hitch a ride back in the jitney that each hotel sent to meet the trains at about 12:30. Another form of amusement that some guests enjoyed was to hire a large touring car and driver to ride around the countryside for several hours. These open cars held up to seven people, plus one or two children on laps, and two families or so could pile in and generally pass a pleasant afternoon.

As the resorts grew, entertainment became a bit more lavish than simple car rides. Murray Posner remembered an early stage in the 1920s when a black singer, Mendel, walked from hotel to hotel: "He knew every Jewish song there was. He would sing and people would pass the hat." Once bitten, you couldn't get the entertainment out of your blood. A woman recalled her 1934–1936 summers at Friedman's Cottage, a kuchalayn. She and her sister teamed up with an existing singing act, the Feder Sisters, and they performed—with their stage being a flat rock in front of a hill. Fifteen years later, on her honeymoon in Livingston Manor, her husband brought his accordion and the two of them spent the weekend singing to the guests. The hotel owner then hired them to return on weekends.

Entertainment in the Catskills started out very nonprofessionally. The owner of the defunct Windsor tells of the early years:

> Well, they had shows in the thirties, but they were minimal. There would be a social director who would get some of the guests and some of the employees, and put up a show. But mostly it was the masquerade ball or the farmers' night or a dance marathon thing, balloon dances and those kinds of things. And then it started to break into have-your-own-staff in the early forties. You had a production man, we had our own scenic man, we had our own comedian, our own singer; in fact, we even kept four girls as a chorus line and some of the guests would participate in shows that the production man would write up. And then it started to bring in some name acts in addition. And eventually these amateur nights sort of died out and it became only professionals.

In addition to amateur nights, mock weddings, and movies, hotels found novel and sometimes no-cost ways to keep the guests entertained. Sometimes a traveling Jewish theater group would perform for whatever they got from passing the hat.

Some hotels avoided most or all of the traditional entertainment, preferring to foster an intellectual and artistic climate rather than the usual vaudevillian style. Chait's in Accord provided classical music, political lectures, and book discussions. As an amateur musician, I was always quite astounded by the high quality of classical music there. Chester's Zunbarg and the South Wind in Woodbourne, Maud's Summer-Ray in North Branch, Skliar's and the Harmony Country Club in Monticello, and the Eager Rose Garden in Bushkill were also noted for that intellectual climate. A friend of Zuni Maud, co-owner of Maud's Summer-Ray, remembered hearing musicians from philharmonic orchestras, listening to important Yiddish writers, and attending Yiddish poetry sessions on the lawn. Zuni Maud, an accomplished artist in many media, covered the hotel's walls with murals based on a 1920s Russian modernist style. So important was Yiddish that a large number of people referred to the hotel by its Yiddish name, Zumeray.

Anne Chester recalled how she was able to get musicians from the major philharmonic orchestras in the country:

Ray Lev, . . . an internationally known pianist, wanted to assemble well-known musicians who liked to play chamber music together and make it an annual vacation at Chester's. Once, when she was up, she suggested this idea, and I said not only didn't I have contacts with these great musicians she mentioned, but I couldn't afford them. "Well," said Ray, "I can get them to come up. They will enjoy the surroundings, we like to play chamber music together, and they will welcome vacations with their musician friends in this friendly atmosphere."

In addition to classical musicians, Anne Chester remembers the talented retinue of others who performed at her hotel: Alan Arkin, Harry Belafonte, Sam Levinson, Anne Bancroft, Zero Mostel, Paul Robeson, Pete Seeger, Dick Cavett, Howard Da Silva, and Barbra Streisand.

At the Vegetarian Hotel in Woodridge, the typical Catskill routines were embellished with both intellectual and health-related activities:

We would entertain the people from the time they got there until they left. People used to get up in the morning, and we'd take them for a hike.

8:30 was breakfast. 10:00 A.M. we did yoga. After that was swimming, boating. Lunch. After lunch we had lectures under the tree of knowledge. We used to get people, chiropractors, [practitioners of] natural health, [who] would lecture on how to eat, how to combine foods. 5:00 P.M. was folk dancing. After that was dinner. After dinner was a band and an MC. We'd have shows and dancing. It was a full day. All *Yiddishkeit.*

As the years progressed, the prevailing mode in Catskill resorts was to provide as much entertainment and instruction as possible. Murray Posner of the Brickman opined:

Sometimes I think to myself, you know, I'm not running a resort hotel. I'm running a school. We teach them how to dance. We teach them how to play tennis. We teach them how to ride a horse. We teach them how to play golf. We teach them how to draw and paint. We have art classes here. And it goes on and on like that. You should get a diploma, not a receipt, when you leave my hotel.

Tummlers

The "tummler" was a social director, a central component of Catskill life, moving its performing arts into a more developed and professional realm. At the Brickman's, the first such staffer signed on in 1925 for the glorious summer salary of $200. Joey Adams, who held such a position, recounts that "a toomler, derived from tumult-maker, is Castilian Yiddish for a fool or noisemaker who does anything and everything to entertain the customers so that they won't squawk about their rooms or food." Entertainment was at first begrudgingly hired, and the owners expected the tummler to do most of it himself. Joey Adams explains:

In the early days, . . . the social director had to be producer, director, writer, actor, song-and-dance man, emcee, comedian, scenic designer, electrician, stage manager, stagehand, and sometimes waiter. After the show he had to mingle with the guests, dance with the fat old women, and romance the 'dogs.' In addition, he was the *shadchon,* or marriage broker. But these were only his evening chores. During daylight he doubled as sports and activities director.

Like everything else in the Catskills, whoever was working was doing so to the utmost, with owners wringing as much as possible out of each staff person. But, also like many Catskill work arrangements, the social macher's job had two sides: "Despite the hardships, social directing was a great opportunity for talent development. Where else could we experiment without restraint, trying out routines, ideas, songs—and with captive audiences who were not only starved for entertainment, but were our fans before we even crept onstage?" Still, "if you die at a nightclub or in a theatre, you can always run home," Adams recalls, but "the roughest thing in the whole world is to lay an egg at a show in the Catskills. There is no place you can hide."

Especially in bad weather, tummlers had to extend themselves to entertain guests. An early favorite was the tummler's ranting and raving, shouting gibberish, and diving fully clothed into the pool or lake. Some tummlers pretended to be other hotel staff, like the maitre d', playing tricks on the guests. Jerry Lewis liked to roll down the stairs. Not all hotel owners could appreciate the crazy antics of the tummlers: "In the Highmount Country Club, I was there in 1950. I worked as a busboy. The owner of the place was noted for a decision he had made a number of years earlier. He had hired Danny Kaye. He was there on a Friday night and they fired him on Saturday. That was his claim to fame. It was the late 1930s. [Kaye] was hired as the tummler. [The owner] fired him because he was crazy." Small hotels could revel later about how their early tummlers had gone on to become world famous; one example was from the daughter of the Irvington's owners, where Red Buttons was the social macher for a while in the 1940s.

Theatrics

In the eyes of John Wiener, a family member from the White Roe, the uniqueness in Catskill entertainment was before World War II, when resorts had their own entertainment. White Roe had thirty entertainers on staff, including Danny Kaye, who worked there for seven years. "We had a casino with dimmer systems, spotlights, everything else a theater would have." It could seat 750. There was also a nightclub with a small orchestra downstairs. The casino put on cut-down versions of musicals. If the shows were not enough, the hotel added other extras, Wiener noted: "They took moving pictures of the guests and drove to New York to get them developed and then showed them to the guests, in the 1940s and 1950s."

Paul's Hotel, grander in the 1920s and 1930s than when I worked there in the 1960s, had four chorus boys, four chorus girls, a prop man, and a wardrobe mistress for putting on major dramatic and comic presentations. Tummlers and their assistants frequently attended the newest Broadway shows to take down verbatim the plot, lines, scenery, and music. Social directors organized these copies, alternating them with original skits, drawing on the labor of many resident staffers. Moss Hart is well-known for his famous extravaganzas at the Flagler, one of the premier resorts of the 1920s and 1930s. His staff of twenty-six, including Dore Schary, staged fine drama as well as knock-offs of Broadway shows.

As Murray Posner, owner of the Brickman Hotel, understood it, the advent of talkie movies in the 1920s put many vaudeville entertainers out of work. They then became inexpensive staff members for the hotels' elaborate theatrical crews. As a young man, Posner enjoyed working alongside the entertainment staff, painting scenery, doing stage carpentry, and acting in skits. He even considered a career in show business, and one season he left the family hotel for a very brief entertaining sojourn at the Windsor Lake Hotel in Greenfield Park. But his father retorted, "Show business is for bums. You're going to college."

Herman Wouk, in *Marjorie Morningstar,* also portrays these elegant productions at his fictional resort, organized by a director of New York City fame. These grand shows by large social staffs declined during and after World War II—social staff were at risk for being drafted, production costs escalated with the growing competition among resorts, and guests tired of the same routines all summer and even in subsequent years. As well, entertainers found new opportunities in summer stock and off-Broadway theater, and in the new TV industry. Those who remained working in the Mountains did so as individual acts, making far more than their seasonal salaries by doing double and triple appearances each night.

Traveling Entertainers

More than one hotel owner claimed responsibility for the shift from resident entertainers to traveling acts. Frank Goldstein said that in the 1930s his Morningside convinced other hotels to stop having their own huge staffs and to have acts circulate through the hotels instead:

Now there were a few hotels we had association with. I said to each individual, I said, "You know, we are very foolish. Each of us spends a lot of money. Why don't we pool our money and have a pool to hire people. You could have instead of one act a night, have five acts. Then these acts would go from one hotel to the other." Well, the system was good. Then, of course, in the 1930s, a lot of actors were very glad to get opportunities. So, they would come up and entertain for very little money. You could get five to six acts, very good acts, to come and play. Say, act number 1 would start at hotel 1. When it was through, in 15–20 minutes, they would be whisked to hotel 2, 3, 4.

For entertainers, this traveling about was a big problem. Doing three shows on a weekend night might mean driving twenty to thirty miles between shows. Once, when leaving the second show of the night, Freddie Roman's car went into a ditch, making it impossible to get to the next show on time:

I got to the third show at a quarter to two. There was nobody left. The owner of the hotel, at a quarter to two, got onto the public address system: "He's here! I told you I booked a show! You bastards, you thought I didn't book a show! I booked a show and he's here!" And sure enough, like little mice, they came back. And at 2:15 in the morning I went on, till 3:00 o'clock.

In addition to hiring acts, some hotels maintained resident entertainers, though not the huge social staffs of the early years. These acts would get free room and board in exchange for one show a week; the rest of the week they were free to play at other hotels. My own parents, always enticing relatives and friends to go to the Mountains, even found people to fit this bill. Our friend Zsu Zsa had left Hungary after the 1956 rebellion, married Freddie Dawson in Canada, and wound up in North Miami Beach. Knowing that they were having a hard time getting their performing careers off the ground, my parents arranged for them to come to Paul's in Swan Lake around 1963 (remember, everyone was going to someday get their break in the Catskills). In their "Don't Stop, Go! Revue," Zsu Zsa played piano, Freddie played horn, both sang, and the difference was made up by a young drummer who also sang a little. These three entertainers, with their intense show business energy, could easily do a show of an hour and a half, and still have strength to drive to a later engagement or two.

People are thrilled to remember having seen famous people before they became famous—in their debuts, or even as children. A Loch Sheldrake owner proudly spoke of having Henny Youngman as the bandleader in the 1920s, along with Danny Kaye as a busboy. One woman recalled fifty-five years back, to 1940, when she was a guest at the Majestic: "That was the year when Danny Lewis was the social director. His wife played the piano, and Jerry Lewis was one of the kids at the hotel." Sneaking a look through the casino at Chester's, one man heard the announcer say, "We have a new entertainer from Brooklyn who's trying out some new material—Sam Levinson." A waiter told me of spending time with Buddy Hackett, shooting rats with a rifle at the hotel's trash dump. I liked that story, since at the age of eleven I had in fact learned to shoot a .22 at a hotel dump, driving there with the handyman and his truck full of garbage. Not all the famous acts fared so well early in their careers. Owners could find themselves furious at the way an act played, as happened at the Irvington:

> Jackie Mason was playing at our hotel. He was known a little, but he wasn't famous as he is now. He was really dirty. They all had a little sexual innuendo, all the comedians. And my uncle, who was not the one who usually took care of the entertainment—he was the kitchen person—came to the show that night, and he was mortified that someone was saying things that were so dirty and he literally got up and pulled him off the stage.

Sullivan and Ulster Counties burst with just such a variety of entertainment in the hotels. Residents of the bungalow colonies and very small hotels, of course, saw the opportunity to get free amusement and spent lots of time crashing shows. Sometimes this was at a nearby resort, since there were so many all over the Mountains. But often people would drive far in search of a good show. The better the hotel, the greater the security had to be to deal with this. I tramped through back woods on occasion to get into top places. Many hotels stamped guests leaving the dining room at night with invisible ink that only appeared under ultraviolet lamps placed at the nightclub entrance. Some places made you show room keys. Smaller places relied on owners, who knew all the guests, patrolling in search of outsiders. In fact, they knew many of the outsiders as longtime vacationers from somewhere down the road, and spoke of how once again they had caught so-and-so trying to get into the show.

Some hotels advertised entertainment to a broad audience, charging admission by the head. This was more likely to be mid-week rock groups or late-night weekend strippers, as opposed to the regular evening shows for guests. In fact, the 1960s phenomenon of rock shows in the larger medium-size hotels was a way of staying alive in a declining resort environment. The Eldorado pioneered in this, bringing acts like Jay and the Americans, The Shirelles, and The Drifters. I loved going to these shows, especially as I never had the chance to hear these groups back in Florida.

Scattered across the two counties' endless resorts were a panoply of entertainment possibilities. Roberta, a hotel owner's daughter, still runs a ballroom in Florida with her husband. Working in the family resort, she recalls: "Irving and I, who are dancers, couldn't wait until evening when we enjoyed dancing in all the large hotels. We knew all of the dance instructors and performers. There was 'Mambo Fiesta Nite' in a different hotel every night. Tuesday, we went to the Waldemere Hotel in Livingston Manor, where 'Mambo Bob' put on a fantastic show; Wednesday night it was Brown's Hotel in the Jerry Lewis Room; Thursday nights, it was the Raleigh Hotel in the Sammy Davis Room."

After-hours pleasure abounded too. I accompanied band members to a motel bar in Monticello where jazz players came to sit after finishing their night's work in the hotels. A variety of such venues dotted the Mountains. As the Excelsior's owners remembered of their excellent pianist, "Mel Powell later played piano for Benny Goodman and became a professor of music on the West Coast. While he was at the Excelsior, musicians used to come by for a jazz session on Monday nights."

Comedian Freddy Roman picked up his soon-to-be-wife, a counselor at the Alamac Country Club in Woodridge, and returned to the Homowack to MC the show. After that show, they went to the late show at the Brown's:

And unbeknownst to me it was jammed. It was Jerry Lewis's birthday, and every comic in the Catskills—and I'm talking Phil Foster and Myron Cohen and Henny Youngman and Jack Carter and Jan Murray—came to celebrate Jerry's birthday that July 4th weekend at the Brown Derby. In the middle of the show, Jerry Lewis crawled in under the tables—he didn't want to upset anything, which was nonsense; everybody was watching him. And every comic in the Mountains got up that night. The show started at one o'clock; at four forty-five in the morning, Jerry took everyone out on the handball court and did Simon Sez. And that's the only way anyone would leave. Now picture this—it's four forty-five, it's my first date with my wife, and she has to be at breakfast with the kids at the Alamac at eight o'clock in the morning. I get her back to the Alamac, it's like 5:30. I drop her off. I go back to the Homowack, it's after 6 o'clock, I'm still in my tuxedo from the night before. The owner of Homowack's name was Irving Blickstein; now I walk into the kitchen at 6:30 in the morning in a tuxedo, and he calls me over and says, "Sonny, I know this is your first job. But for breakfast you could come down in shorts."

For guests and staff not sated by the hotel's shows, there were late-night clubs in town: the Wonderbar in Old Falls, Rainbow Gardens in Monticello, 52 Club in Loch Sheldrake, and Cozy Corners in Loch Sheldrake. The owner of the Gaiety Burlesque told me how his South Fallsburg spot jumped late into the nights for those who wanted striptease acts.

The Casino

Smaller hotels and many bungalow colonies had casinos rather than nightclubs. Casinos could serve many purposes, as this chapter's epigraph reveals: "At Cohen's [bungalow colony] it was a barn. We used the upstairs as a casino, and the downstairs they used to roller skate!" Small hotel casinos had folding wooden chairs, unlike fancier hotel nightclubs. Typically, a hotel would not build a "nightclub" until the hotel could hold 200–250 people, particularly if guests were young enough to be active drinkers. In the more modest resorts, and even in small- to medium-size places with a nightclub, one night there would be a movie, another night bingo. Sunday night was "champagne night," where two dancers took spins with the willing (maybe semi-willing—"Sammy, go ahead, do a little cha-cha with the lady") audience, and the winner decided by applause, walking away with a bottle of champagne. The real "shows" were on Friday and Saturday nights, most often featuring both a singer and a comic.

The casino at the Seven Gables, where my mother cooked for six or seven years, was classic minimalist—large rectangular room with rows of wooden folding chairs. At one end was a stage, at the other a counter across the width—one half a liquor bar with perhaps a dozen stools, the other half a snack bar with about the same number of stools. Everything was ordered from this little spot before and during shows, movies, and other events. Throughout the day, this was the place to get snacks, soda, ice cream, and sundries. For a couple of years, my father ran this establishment, and I helped out behind the counter even at the age of ten. I convinced him that besides toiletries we should stock model plane and car kits, which I wound up assembling myself. Slightly larger hotels had a separate coffee shop, with tables as well as a counter, and 50–100 people might squeeze in for bagels, coffee, and sundaes after the show let out. This reduced the noise level in the casino or nightclub, which reflected a more elabo-rate resort.

Hotel nightclubs differed from casinos in several ways. One, they existed only in hotels with a sizeable enough number of guests to make it worthwhile—say, over 200–250 guests. Two, they had tables and chairs, like a real nightclub, rather than the rows of folding wooden chairs typical of a casino. Three, they were likely to have more modern construction, rather than the creaking wood floors of barn-like casino buildings. Four, with a nightclub, there was a maitre d' who reserved tables, getting tips for front-row tables. This differed dramati-cally from the casino style where people came in quite shortly after dinner to re-serve rows of seats, with either one person sitting there and holding many seats for the rest or by guests throwing jackets over the seats. And nightclub waiters came around taking orders for drinks, rather than guests grabbing their own so-das or drinks at a casino's counter. Five, nightclubs tended to have an attached bar and a coffee shop. The bar was used especially for late shows on weekends where strippers were featured, but also for general late-night drinking, some-times with a musician or two playing lounge music.

At the Karmel, the proprietors tried to drum up a lounge crowd by hiring a guitarist to play in the bar/lounge after the show. Harlan played standards and jazz tunes with his amplified acoustic guitar, and I got to know him. Ultimately he asked me to sit in on piano, and then it became a regular event. I learned a lot of music and got a crack at performing publicly, finally putting to good use the "fake books" that I had been buying from Mountain musicians (I'll explain these fake books later on). But the owners would not pay me for this, saying that I was earning my money as a waiter and that I was only playing the music on my own for enjoyment; they were willing only to give me free drinks.

One Saturday night, the stripper for the late show was so delayed that the house band refused to stay any longer. Harlan, the lounge's guitarist, had packed it in himself. Since I had been playing with Harlan, Perry, the hotel partner who ran the lounge and tended bar (why hire another paid staffer?), said, "Philly, please stay and play for the stripper. I've got guests waiting all night for her." I protested that I didn't want to go afoul of the regular band; I protested that I didn't know the music to play for her. No help—Perry asked till I couldn't refuse; if you spend your life in the hotel business, you can't get in the way of the show going on. Finally the stripper came, a real novice herself, and she was happy to have anyone waiting to play music for her. She was so inexperienced that she asked me how long she should go on with the act. I was worried that I'd be too inadequate a pianist, but her own inexperience gave me enough confidence, and I played a number of blues riffs over and over, as she stripped while holding onto the piano. It was a unique experience for me, one that I never got to repeat.

Sports Figures

A popular post–World War II phenomenon was the hiring of college basketball stars to work as bellhops, waiters, and busboys. At this time, college basketball was more popular than the professional basketball of the National Basketball Association (NBA). These athletes would compete in a hotel circuit on weekends, generating lots of excitement and some wagering as well. Fixers paid off some of the same players in the Mountains as they did in the college season. The hotel basketball league suffered from the 1950–1951 point-shaving scandal, in which star players from the Long Island University (LIU) and City College of New York (CCNY) teams were caught, along with the fixers. To replace the college players, Jack Barsky of the Flagler sought to convince the NBA to let professional players moonlight in the summer. Two teams would play a traveling exhibition tour throughout the Mountains. But the NBA was unwilling to violate its rule against moonlighting, and the effort failed. Stemming from the popularity of the hotel basketball league, resort operators sought to capitalize on the entertainment value of other top sport stars. Their presence alone would be a draw, even without the public demonstrations and classes they might sometimes offer.

Grossinger's was famous for bringing up boxers in training, as well as a host of other athletes. In exchange for high-quality training equipment and the expenses of room and board, the hotel got great publicity. It began with the 1934 training schedule of Barney Ross, an observant Jewish boxer who kept kosher. He was followed by Max Baer, Ingemar Johansson, Michael Spinks, Roberto Duran, and a host of others. But Rocky Marciano was the most identified with Grossinger's, training there for many years; in fact, the robe he wore into the ring at professional bouts said "Grossinger's NY" on the back. Grossinger's sport director Lou Goldstein described his approach: "I made a show out of their training. Every day at 2:30, they'd be sparring. I'd precede that with a detailed explanation of the fighter's techniques, his equipment, his training regimen, every facet of his routine. Then I'd interview the fighter for the guests afterwards, and take their questions. For all this we'd charge a dollar a head, and we always had a few hundred spectators." While Marciano trained at Grossinger's, his 1954 opponent, Ezzard Charles, prepared at Kutsher's, and

Edward R. Murrow interviewed them both for live news coverage from the Catskills. Sonny Liston trained at the Pines for his 1962 title bout with Floyd Patterson. Golf champions like "Slamming Sammy" Snead and tennis stars like Pancho Gonzalez and Jack Kramer graced the links and courts in exhibitions.

Baseball stars made their way up to the Mountains as well. Bob Towers had an ad agency that represented several hotels, and he was also working as an MC at Grossinger's. He teamed up with his friend Arthur Richman, a *New York Mirror* sports columnist and later a longtime publicity director for the New York Mets and then the Yankees. Starting in the 1940s, they brought players like Jackie Robinson, Handsome Jack Kramer, Dick Wakefield, and Dick Williams to Grossinger's, where they would do a question and answer session for 300–400 guests, then sign autographs. Sometimes they would do a trivia quiz, handing out autographed baseballs and game tickets as prizes. By the 1960s, Towers and Richman added the Concord and the Nevele to their routine, often doubling up the ballplayers' appearances at the two hotels on the same day, much like the entertainers. Joe DiMaggio, Pete Rose, Joe Torre, Tom Seaver, Johnny Bench, and Hank Greenberg put in appearances in those days. They were paid $5,000 for such exhibitions.

Hank Greenberg was, of course, a special hero, because he was one of the few Jewish baseball stars. But Willie Mays was pretty revered as well. Around 1974, Mays came to Grossinger's on a Friday night, unannounced. When he entered the dining room, everyone rose to see this great star and to try and press him for autographs. Mays's hosts were worried that he wouldn't have a chance to eat dinner, so Arthur Richman said, "Tell them you're Jewish and can't write on Shabbos." Another time at the Concord, Mays and Greenberg were both in the dining room, and a boy was joking about who was Jewish. Richman told Willie Mays to say he was Jewish, and the boy said, "No, you're not." Mays pulled out the *chai* (a pendant with the Hebrew word for "life") he wore around his neck for good luck, to everyone's surprise.

Kutsher's also promoted athletic figures. A bellhop's recollections offer a glimpse into this milieu:

One of the other things was that Kutsher's sponsored the Maurice Stokes Memorial Basketball game. We had the professional athletes and everyone coming up for the week of the game. I remember the second year I had gotten a program book. I remember going around to everyone there from Wilt Chamberlain to Bill Russell, who wouldn't sign it. He was not nice. There were football, baseball, basketball players. I remember collecting seventy signatures and giving the book to my ten-year-old brother. He was in heaven. This was before people were selling signatures. There was interaction with the athletes. We were like puppy dogs following them around.

I remember one night after the game, I was on my shift and the general manager came over to me and asked if my car was okay. He said, "You got to transport a couple of guys to the airport." Out of the office steps Tommy Heinson, Don Nelson. There were four of them. We all got in the car and they were squeezed. They wanted a place to eat. I took them to Kaplan's Restaurant in Monticello. This was one of the best delis in the world. They were always hopping. The food was good. We had a wonderful time. I did anyway. They were talking about old war stories. Of course these were the days when Don Nelson was still playing. The Celtics were about at the end of the first Dynasty with Red Auerbach. Side note, I dated Red's daughter Randy a couple times. Nothing ever came of it. I considered it at the time a big perk to have bragging rights to that. She probably doesn't remember it, but I do. This night they were really making me feel like I was a definite part of things. We finished dinner. I drove to the airport. As I was letting them out, Tom Heinson comes over and slips a bill in my hand. I finally look at the bill and it was $100. That was the biggest single tip I ever got. I was flying that night.

Gambling and Hustling

Resort areas often are marked by gambling. The Catskills hosted a fair amount of big-time organized crime, a story frequently told in other books on the Catskills and the subject of several essays in *Retrospect*, edited by John Conway, the Sullivan County Historian. The previously mentioned basketball scandal of the 1950–1951 season is a popular legend. So too are the gangland slayings of major organized crime figures. Monticello Raceway's trotters provided a major gambling feature of the area. But there were also lots of local, hotel-based gambling. Concessionaires and hotel owners kept illegal slot machines and ran card games in which players put aside something from the pot from every hand, in exchange for cards, refreshments, and service. Murray Posner of the Brickman recalled that "gambling was wide open," with crap games and roulette wheels. He noted that a hotel could get $6,000 a year from a slot machine owner to locate it in a hotel concession, though he did not say that Brickman's was part of the arrangement. I remember the slot machine that was placed in a small alcove of the Cherry Hill concession when my mother cooked there; everyone assumed that it was acceptable. Bellhops forwarded bets to local bookies. During one of the seasons that my father had a concession, he did, too. One day he was away from the coffee shop when a guest came to place a bet, and I tried to accommodate the guest. I knew the number my father called in the bets to, but was not sure about what to say specifically. I stumbled around, and I worried that they thought I was a cop. I later told my father, who I suppose called to let them know that it was just his confused son.

Hotels didn't require outside bookies and card-game organizers for everything. They found lots of homegrown gaming opportunities. A busboy remembered the gambling and hustling of the 1950s:

> The athletic director had the horse racing concession to himself. He had the bingo. The horse racing he gave to the athletic staff to cut, and because I was big on numbers, I created the odds on horse racing, depending on the bets. That is where we made the money. Horseracing: They laid down a rug with pictures of horses 1–8. They moved on a roll of dice. There were three to four of us on athletic staff, and you could take in five to twenty dollars a night depending on how heavy it was. If you worked it out that nobody bet on a certain horse, and that horse won, you got everything.

Booking Agents

Booking agents handled thousands of comics, singers, bands, dance acts, and other performers necessary to amuse the guests. Joey Adams, in remembering the biggest agent, Charlie Rapp, recounts one owner who demanded a top act from the reluctant agent. The proprietor threatened, "Get me Jack E. Leonard or I can take my account to Tota." "Tota" was Aaron Todah, an agent I knew all my life. I still have the violin Todah sold to my father for me in 1957, when I was an eight-year-old at the Seven Gables in Greenfield Park. Todah provided the acts for the Seven Gables and hung around there a lot, kibbitzing with the owners, one of whom was particularly interested in the entertainment world. When proprietors Harry and Ann Portnoy and Barnie and Bessie Ring complained that Todah gave them an inferior show, Todah promised the coming weekend would be a great show: "I gib you the best this weekend, I gib you." In his agitated Polish accent,

Todah would repeat over and over again, "I gib you." "I gib you" became the trademark with which we teased Todah, and kibbitzed with each other as well. Todah booked shlock houses and small- to small medium-size hotels—to threaten Charlie Rapp with going over to Todah was indeed an insult.

I could not have been more surprised when Todah turned up as a resident agent at the Karmel in 1967, where I was working as a waiter. This arrangement gave him room, board, and a small office in exchange for providing a certain number of free or discount entertainers. Todah's office was a porch-like side room off the dining room, so I saw him all day long. My childhood seemed to be following me through the Mountains. The resident entertainers and resident agents were good examples of the horse-trading element of these small businesses. In the Catskills, so much was patched together with little enough capital, that such arrangements were both necessary and emblematic of that environment.

Bands

Once a hotel had at least a hundred guests, it was necessary to have a band. Larger hotels might have bands of even a dozen members, easily designated as an "orchestra." Actually, four- and five-piece bands were quite ready to call themselves orchestras, too. For the smaller resorts, booking agents assembled three- and four-man bands that had never been together before, sending them up to meet each other at their new job. Other times, musicians assembled at the Brill Building in Manhattan, where they quickly joined together with others, while owners came in to hire them in quite an informal milieu. A sax player who started in the 1930s recalls that contracts were often written on musicians' paper lunch bags.

The quality was, as you might imagine, mixed. But sometimes these pick-up groups clicked and stayed together as a better quality band. At the Cherry Hill in Greenfield Park, I was astounded by the quality of the house band. Each player loved a certain kind of music, but they meshed well. Gary, on bass, was a rock musician at heart; Bob, the drummer, loved "society" music; Dave, the saxophonist, was a jazz aficionado; and the pianist, Joel, preferred classical. Did they put together a band! In addition to doing a great job accompanying the acts, they arranged their own numbers for instrumental presentations of amazing variety. For "Quiet Village," an instrumental popular in the 1960s, they turned off all the lights and played a sensuous "tropical" tune evocative of relaxed Caribbean nights, with haunting vibes and vocal bird sounds (produced from Gary's mouth).

As a child of twelve and thirteen, I gravitated to these musicians. I ate with them in the main dining room, picking up lots of information on music and college life. I played an ongoing Ping-Pong tournament all summer with Gary, the bassman, totaling hundreds of games recorded in our heads. A music student, I got innumerable tips and access to exotic instruments like vibes. Often they let me play timbales when they did poolside Latin music in the afternoon. Once or twice a year they let me sit in with them on a rock tune while they were playing dance tunes before the show started. These and other musicians in other hotels introduced me to the "fake books," bootlegged compilations with hundreds of pages of songs with melody lines and chords. I quickly obtained what were simply called "#1," "#2," "#3," and the "Latin fake book." Each page might have three or four tunes in small print, a total violation of copyright laws but the staple of performing bands. Such books are more widely available these days, but at that time you had to know the right people in order to buy them. Band members taught me to make chords to the abbreviated chord symbols— and gave me a musical education I could never get from my classical teachers back in Florida.

A veteran sax player reminisced: "Because there were that many hotels, and every hotel had to have a band—you couldn't function as a hotel without a band—there were jobs for anybody, because multiply the hotels by four, you had [that] number of musicians." But apparently, the musicians' employment was not always guaranteed. This saxophonist's first stint was at the Linden Lawn Hotel in Mountaindale in 1935, but "at the end of four weeks Mr. Silver said to us, 'I'm sorry, boys. I'm not getting enough business to pay the band.'" Luckily, the saxophonist's family had a country home down the road, so he spent the rest of the summer there.

Owners got as much as they could from all their staff, including the band. As a tenor sax player recounted, "You had to play for lunch in addition to playing in the evening, although I think the guests would have been so grateful if we just shut up and let them eat. But the owner wanted to get his money's worth." This musician, like any self-respecting mountain staffer, complained about the food. In this case the band was not eating in the main dining room:

> We were once playing at a hotel where we thought the guests were getting better food and more to eat than we were. One of the things we didn't get at our table was sweet cream. So we got up a delegation and went into the kitchen and said to the boss, "We demand sweet cream." He was no fool. He said to us, "OK, you pick out the sweet cream and

you got it." We didn't know what sweet cream was. It was a demand, but none of us had ever had it before.

But if the boss could put one over on this band, they could get back as well:

Very early on in the second job that I had, at the Hotel Turey in Harris, we were all progressive and we got word that the Friends of Soviet Russia were having a benefit in Monticello, and they heard about our band and they asked if we would come and play for the benefit. So after we finished playing that night, we packed up and got in the car and went to Monticello and we played. It turned out that that was a very busy weekend, and when we got back—we slept in the social hall—there was a sign on the door, "Sorry, boys, we're filled up for the weekend. You'll have to shift for yourself." So the next day, we went in and we quit and we went down the road to Monticello and went into the employment agency. We were there just an hour, and he says to us, "I have something for you in White Sulphur Springs House. So we went there, and there we made seven dollars compared to the four dollars we were making at Turey. But there, too, at the end of two weeks, the owner came to us and said, "Look boys, you outnumber my guests." So we made our way back to Monticello, and without telling them [at Turey] that we were now out of a job, we got them to up the ante to seven dollars, and they brought us back on the condition that we had rooms of our own to sleep in.

This particular band was clearly fussy about their working conditions, as this tale attests:

One time we wanted to get fired. Beginning in 1936 or 1937, we played in a bigger hotel. We also played tennis, so the idea was you had to find a place that had good tennis courts. Well, we found this hotel, the Saxon, outside of Monticello and after four weeks we didn't like the tennis courts so we decided we had to get fired. You couldn't quit. The owner could fire you but you couldn't quit. That's what was written on the paper bag. So we decided that on Saturday night, at the height of the festivities, each of us took out a different number. One took out a waltz, one took out a fox trot, one took out a tango, one took out a rhumba—there were four rhythms—and we let out this cacophony of sound, in the middle of which the owner comes walking into the social hall, you got to visualize, with his favorite guest on his arm. And he walks in and he listens, and he turns to the guest and he says, "You see, when they want to, they can play!"

In the 1930s and 1940s, bands provided more than just music in some small hotels. Henry Foner, a veteran of that era, recalls:

Hotel owners—usually two partners, who, by summer's end, were no longer speaking to each other—felt that, once they had hired an orchestra, they had discharged their obligation to provide their guests with entertainment. Thus, it devolved upon the band to furnish not only music, but other types of diversion as well. These usually took the form of "skits" or "blackouts"—sketches whose origin is probably found in burlesque.

Foner's band took the opportunity to write some of their own songs, including "Shoot the Strudel to Me, Yudel," in honor of the Arrowhead's owner.

Throughout the years of listening to bands and singers doing classic Yiddish tunes, I usually found them hackneyed. Now, I enjoy them and play them myself. It's just another example of how young Jews at that time were resisting elements of their own culture, only to have it return later. But, clearly, the melodies and lyrics seeped into my consciousness, for even as a teenager I knew many of them and sang them to myself. "My Yiddishe Mama," "Oifn Pripitchek," and "Vie a Hien Zol Ich Gayn?" were etched into the musical center of my brain, along with numerous *freilachs, bulgars, shers,* and other dances.

Musicians' recollections of their glory days were frequently in superlatives:

I played tenor sax in Ben Tobin's Orchestra from 1930 to 1935. We were known as the biggest little band in the world because we consisted of only six pieces—piano, drums, trumpet, two saxes, and guitar (banjo at first). In 1930 we played at Loch Sheldrake Rest. In 1931 we played at the Flagler Hotel in South Fallsburg. Prior to our playing there, the Flagler always had a big band—ten pieces or more. Our sound was so full that Mr. Fleischer had no qualms about hiring us. During that time, in lieu of larger salaries, the owners allowed their bands to have one night during the season called "Band Night." Tickets were sold for admission, and the band kept all the profits to divide among the members. To draw a crowd, a band contest was held and all bands from the area were invited to try to win the prize—a trophy loving cup. Our band participated in many contests and won every one.

Another sax player who started band work in 1935 gave me a similar story of winning lots of Flagler contests, based on the fact that their band played many tunes they wrote themselves.

Many band members fondly recall those band contests. Another tenor man remembers such competitions in the mid 1930s at the Nutshell Hotel in Lake Huntington, which he claims "had the largest dance floor in Sullivan County. We could put 1,000 couples on the floor." This gentile musician also recalls learning to drink tea from a glass and watching in fascination as the *schochet* slaughtered cows at the butcher shop next to the casino.

People were proud of the successes of their band members. A piano player in 1930 saw his trumpeter get in the New York Philharmonic and his trombonist make the Philadelphia Orchestra. He also recounted this story: "I remember a skinny kid coming up and [he] asked if he could sit in with our band. He had a squeaky thin voice and his name was Sonny Schuyler. The very next year he was responsible for "Besame Mucho," which is still heard once in a while." Indeed, that song was a major standard Latin tune for all the years I spent in the Mountains, and one I remember playing myself on many occasions.

The following recollection of playing in bungalow colonies gives us a glimpse of the declining glamour at the end of the Catskills' golden era:

During the summers of 1971, 1972, and 1973 [when he was 19–21], while many friends worked as summer camp counselors for a few hundred dollars, three of us piled into the drummer's van and drove Saturday afternoons to Monticello, South Fallsburg, or Liberty. The band earned four hundred dollars a night and played four hours for crowds from Queens, Brooklyn, or the Bronx, lots of New York taxi drivers and their families. The highlight of the evening was a special show by a guest talent not good enough for the hotels. By the 1970s, that meant you were pretty bad. I vividly remember Aida the belly dancer, somewhere in her late forties, trying to look sexy under fluorescent lights [with] flypaper hanging against the walls of the stage. . . . The bungalow colonies would rarely put you up for the night. At two in the morning, we would either drive the four hours home [to Long Island] or head for a campground, or if the manager and the weather agreed, sleep in chaises by the pool in our sleeping bags.

Chapter 6

"Mountain Rats": The More Skilled Workers and Other Veterans

"Your father always dragged me back to the Mountains.
Come May, we closed up the business
or left our jobs and went to the Mountains."

Mountain Rats like my family had it in their blood; they couldn't stay away. Chefs, maitre d's, bakers, saladmen, and other top echelon workers, as well as concessionaires and older waiters, were an older generation, in their forties through sixties during the 1950s and 1960s. This breed of migrant workers often held similar jobs in Miami Beach in the winter, sometimes with fall stopovers in New Jersey resort areas such as Lakewood. Others returned to New York City. Mountain Rats were different from the young staff, who worked only a limited number of years. Mountain Rats were not having the "formative" experience of the waiters, busboys, counselors, musicians, and bellhops who returned to college on their climb up the mobility ladder. Instead, Mountain Rats were stuck in dead-end jobs of twelve-, even fourteen-hour days, seven days a week. The good pay was only relative, if you figured it out on an hourly basis. It got worse when you saw how it drained these people of their health.

Still the Mountain Rats kept returning. They became habituated to their routine and dwelled in a loyal camaraderie with their itinerant coworkers. Jimmy Ferrazano, cooking at a sleep-away camp, drove many miles each Saturday night to help my father out in his coffee shop for a couple of hours, no matter how hard he had worked that day. Saturday night at SGS Bungalows in Swan

Lake included a bar set-up and carved meat spread, requiring lots of quick slicing and serving. Who else but a trusted old friend, also in the business, would work for those few hours? Jimmy, younger and healthier than my father, would stride in, full of energy, refusing to even let my father help out in his own coffee shop: "Sit down, Bill, I can take care of it. Take a rest." Jimmy wouldn't take a penny for this, just a meal and some candy bars.

From all their years in the Catskills, these Mountain Rats were the insiders who really knew the scene. People had their favorite local bars and restaurants for hanging out after a day of hard work, where conversations typically turned to who was working where this year. The chatting and hanging out continued in Florida in the winter, where they met friends in Dubrow's Cafeteria on Miami Beach's Lincoln Road and reminisced about last summer in the Mountains. That magic pulled them back the next summer, and they grew old and infirm, along with the Catskills themselves. As the region declined in the 1970s, the Mountain Rats competed for fewer jobs, and many had trouble setting up permanent roots. Cubans displaced them in the Miami Beach hotels.

Someday, they hoped, there would be a break. A person might land a substantial year-round position. A small business that opened in the winter might survive past the spring. For my parents, each such attempt failed, often merely by virtue of closing up the store or restaurant in Florida from mid-May till mid- or late September. The Mountains drew them magnetically, these veterans who were automatons on other people's calendars. As my mother often told me, "Your father always dragged me back to the Mountains. Come May, we closed up the business or left our jobs and went to the Mountains." What a price to pay!—My parents left Florida in May to get to the Mountains for Memorial Day (colloquially called Decoration Day in New York) and worked in the dreary, preseason June of near-empty resorts. Hotels wanted their chef in place by Decoration Day so they were guaranteed having that single most key worker, and also because the kitchen had to be opened, supplies ordered, and much food prepared for freezing.

That meant I left school in Florida a few weeks before its regular early end, and I had to finish up five or six weeks in a strange new school. In this brief period of time, I was supposed to learn curriculum that often differed substantially, especially the local and state history and government material. Another hotel child recounted this same kind of experience: "We lived in Flatbush for the winter. We'd come up here in March and go to school up here. Start school here in September and in November we'd go back to school in the city. No one thought it was psychologically good or bad, you just did it and accepted it." Some years I went to school in Ellenville, nearer to the hotel where my mother worked, and where we all lived. Other years I went to school in Monticello, either because my mother worked closer to there or because my father worked in the employment agency there and could take me to and from the hotel to school. One year I stayed with relatives in Queens to finish school, since my parents didn't have their jobs in place yet. Then, the end of the season caused further disruptions—my parents put me alone on a plane right after Labor Day, to return to Florida and start school while living with a changing retinue of friends and relatives. Some of these people had never had children and were not too sure what to do with me. At the time, I was excited by this, even when my temporary home was uncomfortable. At least on this end of the Catskill-Florida commute, I was going to a school I would stay in until I was pulled out in May for another strange school.

Even when my parents arrived, our living situation was often unsettled, since we didn't own a house until I was in fifth grade. Because my parents didn't want to pay rent for the months we were in the Mountains, they often rented different apartments each year. For my senior year in high school, I successfully insisted that I would live alone in our own house for the month until my parents arrived. As soon as I got to the airport, I took a cab to a used car dealer my father knew and for $125 bought an ancient Studebaker, learning the stick shift in the car lot before driving away on the expressway with great trepidation. My friends, like me, thought this was very exciting to be living alone, and it was. But overall, it took decades to really grasp how disorienting and lonely this lifestyle was, which so casually uprooted people with the season's progress. Magic has a downside—Catskill glamour was built on the hard work of many people who did not reap its rewards. Yet, they, too, sensed the magic, trying to hang on to it as long as they could.

What could get these Mountain Rats to come back year after year? For some, it was a great pride in their work and the appreciation they received, as Jack Nachowitz, a baker, recalled:

> There's something in your blood. I loved the mountains. It was a challenge. It's nice to hear compliments. You'd be sitting in the lobby, and you hear them talking about the cake. Sometimes they talk about the food, but most of the time the dessert. Chicken was OK, the steak was steak. You know, it's good. But the cake, "He makes different cake from everybody else."

Sol Eagle, a lifelong Catskill veteran and dear family friend, worked as a waiter, head waiter, saladman, and farmer, and he still lives in the Mountains. He puts it like this:

> Once it gets into your blood, there's no other place like it. I went an entire winter in Europe, and came May, oh the pull was so great we had to get back. I was offered jobs in Europe—catering jobs, and in Israel at the King David Hotel, the manager wanted to give me a job as his assistant manager, but I refused that because I had to get back to the Catskills.

But at the same time, Sol's wife, Dorothy told me, "It was so tough that before the season when I had to go I used to say, 'God, I hope I don't make it. I'd like to die before the season opens.' Many times I heard your mother say the same thing."

The Mountain Rats didn't only come to Florida, they also came to our house. Sol and Dorothy came to Florida in the winter and once stayed with us. Though this was done to help out friends, at other times my parents rented out a room of our house that had a bathroom attached to it, for the extra income, just like at a Catskill boardinghouse. Despite working in the overeating and generally unhealthy food environment of the Catskills, Sol and Dorothy Eagle were into natural foods in the 1950s, the first whole-foods aficionados I ever met. They traveled with a tremendously large juice extractor for making every kind of vegetable juice and carried with them sacks of every kind of grain and bean imaginable. Other Mountain Rats dropped in throughout the winter. Some years, my parents worked at Miami Beach hotels that were owned by Catskill resort operators, such as the Haddon Hall in South Beach (owned by Kutsher's). The hotel people, owners and staff alike, were our circle of friends. On the way from Florida through New York City to the Mountains, we stayed in Jackson Heights, Queens, with Ann Gotkin, the Seven Gables' children's dining room waitress; her husband, Jack; and their children, Paul and Ilene (who were a waiter and counselor, respectively, for many years). When my mother recovered from major surgery in New York, she stayed at the Gotkins' house. When Ann and Jack moved to Florida, they were frequent visitors, and my parents spent long hours helping Ann rehabilitate from a stroke. Seven Gables owners Ann and Harry Portnoy and Barnie and Bessie Ring, along with their children and grandchildren, also remained steady features of our Florida and New York life. We could never get too far away from the Catskills. The North Miami Beach neighborhood near us, where our synagogue was located, was even called Monticello Park, a legacy of the early settlers who came from the Catskills and elsewhere, buying into the land developed by Sullivan County Development in Florida, Inc. I often wondered if that was why my parents moved there from Miami Beach, across Biscayne Bay.

Life was not easy in the Mountains. One year we were ripped off of a summer's earnings when Paul's Hotel went bankrupt and my mother's as yet uncashed checks in the vault became worthless. Likewise, my father's account was dipped into, because the hotel had taken out of staff paychecks the amounts staffers had charged in the concession. The following April, we had to drive from Florida to the Mountains just to work Passover. I was pulled out of high school in the middle of the year to do so. Each of us worked in a different hotel and met up again after the eight-day holiday to drive home. Waiting for acceptance letters from college, I had mail forwarded by a friend in Florida and learned I got a full scholarship to Long Island University. This, by the way, was truly a shlock college, so appropriate somehow for a boy brought up in hotels, some of which were shlock houses. So even that key event in my life happened in the Catskills.

During job interviews, my mother insisted to owners that our family be given a guestroom rather than living in the staff quarters. As she put it, she didn't want me to grow up feeling second-rate. I remember one hotel where I sat in the car while she interviewed, and the key obstacle to the job was the owners' unwillingness to provide a good room for us. Even in the guestrooms we were able to occupy, the setting was far from comfortable. In the usual course of events, we were given guestrooms at the bottom of the scale. Most typically our room measured eight-by-ten, into which was crammed a double bed, a single bed, one dresser, a closet, and a sink. The few suitcases that held all our belongings for May through early September were slid under the beds and on shelves above the sink and closet. Remaining floor space measured about three-by-five, and it was virtually impossible for the three of us to be in the room at the same time for more than a few minutes. The demand for a guestroom didn't always work. At the Cherry Hill and at Paul's, my parents had staff rooms, but they were very large and even had private baths by virtue of some past effort at carving up old buildings into staff quarters. These were closer-in buildings where counselors, band members, and other non–dining room staff lived. Waiters and busboys were usually up on a hill somewhere, in more primitive buildings.

Kitchen Professionals

The Chef

The kitchen staff worked a long day. My mother's cooking schedule had her up at 5:30 in the morning, working almost all day till around 9:00 at night, with a slight rest between meals. But her loyalty and friendship to the Seven Gables owners, who had become friends, led her to sometimes forsake afternoon naps and plant flowerbeds on her knees after lunch. To show off her talents, she would other times skip that nap to hand-roll *kreplach* (a Jewish meat ravioli), even though many chefs obtained them ready made. Sylvia Brown was proud of this one thing in life she could do well, and she treasured two clippings from a *New York Post* entertainment columnist who praised her cooking. Her menus were always far more elaborate and full of more choices than any other hotels of that size. I know from working large houses like Brickman's and the Nemerson that her menus were on that par. In 1951, however, a handwritten menu from my parents' hotel (printed on p. 98 of this book) is far more modest.

During most of the years my mother worked at Chait's, she wrote weekly poems to Annette Finestone, the owner, with whom she had become very close; sometimes she wrote them to Max Finestone as well. Annette sent these to me in the course of my writing this book. These lines were penned on the back of sheets of paper bearing Sylvia Brown's handwritten food orders for the week. The juxtaposition of food orders and poems to an owner/friend exemplifies the ambivalent life my mother lived in the Mountains. Sylvia always called them "pomes," and, along with occasional prose comments, they spoke of her hot-headedness, her tiredness, her relations with her bosses/friends. My mother often threatened to quit—on one food order there is a preface, "I suppose I'll be talking with you before you order. But just in case you brought a fabulous Continental chef with you and no longer require my services—until he (or she) takes over and checks our inventory, this is what we'll be needing—based on a premise of 100 people."

In one poem, Sylvia wrote of her relenting, following a threat to leave:

> *By now you should have had your fill*
> *Of my second handed poetic swill*
> *No swell-head—I've kept my job*

Surprised!—I'm just a culinary snob!
Who yearns to go—but forced to stay
And toil again another day

The underlying tension between boss and friend was also played out in these lines:

I think I shall no longer write
Pomes for Annette's delight
You show them round and folks will think
That I'm some kind of kookie fink
Who writes love poems to other girls
And carries on with tizzy whirls
I'm really just a lousy poet
And really mind if others know it
This love affair between we two
Is really just a tete a deux
The only reason I write them, honey
Is, on the other side, I'm spending money [the shopping list is on the reverse]
And while you read them, you can think
That I make Blue Mondays turn out pink
Cause even while I spend your dough
I cheer you with a rosy glow
For poems are made by fools like me
To captivate my boss, you see?

[August 10, 1970]

Late one August, the tiredness of the season caught up with my mother:

There was a big fat girl with a lot of messy curl
Stuck up under a chef's cap
And at half past 2 all she cared to do
Was not to write pomes, poems, or menus
But to take a long delicious nap.

Tho I've been called by names like Greta Garnish
And others with a sound of tarnish

As the praises fall so thick and heavy
On the noises I'd declare a levee
As the clock strikes 2, all the hell I want to do
Is crawl into my mattress and vanish
                              [August 22, 1971]

With Labor Day and the season's close just around the corner, Sylvia wrote this one:

The storm and stress and strain are nearly past
And now you won't be nearly so harassed
And once again you'll smile a smile so wide
And maybe not say things so really snide
And skies above may get so really blue
That one and one may almost equal two
Oh, welcome, Fall! that brings surcease and quiet
You pray it might be a year-round diet
And unlike Clancy, you won't have to lower the boom
As the lights go off for good in the children's dining room
                              [August 29, 1971]

Loyalty—perhaps combined with drivenness and the need for distraction from other pains—shone through in sickness and death. Twice in those years at the Seven Gables, gas ranges exploded in my mother's face. She returned from the hospital the same day, wrapped like a mummy and quite scary to a little child. But she was back in the kitchen to finish the day's work. My father, too, suffered a gas explosion from a coffee urn in his concession, though less severe. Years later, when my father died at Chait's, my mother was back in the kitchen hours later. In true Catskill fashion, when I spent a week there after my father died, I, too, was pressed into service behind the salad counter.

At the Seven Gables, my father returned from his job at Dependable Employment Agency and immediately ran into the kitchen and helped serve dinner. But I wanted a piece of him before I lost him to the omnipresent maw of the kitchen— around 6:00, I would begin waiting for my father to return. I went to the edge of the hill overlooking Route 52, spotted my father's car, and ran to the driveway that wound up the hill. I jumped in and drove with him the short distance to where we parked behind the kitchen, and then begged him to play catch with me for a few minutes before he went to help my mother in the kitchen.

The years he had the concession, he would do the same. Every additional hand helped in the kitchen—if a plate had meat, sauce, two vegetables, and a garnish or two, the main line moved fastest if there was one person for each of these items; but hotels couldn't pay people for that brief period of time, nor drag them in from other duties. Bill Brown was obviously not paid for this, but it was his way of helping out my mother. And after all this, my parents often played poker, and didn't get to sleep till midnight.

Even in her later years, after my father died and she had stopped working the full season, my mother would let her owner friends at Chait's talk her into driving from Cambridge to Accord for weekends and holidays. It was a four-hour haul, and by then Sylvia Brown was broken down from years of work, and she more and more frequently wound up in the hospital with heart and lung problems. This loyalty was interesting—it kept the small hotels alive, operating on shoestrings, guilt, and labor beyond the regular salary. It also helped form the communities that were so integral to this curious world of Catskill culture.

Each meal was served separately for staff, guests, and children, a total of nine different meals a day. Plus, other people would crop up from time to time: late-arriving guests, owners' friends, entertainers needing food before going on stage. Higher level staff (especially chefs and saladmen) resented waiters and busboys, partly due to their own skill as chefs and saladmen, and partly due to class antagonism with the typically upwardly mobile dining room staff. The chef, steward, and saladman were in charge, but had to get the waiters and busboys to follow their management.

Chefs were notoriously temperamental, and most of them yelled all the time. They had very definite ideas about how waiters should order and pick up meals. For instance, you couldn't stand at the range and say, "I want a boiled chicken, dark meat only, with no vegetables." Rather, you had to yell definitively, "Ordering, a boiled bottom naked!" You had to snap out the whole order very quickly, not stumbling or changing your mind about what garnish, sauce, or vegetable was held back, or how well-done a steak was to be. If you goofed in this process, you were lucky to be merely embarrassed by being scolded: "How did you get to be a waiter? You know less than a busboy!" The worst outcome was that the chef autocratically threw you off the line, hopelessly jamming up all your meal orders. Working as a fifteen-year-old waiter at Paul's, where my mother was the chef, was perhaps unwise. My mother spared me no angry shouts. Because that was my first waiting job, I tried hard to do it right—the combination of a mother's yelling and a chef's scolding was too much to bear.

Sylvia Brown took cooking dead-seriously. Her plates had to be beautifully garnished. That meant sending busboys and waiters out on the hotel grounds to pick crabapples and ferns for decorating the main dishes, an assignment that often brought the staff in earlier than they would have liked. When the plates were being assembled, each vegetable and each garnish (there might easily be two or three) had to be in place, and with no sauce dripping over the edge. If a "vegetable man" goofed here or if a waitress smudged a dish when putting on a hot cover to stack on her tray, there was lots of shouting. Though I have never been in an airport control tower, I cannot imagine it being a tenser place than the main line.

From the chef's standpoint, it was a terrible crime if you left the range with hot food and then went to the salad counter to pick up cold food at lunch. It was imperative to get cold food first so the hot food would not lose its peak temperature. The chef would scream, "What are you doing with my food, letting it get cold while you go to the saladman? Get out of here!" And you would be forced to leave the kitchen without the cold main dishes, such as Hawaiian salads, bananas and cream, or herring salad platters. That meant wasting a whole trip back to get the cold dishes, while your guests were sitting at their table with some people missing their food. Partly this was the chef's pride, and partly it was to avoid having the owner yell at the chef for wasting food. Plus, it was a logical outcome of working so hard behind sweltering ranges for hours at a time, trying to coordinate many hundreds of dishes in a fairly small area.

Tempers were raised in large part from the sweltering heat of the kitchen's many ranges going at full blast. The space between the ranges and counters trapped heat, and ventilation fans were few and weak. My mother, like many chefs, kept a bucket of ice water on the range, dipping a glass in it all the time to cool down and rehydrate. A basin of rags sitting in water provided a constant source of cooling bandanas to wrap around her face. Waiters and busboys suffered from this heat in two ways: The constant transition from the air-conditioned dining room to the stifling hot kitchen was very uncomfortable. Also, if you had shaved as recently as one hour before dinner (maitre d's often wanted us to have a second shave of the day so the five-o'clock-shadow would not make us appear grungy), sweat invaded nicks that you never knew you had, and your face and neck burned for the whole meal.

CHAPTER 6

The Saladman

All cold foods were the bailiwick of the saladman, except cold borscht and schav (a cold potato and sorrel soup). Cold foods included all vegetable salads and "livestock" products, such as milk, butter, coleslaw, pickles, lemon slices, and pickled tomatoes (livestock is "live" because it is still useable, not to be thrown out). Saladmen, maitre d's, and owners traditionally yelled at waiters to "get the damned livestock in!" after meals. The saladman's interest was clear—so that he could pack it all away and close up the salad counter. The owner wanted to make sure the livestock didn't get thrown out, which was more likely if it didn't get returned promptly. And the maitre d' yelled about this because the saladman and boss wanted him to police the waiters. Waiters tended to dilly-dally after meals, sitting around in the empty dining room; other times they might set tables for the next meal before bringing the livestock in. Sam, the saladman in the wonderful film *Sweet Lorraine,* provides a typical example of the resort milieu. His assistant, Molly, tries to get him to ask the waiters nicely, upon which he says that he will leave early and let her attend to the problem of getting the livestock packed away. When Sam leaves, she tries to be nice but fairly soon winds up shouting at the recalcitrant waiters.

The saladman's charge also included the fruit cups or sliced melons or glasses of juice that were placed at each setting before the guests entered the dining room. Also in the saladman's realm were the many varieties of herring and fish that made up a large chunk of Catskill cuisine. The saladman was especially busy at lunch, since many of the dishes were fruit salads, fruit and sour cream, cottage cheese and sour cream, egg salad and tuna salad plates, and the like. Virtually all these dishes were available as "mains" or "sides," and guests often ate several different items. The salad counter was a veritable mountain of plates. Many of these plates were "dummy plates," fully garnished and prepared with pepper slices, tomato wedges, a bed of lettuce, fancy-cut radishes, and a mound of potato salad. They merely waited for a specific order, at which point a large scoop of tuna salad, herring salad, or a small can of salmon was put in the very middle. A smart saladman could gauge how much was needed, partly by what the guests typically ordered and partly by the desirability of the chef's hot choices.

Mark Hutter recounts how dining room staff got back at a mean saladman:

He was a particularly nasty individual, and we decided to give him the works. We told the guests that the best thing on the menu was the

"Hawaiian salad," a particularly time-consuming one to make [the Hawaiian salad was a scoop of cottage cheese sitting atop a pineapple ring and crowned by a maraschino cherry, surrounded by canned pears and peaches, slices of melon, and sometimes Jell-O cubes]; usually there were only four or five orders for it. One day, because we pushed this salad, there were approximately thirty-five orders. The saladman was "really bombed." We estimated that he lost ten pounds during the meal. The next day, he made about twenty such salads beforehand, anticipating the same demand. Accordingly, we changed our tactics; we did not push the salad, and he was caught with fifteen extras at the end of the meal, which he had to "break-down."

I remember the impressive salad counter at the Stevensville; it had perhaps eight to ten helpers, including some young Japanese men whose giant knives truly flew through the air, slicing a huge watermelon into twenty serving-sized slices about as fast as I could cut an apple into quarters. The larger and better the hotel, the more artistic the saladman was expected to be. The *garmigiere* work included large presentations for midnight suppers and other special events: exotic sculptures of chopped liver shaped into a chicken, extravagant boats based on hollowed-out watermelons filled with cantaloupe and honeydew balls, and multilayered vegetable platters full of sliced tomato constructions, radish flowers, and cucumber fabrications. Sol Eagle's beautiful designs graced my bar mitzvah table, catered by my mother at our house in Florida. Sometimes even individual pieces were highly labor-intensive and decorative, such as chopped liver swans made for each guest's seat on Friday night, sporting wings made of bread or wafers and beaks of *mandlen* (bread-like soup nuts). My mother, when cooking in small hotels that sometimes lacked an inspired, creative saladman, frequently did much of that fancywork herself.

Creative saladmen needed to be freed up from the mundane work of simple chopping and scooping in order to design and produce their delightful creations. Unfortunately, saladmen often did not have enough helpers. In the 1940s, at the Olympic, waiters and busboys were required to help out at the salad counter. One veteran of many years recalled how his wife sometimes helped out—for no pay. In the early years, many small-hotel owners expected one person to be both saladman and steward, and even to look in on the dining room since they didn't have a maitre d', but only a boss taking over some of that task.

Running the salad counter was a demanding job. As one saladman recalls: "I'd be the first one in, [at] six in the morning, work all day, have two hours off in the afternoon, come back for dinner, and be the last one out of the place at 9:30." Much of the work involved making food from scratch, even cleaning whole herring before making *matjes,* pickled, and creamed herring:

> I used to make a barrel of half-sour pickles. You know how many pickles go into a barrel? A big barrel—300 bushels, each bushel has 330 or 340 Kirby pickles. It was so good they finished it—it should be enough for two weeks—they finished it in one week. I used to make three or four boxes of cabbage [coleslaw], maybe 80 pounds to a box. Maybe for two times [it would last]. The boss would say, "Don't make it so good." I made a busbox of vegetarian chopped liver. Every morning slicing lox myself. Pickled lox I made.

One Passover provides another example of how demanding this job could be: At a hotel with seventy-five tables, each couple wanted their own Passover plate with the ritual foods. This required preparing three hundred plates.

The Baker

A good baker contributed a lot to the interesting looks and tastes of the meals. As one hotel owner recalled, "We had a baker. He had a repertoire! A whole season, he never repeated a cake twice!" The baker got up at 4:00 or 4:30 A.M. to make huge amounts of dough and to bake breakfast rolls. He ran his own private principality, parallel to the chef, though not as prestigious. He may have had one helper at a typical small hotel, but that's it. At a larger place, such as Brickman's, the baker had seven workers. At one medium-size hotel, the baker shlepped 100-pound bags of flour and sugar on his shoulders and carried 110-pound cans of shortening. He didn't even have a hand-truck. When the hotel finally gave him a helper, who was inexperienced, the helper came in hours late. So the baker started recruiting students from the Food Trades High School, whom he taught during the year.

Bakers were responsible for all the rolls, cakes, and pies. Except for *challah,* bread was often brought in because there was a limit to how much the baker could do in his small bakery, given the time constraints and the number of ovens available. Bakery trucks were always plying the roads of the Catskills, servicing the endless resorts—Katz's in Liberty, Mortman's in Woodridge, Madnick's in Fallsburg.

Getting up so early was quite tiring, according to Jack Nachowitz, who baked at the Aladdin from 1953 to 1972. Rather than start making dough at five in the morning,

> In later years I would make the dough for the rolls the day before and refrigerate the dough. Then I'd have the night man—who washed the floors and then walked around checking everything—I'd have him light the ovens and at a certain time take the dough out of the refrigerator and put it on the table—it was on sheet pans. Then when I came in, the dough was fully risen and all I had to do was divide it on the divider and shape the rolls. When it was very busy, I would make the rolls the night before, put them on the pans, and put them in the refrigerator unbaked. And then I would have the night man take them out and put them in the steam cabinet, without steam. When I would come in, I would light up the steam cabinet and then in a manner of minutes they would be risen and the oven was hot already and they would be ready to go into the oven.

Like so many of the upper-echelon hotel professionals, Jack took great pride in his work. Every week for Sunday dinner, he would make apple strudel:

> I used to pull my own dough. I tried using the ready-made dough, and, depending on whom you bought it from, sometimes you couldn't open the leaves up. I had a table that was nine feet long, two-and-a-half this way, and I would get sixty portions of strudel from one table of pulled out dough. So I used to make anywheres between five and eight tables of dough.

Having watched my mother pull strudel in the Catskills—many bakers didn't have that skill, and she was always willing to put out extra effort to grace the hotel's tables—I understand how labor intensive this work is.

Like the chef overseeing the distribution of meals, the baker carefully tended his dessert counter at lunch and supper. He might have been working on these delicacies since early in the morning, while also baking rolls. It seemed a rule of Mountain life that there were never enough onion rolls; while setting up for breakfast we tried to grab as many as we could, since the guests ate them at once and requested more. Getting friendly with the baker meant he would throw some tasty pie or cake slice your way, a more likely bet than getting food snippets from the chef, in part because the bakery was watched less cautiously by the steward and owners, and in part because bakers seemed always to be much friendlier than chefs. It was a great treat to get yesterday's leftover deserts—in some hotels they were nicely laid out for the staff to take. Sometimes you even got the current dessert from the baker, as this baker's tale reveals:

With the kids I was OK. I used to make ice cream cakes, the ice cream logs, and I had a big ice cream knife that was like a machete, and I'd have a heavy board, and I'd chop it. And of course the kids wanted to get the ends to eat. I said, "Don't touch anything until I'm through chopping or your hand is going to be on a plate." I was counting as I was dishing it out. And if a kid told me he needs twenty, I'd give him twenty-two, one for him and one for the busboy. And some of them would try to con me and say, "You only gave me eighteen."

Like chefs, bakers were often subject to the caprices of the owner. One baker recalled of a boss: "He would make up the menu at eleven at night. I would have to come down and check the menu, and if he had danish on, I would have to—eleven o'clock at night—mix the dough because that dough has to rest and relax, and you got to roll it in." Other bosses would give more leeway:

We'd get a copy of the menu, and then I would bake accordingly. She had lemon pie on the menu, and I made the lemon pie, and I was dishing it out on a table in the kitchen, and she calls me over and says, "What's this?" I said, "Lemon pie." She says, "Where's the meringue?" So I took the menu and I said, "Does it say meringue here? That's a two-crust lemon pie. You want meringue, you put it on the menu. Lemon meringue pie." She says, "From now on, make up your own menu." And that's what we did, and it worked out fine. There were no complaints after that.

Working together in a tense kitchen, it was imperative for the baker, chef, and saladman to get along. The exchange of food was a part of this: "They all liked cake. They had a saladman [who] would take a pound cake and eat it like a lollypop. We had a chef; I used to make long sticks of coffeecake, the size of a sheet pan; he would take a half of one of those and walk around and eat it like you would eat a fudgsicle."

Yet stories abounded of less friendly relations:

They had one chef there that trusted me. He would make his gefilte fish in my mixing machine. He had an experience once—his mother was a chef also—and he called her up one day; he said, "My gefilte fish fell apart." She said, "Where did you mix it?" He said, "In the baker's machine." This was another baker at another time. She says, "Do you get along with the baker?" He says, "Not really." She says, "He must have put a handful of baking powder in your fish and it just blew it apart."

The Steward

Smaller hotels did not have a steward, since that was too costly a position given the size of the operation. One of the owners would take care of the steward functions, in tandem with the overworked chef and the saladman. Well within the tradition of multiple jobs, I spoke with one steward who also chauffeured guests and assisted the owner in renting rooms on Sundays. In the more sizeable medium- and the large-size hotels, the steward had a lot of responsibility. Stewards were in charge of ordering all food, following discussions with the chef, saladman, and baker about the menu. They had to walk a fine line between pleasing these various people, especially the chef. Stewards also had to take delivery of food from many suppliers and make sure it was stored in the proper location. For example, meat was often delivered as large sides of beef or as whole-dressed lambs. The meat was then taken to an adjoining room or building containing additional refrigerators and a bandsaw for the chef—or steward—to cut as he or she desired (only in large hotels was there a resident butcher).

The steward needed to make sure that food was kept properly and appropriately reused, not wasted—for example, pats of butter that had melted could not be placed on dining room tables but could be put into a large dish for use in cooking. It was also the steward's task to oversee the work of the dishwashers, glasswashers, and potwashers, each of these tasks being conducted in separate alcoves or rooms. The steward made sure there were enough dishes ready for meals and checked that the waitstaff cleaned their silverware. As well, he made sure that meat and dairy dishes were kept separate—it was amazing how often they got mixed up by dining room staff and dishwashers. Plus, the steward had to make sure that all dairy and meat foods were separate, since, in the words of one veteran, "The *meshgiach* [rabbi in charge of enforcing kosher laws] used to walk around constantly." And the steward had authority over the waiters and busboys when they were in the kitchen.

As one steward recalled, he began his day "way before 5:30." He recalls, "I was the first man in the kitchen, and I was the last man out." With so many tasks to carry out, the steward seemed to never have time off:

> And the only time off that I had was after lunch. After lunch I took off for I would say between 2:00, 2:30 and I didn't get back until almost 5:00. And that wasn't always that secure for me that I could go to sleep or do anything because there were always deliveries, deliveries from everybody, groceries, butchers, vegetables. In the first year, I took all that. I used to be in my bathing trunks; they used to call me or page me over the phone and say, "Kurt, you have a delivery," and I had to run and accept whatever there was, and the second year I stopped all that. I said there will be no delivery between these hours. That's how I really scheduled it so I'd at least have a couple of hours off.

Another steward spoke of the drama of the job:

> As soon as I went to the kitchen, there was an extraordinary fascination. I loved it. I couldn't believe that I was going to play the key role in producing all these meals. . . . Everybody said it—feeding people in the Catskills was the toughest job in the world. There were the most demanding quantities. It was like going right into the Olympics. . . . One of the major challenges of those kitchens was not to run out. Running out of an item in the Catskills was almost like a terrorist assault.

He further described an incident of this seasonal drama:

> I remember once on a Jewish holiday running out of horseradish. You could never forget this. What had happened was that the saladman had put the used horseradish back in the original case. He had been conservative. I assumed that we had two cases. It turns out, we didn't have three bottles. We ran out. The dairy man was at *shul*. He was orthodox. He had a slow manner. I asked him to give me access to horseradish. He didn't want to do business on *yuntiv* [religious holiday]. I escalated this to a national emergency. You needed a capacity for drama. "I'm not going to kill myself, but I'm close. Look, you've got to open the door to the store. How much money do you need?" I rushed into town and picked up cases just before the great revolution would have started.

The Maitre D'

A maitre d' with twenty-five years of experience at a large hotel remarked, "I looked around at the old-time waiters. I didn't want to be an old-time waiter, so I went looking for a job as a maitre d'." As one of the most important jobs in the hotel, this position carried prestige and the possibility of good money, depending on how resourceful the person was.

The maitre d' held an interesting and complex position. He had to be a stern supervisor to the waiters and busboys and a trusted lieutenant of the boss. To the chef, he had to show that he could control the waiters, preventing them from acting inept or foolish and hence disrupting the kitchen routine. Yet he could not alienate the waiters and busboys too much, lest they begin to give shoddy service and drop nasty comments to the guests.

To the guests, he had to be a pleasing servant and a conniving manager—one who got them to make his life easier by accepting certain seating positions, but sometimes he needed to accommodate requests. Of course, tips could garner the maitre d's favoritism in seating, and in getting special foods not on the menu (e.g., sturgeon or chicken livers). In his social role, the maitre d' had to facilitate singles meeting each other and group people by age—couples in their thirties didn't want to sit with people twice their age. The maitre d' received guests' complaints about the waiters and busboys, sometimes merely placating the guests but other times disciplining the staff.

In Vivian Gornick's essay about her waitress years in the Catskills, she recounts one New Year's Eve where a multicourse midnight banquet was served, with no choices on the menu. It was so frantic, with waiters and waitresses pushing each other at the counter, that Gornick panicked. Another waitress said, "Skip the chow mein, they'll never know the difference. Go on to the next course, there's no one on the line over there." Too late, Gornick realized the problem: "It didn't occur to either of us that she, as it happened, had only drunken singles at her table, who of course wouldn't know the difference, but I had married couples who wanted everything that was coming to them." Sure enough, a guest called the maitre d' to the table and complained: "'Where's the chow mein?' he asked quietly, jerking his thumb back at my tables, across the head of the woman whose blue-lidded eyes never left his face." Gornick simply replied, "I couldn't get to it. The kitchen is a madhouse. The line was impossible." As the maitre d' raised his voice to a yell, Gornick took in that he, too, was afraid, fearful of the guest who demanded retribution. And so, the maitre d' said, "You're fired. Serve your morning meal and clear out." After she took in the immensity of this, she stepped back in her mind:

> Then I realized that tomorrow morning my regular guests would be back in these seats, most of them leaving after breakfast, and I, of course, would receive my full tips exactly as though none of this had happened. The headwaiter was not really punishing me. He knew it, and now I knew it. Only the blond woman didn't know it. She required my dismissal for the appeasement of her lousy life—her lined face, her hated husband, her disappointed New Year's Eve—and he, the head- waiter, was required to deliver it up to her.

The maitre d' deflected his direct power by having his captain of the wait- ers conduct much of the routine inspection and assignment of tasks. Sometimes a busboy captain directly supervised the other busboys. For waiters and busboys to "check out," they had to show clean side stands—with the metal silverware chutes in those stands cleaned of food particles by steel wool—clean and orderly set tables, chairs tucked in just right, and extra "side jobs" (such as refilling ketchup bottles, sorting dirty linen) accounted for. This checking-out routine was often a miniature battle. You had to strategize how much you could get away with before calling over to the maitre d' or captain to "check me out" (very small hotels might not have a captain, so the maitre d' himself would check out the staff). The most demanding ones would run their fingers over the silverware chute, trying to detect the smallest dried-on flakes of food; they would lift the silver bucket to ensure the wood shelf on which it rested was clean and dry; they would rummage through the silver drawers to make sure you had no personal items, such as combs, that would contaminate the silverware. If they were displeased with the sanitary and esthetic condition of your station, they would likely make you do more than usual in order get out. Often you would bargain with them, claiming that you had done some extra side job that took up a lot of time and that you deserved to get out early; or, you had a date and didn't want to keep the girl waiting. These exchanges ranged from a rou- tine banter of coworkers to the harsh words of control. In exchange for the un- paid, foreman-like tasks of regulating the waiters and busboys, the captains got window stations and were given guests who were known to be high tippers, as well as full stations even in slack times.

Owners told the maitre d' how they wanted things done, such as the pre- sentation of the table (fanciful folded-cloth napkins at dinner, neat table settings), the appearance of the waiters ("tux" pants and cummerbunds, clean shirts, polished shoes). Often the maitre d' could not completely meet these requirements. If the laundry service failed to deliver enough clean jackets, waiters and busboys might wind up serving in stained ones. If tablecloths were in scarce supply (either because the linen truck goofed or the owner economized), the maitre d' might instruct waiters to place clean napkins over stained areas of the tablecloth. One or two of these on a table might not be too noticeable, given all the plates, silverware, glasses, condiments, pickles, and other items. But there was a limit to how far this could go before it looked too shlocky.

One season my father landed a job as a maitre d' in a small hotel, the name of which I sadly do not remember. At first it seemed to him a desirable reprieve from the other work he had been doing, especially running coffee shops. But it kept him on his feet far more than his poor circulation could handle, and he lasted only that one summer. I visited him the day he started at the job, and he asked my help in figuring out how to keep track of guest seating, since I had been continually working in dining rooms for some years and he had not done so for quite a while. I was so glad for him to have this job, which was more important than others he usually performed, and I treasure a photograph of him in that dining room.

Other Workers

Not all workers were trapped in the Mountains without a separate career. There were many teachers and others with seasonal jobs in New York who would come up every summer to be camp directors, athletic directors, and even musicians and entertainers. Camp directors in particular were invariably schoolteachers. These staff did not depend on the Catskills for their livelihood, as much as they wanted a paid vacation. Their experience was thus quite different in that they could easily shift back to their regular jobs, and they were not particularly harmed by the dramatic decline of Catskill hotels beginning in the late 1960s. As well, many of these workers, such as camp directors ("head counselors") and athletic directors, got to bring their families with them, and they were treated more like guests than like staff.

Chambermaids had far less status than the more professional groups. Often they were local residents, often older women, though frequently enough they were young Irish women from New York. Chambermaids worked long hours for much smaller tips than did the dining room staff, and they didn't hang around that much with the waiters, busboys, and other such staff. Larger hotels would have a housekeeper who was in charge of the maids and whose position was considerably more important than her staff.

The Employment Agency and the "Bimmies"

For a long stretch of time, my father worked the desk at the Dependable Employment Agency in Monticello, one of the two major employment agencies in the Catskills. Bill Brown took calls from owners, maitre d's, camp directors, and stewards seeking staff, and from job seekers themselves. Much of the time, he was on the road, driving workers to hotels all over the mountains, often with me along for the ride. How he remembered the routes to countless hotels always amazed me! And he knew all these people everywhere! To a naive child, access to these endless kitchen doors and hotel offices seemed magical. It was, of course, just the drab reality of being a driver.

Sure enough, most of the people my father drove to new positions were the dishwashers, potwashers, glasswashers, handymen, countermen, vegetable men, third cooks, and saladmen's helpers who had no cars. They were mostly alcoholics, often recruited from Bowery flophouses. (Waiters, counselors, chefs, and lifeguards either had cars or made their own way to their jobs.) These unfortunate souls who did the dirty work in the hotel industry we disparagingly called "bimmies" (reputedly a Yiddishization of "bum"), and they were the butt of humor. When bosses and maitre d's yelled at us waiters, we took out our verbal licks on the bimmies. When one of our number goofed up, we called him a bimmy. These men were truly downcast. They got advances on their low pay, or merely credit, that often would be spent on food and beer in the hotel concession, and by payday they had nothing left. Two weeks sober might be the best to hope for—state law required paying all staff every two weeks—before a binge finished them off and they departed in the middle of a job or were dumped in the drunk tank by the local police.

Every hotel had at least one story about a bimmy who was a down-and-out person who had previously been a success. My mother, an opera lover, delighted in speaking of a "kitchen man" (a generic term for the lower-level staff assisting in the kitchen) who had been an opera singer. Here is how one owner's son remembers these workers:

Many of them were seamen who wanted a little time on land. All usually had different stories to tell. I remember a comptroller from a well-known university, a United Press International journalist who was stationed in Berlin, officers in important companies who couldn't handle the stress of work and family, ex-cons who had spent time in the most prestigious of jails, a chef who was a dishwasher because of his inability to handle wine, several foreign-speaking people who couldn't make a go of it because of language barriers, and many others with a variety of backgrounds.

Bimmies were sometimes white, though more often they were black, Latino, Chinese, and Arabic. They were the only part of the hotel workforce that was totally gentile. In a way, they were one big collective "Shabbos goy," the gentile who performs labor on the Sabbath which is forbidden to Jews. These men rarely socialized with other hotel staff, and in hotels that permitted staff members to use the pool and other facilities, the bimmies were the only part of the workforce that were not welcome. Other hotel workers were making decent or even excellent money, but the bimmies were the one category that failed to benefit from the resorts' opportunities. The exploitation of these workers was one of the main negative features of the Catskills.

Everyone treated the bimmies like dirt, though there was always the threat that one might turn in anger, such as in the heat of the dinner "rush," when tempers flared if a waiter didn't immediately get a requested, "Side of carrots! I need it now before my tray gets cold!" I once grabbed the rails where trays rested in front of the range, threatening to vault over the counter, only to have the vegetable man move a gigantic kitchen knife to the vertical.

But back to the employment agency. The bimmies set the tone of the place. They congregated outside in a cement-covered yard or in one large room, waiting for jobs. While waiting, they drank, yelled, fought, threw up, and cursed. It was often hard to tell who was looking for work and who was just hanging out. As expected, the cops were frequent visitors. Applicants for higher-level positions had a smaller, separate room, which was attached to the area where the two owners and their two assistants (my father was one) sat. Down a little corridor were small rooms—about six-by-six—for bosses to interview more skilled job seekers such as chefs, maitre d's, and saladmen.

This was no place for a child, but I spent enormous amounts of time there during the years I finished the school year in Monticello, mostly during school lunch periods and after school. I was fascinated and repelled simultaneously. At the time, I was just trying to be where my dad worked. Later, I thought I was learning about the gritty undersides of life. Since I couldn't go home to the hotel until my father finished work, I usually wandered around town and hung out at the employment agency until 5:00 or 5:30. Down the piss-smelling alley to the agency, sidestepping drunks on the pavement outside, I entered this bizarre form of after-school.

The employment agency owners—Harold Streiffer and Dave and Charlotte Moroch—became friends of the family, and Dave became part of the winter-time Florida crew we associated with. Imagine how nasty you could get running a business like this—that was Harold's reputation: screaming at the bimmies, calling the cops, wheedling employment fees out of people, lying to hotel owners about people's qualifications. When the Mountains really began dying in earnest, it was time to close the business. Surprise of surprises, hard-nosed Harold took up painting and created sensitive canvases of Vietnamese peasants fleeing American tanks. None of us could figure out this transformation, but my parents, always interested in acquiring low-cost original art by friends, bought a few of his works.

Down and out workers found their way to hotels through other devices as well. When he was a Liberty police judge, Abraham Kleinman found a solution to jail overcrowding: "When the jail began to fill up, I'd call up the hotels and ask them if they needed a dishwasher or two. Sure enough, they'd send someone down to pay the fine and take the guy to work. Then we wouldn't see the fellow for a couple of weeks or until the next payday." This was a variant of the off-season "Mountain justice" that reigned in an informal community, as remembered by the son of one longtime Catskill lawyer:

> Sometimes an alcoholic would show up in one of the towns. And if he got arrested in Woodridge, he wasn't really arrested. The police chief, who was essentially the only policeman, would put him in the back of the car and haul him into Mountaindale. And Mountaindale would pick him up and haul him [elsewhere]. The guy was really well-traveled. If someone wound up in that loop, he'd never get out. He sobered up in the back seat of a police car.

If the drunk got as far as court, there was another option:

> One of my favorite things was to go to Friday night Justice's Court with my father. It was entertaining. The town justice was less like a judge and more like the old, sage rabbi. There was a war between two taxi companies in Fallsburg. They would get out of hand—I don't remem-

ber what the incident was; one night they wound up in court. It was the trial between Mendel's Taxi Company and Beerman's Taxi Company. The place was jammed. People were stacked in the place. People were sitting up on the raised windowsills. There was no place to sit. Clearly it violated fire safety rules. First there was the parade of drunks. They didn't really hand out sentences, so people didn't have criminal records. If you were a drunk, they gave you a bus ticket to go out of town and told you never to come back. It was more a social justice than a legal justice. That was mountain justice.

The Concession

My father's other Mountain-Rat occupation was running concessions, a central part of any Catskill resort. On a number of occasions, my mother made a deal that my father could rent the concession at the hotel where she cooked. This worked out for some of the years we spent at the Seven Gables in Greenfield Park, and at Chait's in Accord. The years my father worked for the employment agency, he lived with us in the hotel. Other years, my parents had to work in separate hotels. One year, my father ran a concession at the SGS Bungalows, while my mother cooked at Maxie Schmidt's Grand Hotel in Parksville, just beyond Liberty. Tired as she was after a workday that began at 5:30 A.M., she came over several nights a week to visit my father and me, and to bring food from the kitchen at the Grand. My father bought food from Maxie—an important item was potatoes that had been put through the automatic peeling machine, thus saving a lot of labor for us as we made our well-liked homemade French fries. Other food items were available at wholesale prices lower than the small concession could bargain for at food dealers. And, being a good Jewish mother and a Catskill chef, Sylvia brought us prepared food to eat, since we were otherwise subsisting on coffee shop cuisine.

Some summers when I could have made good money waiting tables, I gave in and worked for my father in his concessions, putting in more hours than when I was a waiter, and refusing to take very much money from him for it. Some years I put my foot down—at least halfway—and worked as a waiter all day and then worked in his concession at night. Some years this might be in the same hotel, but other years I traveled twenty miles each way to do this, from Loch Sheldrake to Swan Lake. In my last year of college, I insisted that I would not go the Mountains, but my mother convinced me that my father couldn't afford to hire the help he'd need to run the concession. So I compromised: I remained in Brooklyn, driving a cab three days a week and seeing my friends. On Thursday mornings, I took a bus to the Mountains, worked there until Sunday, and a weekend husband returned me to the city on Sunday night. I loved the years when my father worked at Dependable or was a maitre d', and the one season he was actually hired to manage the Stevensville coffee shop (which the hotel ran itself), a very large operation that didn't require him to press for my services.

When I was younger and my father had concessions, I would love to go to the wholesale distributors, either in South Fallsburg (Mountain Candy) or Liberty (Briker's), where we bought candy, cigarettes, toiletries, and paper goods for the business. These dealers were in huge warehouses, packed floor to ceiling with everything imaginable to run a coffee shop. They smelled of two main ingredients—tobacco and candy. Later, when I was older, I sometimes ran this errand myself, though my father liked doing this during the off times of the day since he got to gab with people. He would drive to Monticello every other day to "get bagel" for the same reason, and he would stop off to visit old friends. Drakes Cakes—individually wrapped slices of yellow or marble pound cakes, small crumb-covered coffee cakes, and Devil Dogs, i.e., cream-filled logs of devil's food cake—were some of the more popular snack items in the concession. The problem was that the distributor, solely selling Drakes Cakes, came around in his truck very sporadically. We were not a large enough buyer to warrant his driving miles out of his way, so often my father would cruise the main roads looking to snag the distributor's truck on its way to a hotel, and then they would do business on the side of the road.

As I got older, I hated working at the concession. It was a less "important" job than waiting tables, and usually done by people with skills so poor that they couldn't get into the dining room. I only did it because my father ran these coffee shops and he got my mother to press me into service. It was hard to hire people to work the coffee shop, since the pay was low and nights were taken up. My father worried that people would steal from the cash register when he was out getting supplies or even in the bustle of the evening rush. I was not only the trustworthiest alternative, but I was very good and extremely fast at this and could easily do the work of two people. My dining room experience, combined with a lifetime of hanging around ranges and salad counters, taught me proper food presentation, so that our sandwiches and other plates looked substantial and not like greasy-spoon food. Plus, I could run around the side of the counter and serve the food after preparing it.

In the smallest concession Bill Brown ever ran—at Chait's—he had a six-foot-long counter, with an equal number of stools, and perhaps four tables. That was in his last year of life, when his feet were so bad he could hardly stand, and the small amount of money he earned was at least enough to give him the dignity of earning his living. His earliest concession was at the Seven Gables. The concession there had a counter that ran the thirty-foot width of the casino, set off by nothing except the stools in front of it. One half was the bar and the other half was the soda fountain, divided by the counter-gate used to get inside. There were no tables to sit at, since the rest of the casino was filled with folding wooden chairs for shows, movies, and amateur nights. In the middle of a show, it was hard to control the noise of people ordering things, though we would of course not run a malted machine while a comic tried for laughs.

Paul's was the largest concession Bill Brown ever ran. It included a coffee shop and a separate bar and nightclub, as well as a room with pinball machines (I was quite good at pinball, styling myself "Captain Flipper"). My father had to have a bartender and cocktail waiters and waitresses for that large operation, and even so he was constantly running back and forth from the coffee shop to the bar. Worried that the bartender would steal money—a common occurrence—he took the cash in himself until the very end of the show when little was served at the bar and the action moved back to the coffee shop.

At one small Swan Lake hotel, my father ran a concession without a bar; this was the place I drove to from my waiting job at the Karmel. The casino was across the road and had a bar in back that I would open up for a brief hour, hoping to pull in a few extra dollars. I would load a busbox with about a dozen bottles of liquor and mixes and trot over, then come back for another busbox of cold beer. It hardly seemed worth it, since I usually only managed to sell about ten beers and half that many drinks, but my father couldn't stop himself from the effort.

Whether in a hotel or a bungalow colony, much of the daytime business in the concessions was on charge accounts. Each guest family or individual staff member had a page in a loose-leaf or composition book. We wrote in pencil the amount, and, if they were particularly fussy, the item as well. At the end of the week, we added this up and collected from them. Frequently there were disputes over whether we had marked anything extra, since people often felt they "couldn't possibly have charged all that much." We had to remember what items children were allowed to charge, and if they had misbehaved and were forbidden to charge we had to enforce that, too. Parents would often come by from the pool or softball game to check on what their children had bought. At

SGS Bungalows, some families left standing lunch orders for their children so they wouldn't have to cook in the middle of the day for them. In the words of a woman who spent 1958 to 1964 in a bungalow colony, "I would go to the luncheonette and for one dollar I'd get a hotdog, French fries, and a coke and a nickel back to play the pinball machine." Adults, too, liked the idea of a short meal that they didn't prepare, so we had at least one special each day, such as stuffed shells, meatloaf, or lasagna. More often, though, sandwiches and fries were the food of choice.

At hotels, staff members ate a lot of food in the coffee shop for several reasons. One, they didn't like the lousy leftovers they got in the kitchen, and my father could put out better food for them. Two, the concession was not kosher, so the staff could get cheeseburgers and BLTs. Three, the coffee shop was a friendly hang out, relatively removed from the bosses' reach. There were discounted "staff prices," and it was necessary to remember the regular and staff prices for all items so as not to make errors in the charge book. Staffers were often trying to get us to lower their prices even more—everyone bargained in the Mountains. Bosses and upper-level workers might frequent the concession as well. At the Aladdin, there was even an "owner's table." The baker recalls eating a Yankee Doodle cup cake there: "And she [the concessionaire] yells, 'People, people, this is your baker! Look what he's eating!' She holds it up; everybody's laughing."

One of the central coffee-shop skills to learn was making an egg cream. This drink, native to New York City and rarely served elsewhere, is essentially the soda part of an ice cream soda: chocolate syrup, milk, and seltzer. There are endless permutations of the preparation of an egg cream, including the order of the three ingredients, the slope of the glass, the strength of the seltzer from the soda fountain, the vigor of the stirring spoon, and the proper amount of foam to leave on top. The most frequent intrusion from customers at the counter concerned the proper way to perform this quasi-sacred food preparation.

Julie Beckendorf, with his partner, Laibel, ran a local vending machine business. Once a week he would visit each hotel or bungalow colony. Julie would take all the money out of our machines and bring my father and I into a far corner of the concession where he would divide it, half-and-half, with a drop extra to us as proprietors. When I was younger, Julie would toss four or five quarters to me. I felt that Julie was an old friend, a completely routine part of the Mountains. Even in years when my father did not have a concession, and hence I was not working in one, I would see Julie all over on the roads, with pinball machines in his pickup truck. Fairly often I would hitch rides with him—when

I didn't have a car, I spent lots of time hitching around between lunch and supper to pick up girls.

During the day, in hotels that had a beer or liquor license, the concession often hosted the bimmies when they were not at work, or even when they were supposed to be at work. Bimmies drank enormous amounts of beer (at thirty-five cents a bottle, three bottles for a dollar) even in the middle of the day. On innumerable occasions, the hotel owner would come charging in, yelling at my father, "Bill, what are you doing, getting my men drunk in the daytime?" And turning to the men—and the women, the chambermaids—he would yell, "Get out of here. I'm not paying you to sit in Bill's concession drinking beer!" From time to time, the owner and my father would negotiate a certain brief period in which beer drinking was OK. But like other truces, this one was frequently disobeyed.

There was always a mid-afternoon busy period, but the busiest time began after dinner when people hung around eating, buying cigarettes, and playing pinball and the jukebox. Then it plunged ahead until after the night's entertainment ended, when hordes of people descended at once, all wanting their late night snacks instantaneously. At Paul's, the counter area only sat about six people and the coffee shop ran a narrow length with about twelve four-person tables. Clearly, not all the guests who wanted to could fit in there. Not surprisingly, we wanted the customers who would have a pastrami sandwich, fries, and a milk shake. Some guests were content to nurse a cup of coffee or tea for an hour after the show, and we implemented a minimum charge so that the tables would not be taken up that way. The minimum was not that high—I think a dollar a person in the 1960s, but we did get some complaints. It was just another of the many bargaining issues that permeated the resorts. At Paul's and at the Commodore, I cooked and waited simultaneously, working at a pace that often exceeded the dining room's frenetic level. For me, this was often additional work; at Paul's I worked a full day in the dining room and voluntarily helped my father out between meals and in the evening. We did recruit regular dining room staff to work for the extra tips and small pay we gave, though most would only do it on an occasional basis. At the Commodore, in Swan Lake, Saturday nights featured a late show with Velvet, the stripper, and there was an additional rush after her last piece of flesh was bared. We were bleary-eyed by then, having already had the Saturday after-show crowd in our large coffee shop, but we had to stay awake for one last rush.

For the rent, concessionaires often got the right to run card games (this meant poker; gin rummy, bridge, canasta, and other such games were not considered major gambling games). Except for staff games, which were exempt, it was expected that guests would play in the "card room." From each hand, a percentage of the money was taken from the pot and put into a kitty that went to the concession operator. In exchange, players received new cards and all the food and drink they wanted during the game. The kitty depended on the stakes of the game. A "ten and twenty" game, with bets of ten cents and twenty cents, might result in a pot of ten dollars, so the kitty might get two dollars of that. There were often several games going at the same time. Over the course of a night, this added up pretty well and the concessionaire did good, even after paying off the bellhops who typically handled the games. If the concessionaire felt the kitty was too small, he let the players know quite clearly about it. Along with pinball machines, jukeboxes, and sometimes even illegal slot machines, card playing contributed as much or more to the concessionaire's income as did food and other products.

Once in between lunch and dinner at the Karmel, I visited Ann Portnoy, who had been a partner at the Seven Gables and who remained our family friend for years, as did her children and grandchildren. Ann, then probably in her seventies, had taken the concession that year at the Monterey in Woodbourne, a small one-person concession operation of which the only saving grace was the card games. She was so busy that day with games that she begged a favor— would I drive a mile to town to get some change for her?

Sure I would—across the generations, from one Mountain Rat to another.

Me with college girlfriend Via Friedman when I worked at the Commodore Hotel in Swan Lake, 1966. *(Photo by William Brown.)*

Me at Evans Kiamesha, 1961, at age twelve. *(Photo by William Brown.)*

Kitchen at the Karmel Hotel in Loch Sheldrake where I worked for several years as a waiter. *(Photo by the author.)*

Me fooling around on drums at the Seven Gables Hotel when I was around eight years old. *(Photo by William Brown.)*

Me at the Commodore Hotel, 1966.
(Photo by William Brown.)

Kilcoin's in Swan Lake, a favorite hangout for hotel staff. *(Photo by the author.)*

Good Afternoon...

Brown's HOTEL ROYAL

on beautiful White Lake

Menu

May We Suggest

Stuffed Peach Salad
Uneeda Biscuits & Jam

Sour Cream
Blueberries – Chopped Vegetables – Pot Cheese

Cream of Tomatoe Soup

Choice of
Lox Puff

Baked Potatoe   Buttered Beets
Garden Vegetable Plate
Onion Omelette

Lemon Sponge Cups

Coffee – Tea – Milk – Buttermilk

Sylvia Brown's hand-written menu at Brown's Hotel Royal, 1951. It shows less variety than she would later have at larger hotels.

Going Out Tonight? BY MARTIN BURDEN

Shine's serves its complete Sunday dinner at half price for children under 10 . . . Pianist George Sterney is the entertainment attraction at Mori's in Scarsdale . . . Belgian pianist Francy Boland and Dutch bassist Eddie de Hass have joined the show at Julius Monk's Upstairs Room . . . Thelonious Monk and his quartet are at the Five Spot Cafe, their first local date in five years . . . "Carioca Carnival" is on view at Benito Collada's El Chico Wednesdays through Saturdays . . . Pianist Laura Leeds has opened at the Beau Brummel.

Angie Gulotty is back as owner-host at the Rockville Centre restaurant bearing his name . . . The final round in the selection of the Brooklyn Summer Cocktail will be held today at the Hotel St. George . . . Jazz pianist Charlie Queener has joined the Tony Parenti group at the Cafe Metropole . . . Greek pantomimist Sophia Pantages makes her American debut tomorrow at the Bowlero, in Clifton, N. J. . . . Anthony P. Tuffaro will mark the ninth anniversary of his Queens restaurant with a week of festivities in September.

MENU MAGIC: Baked chicken at the Cafe Grinzing; Sylvia Brown's baked eggplant Milanese at the Seven Gables Hotel, Greenfield Park.

Paddy White is enlarging kitchen at Paddy's Clam House to prepare frozen seafood dinner for take-home use . . . The Polonaise plays host tonight to the National Gourmet Society . . . Singer Portia Nelson, now at the Red Carpet, has written several songs for the forthcoming Broadway musical, "Nine O'Clock Revue" . . . The Sirloin Room at Walsh's Steak House has been redecorated for the fall banquet and party season . . . Robert Remacle, formerly of the Waldorf Astoria, is now maitre d' at Craig's restaurant in Great Neck.

George Jessel marks his 50 year in show business Aug. with a party at the Coral Reef Beach Club, Lido Beach . . . Rudy Wassenaar, bartender at Pete's Backyard, is an auto racer and has competed at most of the famed American tracks . . . Jodie Sands is the top attraction at Shell House this week; John Mathis returns for

GULOTTY

beginning Aug. 20 . . . Frank Cerutti's daughter-in-law, Mrs. Louis Cerutti, is in Europe buying wines for the restaurant . . . The College of Complexes, "a night club devoted to the intellectual set," has started a "Brains and Beauty" contest.

JOHNSON

The Mariners bow into the Stage Coach Inn this week-end. Coming attractions: Jodie Sands and Cab Calloway . . . George D. Johnson, general manager of the Hotel McAlpin, has instituted the combination Town Room and Minute Chef, serving everything from a quick snack to a full meal . . . Singer-pianist Lucille Jaret is at the Pygmalion . . . Alex Alstone, pianist at the Casanova, has had his two newest tunes recorded by Pat Boone and Dean Martin . . . Timmie Rogers, star of "No Time for Squares" (now in Atlantic City), is co-owner of the 40-man show.

The Vogue Room serves "mint champagne"—champagne in a frosted julep glass with crushed mint . . . The Flight Deck, an outdoor patio just opened at the LaGuardia Hotel, features a light summer menu . . . The Mary Lou Williams trio opens at the Composer Aug. 22, joining the Marian McPartland group . . . Jack Wallace's orchestra will be at the Harrison Island Yacht Club, New Rochelle, till Labor Day.

New York Post column on Sylvia Brown's cooking, Seven Gables Hotel, 1957. My mother proudly carried this around in her wallet all her life.

Another of my parents short-lived restaurants in Ft. Pierce, Florida, 1956.

My father at one of his short-lived Ft. Pierce, Florida, restaurants, 1955. They thought Jews driving down to Miami Beach would welcome a Jewish restaurant. The business didn't last long. One winter, Harry and Ann Portnoy stopped in and wound up hiring my mother to cook at the Seven Gables in Greenfield Park, where she worked for six years.

My mother, chef at Chaits in Accord, with an unidentified individual, around 1978.

My mother as chef at the Seven Gables, around 1959.

My father as maitre d', unknown hotel, around 1967. The pink shirt and shiny gray tie were typical evening attire for maitre d's in smaller hotels.

My father in front of his concession at the Seven Gables, around 1959. The concession was in the casino, in a building attached to the kitchen, dining room, and children's dining room. Uncommonly, the main house was at some distance from this location. *(Photo by the author.)*

Chapter 7

Young Workers: Waiters,
Busboys, Counselors,
Bellhops, and Others

"Probably the best education that I ever received
was waiting on people."

I grew up in hotel kitchens and dining rooms. To be near my parents when I was between the ages of five and ten, I sat at the "owners' table" in the Seven Gables kitchen, where the bosses held court, and where my mother as chef sat during the rare moments she was not working. Even though the hotel had an office in the Main House, it seemed that most business was conducted from this round table in the corner of the kitchen. Deliverymen came to get their orders signed, the talent booker came by to arrange entertainment, and key staff people sat down to go over work issues. Guests who were friendly with the owners, from years of vacationing there, would even walk in to chat. All sorts of food popped up there, especially bits of whatever was currently being prepared at the stove.

I was fascinated by the bustle of the place and learned hotel life as a preadolescent ethnographer. I learned to set tables by helping out the waiters. Running errands for Paul, the saladman, taught me the rudiments of *garmigiere* work—artful food presentation. Watching food dished out at the range showed me how the kitchen ran. When my father had the concession at the Seven Gables, I sold soda and beer in the dining room at dinner. Helping at the soda fountain while still under age ten gave me a talent for fast work in the short-order mode.

Being a "staff kid" was a mixed bag. I had the run of the hotel and, by about age ten, ate in the main dining room at the "staff table"—with the lifeguard, camp director, bookkeeper, and band members, who were always my favorite. One Labor Day, when I was around ten, after everyone checked out, the bookkeeper's daughter and I decided to rummage through all the guestrooms to see what people had left behind. We turned up tennis rackets, baseballs, and other little treasures in several hours of hunting. This seemed our due after tolerating a whole season of guests dominating our lives.

But no matter how much fun, I felt like an outsider—neither guest nor staff, and of a lower class; even if many people at this hotel were of modest means, we were the ones having to work there to serve them. Tania Grossinger, whose mother worked as a social hostess at her relatives' hotel, writes extensively of the "in-betweeness" of this staff-child status. Even being an owner's child or relative had drawbacks:

> At the end of every week, the counselors at the day camp used to have a little ceremony and give out a "Camper of the Week" award. I used to cry every time I did not get it (which was, of course, every time). No matter how carefully it was explained to me that I could not get the award because I was "one of the owners," my competitive nature compelled me to try to win that little trophy.

I always yearned to get into a dining room job, where I would be my own person. When I was thirteen, at the Cherry Hill, a busboy who was missing at the last moment on a busy weekend late in the season gave me the opportunity of a lifetime—a half-hour before dinner, I grabbed a cutaway jacket and bow tie and then went to work full-time for the remaining two weeks of the season. From then on, I worked the Mountains every summer, till the end of college. At the age of fourteen, I felt I knew enough to be a waiter, having helped out other dining room staff for years, but no hotel owner could swallow the idea of a fourteen-year-old waiter. Given my connections, I only needed a year of that apprenticeship, and at fifteen I was a waiter.

Working the Dining Room

Every meal had a "shape," a way that it went—a good meal, a bomb, a breeze. A "good meal" was what you could usually hope for—a fairly routine event.

When the meal was a "breeze," you had waltzed through it without a care, always being ahead of the pack, with no complaints from guests. The worst, a "bomb," was when you were "hung up" and could never catch up with the guests' demands or the kitchen's schedule. One of the measures of how well a meal went was how early you got out of the dining room. If you could "check out" with the waiter captain and the maitre d' while most others had as much as fifteen minutes more labor in setting up, you felt you had done well. The amount of sweat was also a good way to judge how well the meal went—if you were excessively drenched in sweat, compared to what you usually were, then you had run too fast, made too many extra trips, worried too much about being "hung up." A gauge of success, in the middle of the meal, was how close you were to the front of the line to pick up each course, especially main dishes.

Serving lunch and, even more so, dinner, the key thing was to get on the "main line" early. Guests might have drifted in and leisurely eaten appetizers and soups, which were easy to pick up in the kitchen. Busboys were not allowed to pick up appetizers and soups themselves, as captured in Sydney Offit's novel: "Danny Rose picked up the mushroom and barley soup. The chef knew he was not a waiter and shouted loud enough for everybody to hear, 'I'll cut off the hands of the next busboy I see picking up on this side of the stove.'" If you didn't get caught by an irate owner who felt you, the waiter, should be doing the serving, you could even pick the food up and hand it immediately to your busboy, poised beside you, for delivery to the guests. The chef and steward might be tolerant with soups and appetizers, but they got frenetic and deadly serious with mains (main dishes), which only waiters were allowed to handle. Partly this was because mains were more expensive, there were more choices, various options about how well cooked, and what vegetables and garnishes were accompanying. Mains were large, and, unlike soup, you couldn't get enough on your tray to serve your whole station at once. If you were at the head of the line for your first trip, you'd be back quickly for the next trip or two. You wanted to get mains out early since you didn't want your guests complaining that other people were being served first.

It was possible to get "hung up" during any course, but once you were late with mains you completely lost control of the meal. Some waiters routinely got hung up because they couldn't organize their work habits and let guests send them to the kitchen too often. The trick was to not make extra trips for a single request, since then you'd never stop running. You bided time until several requests were pending or you had finished serving the current course. Waiters prone to getting hung up never learned to manage themselves or others. The frenzy of hung up waiters was pathetic; they would be running around, dripping sweat, asking other waiters for any extra dishes, whining at their busboys to help out.

Waiting tables at the Karmel in Loch Sheldrake, I had to put up with Julie, one of the owners. As with many hotels, two couples owned the place, typically in-laws. Julie's fiefdom, as the quasi-steward, was the kitchen, where he supervised meals wearing a white apron over his regular office clothes and brandishing a giant serving spoon, which was used for dishing out vegetables. He yelled all the time and, when really angry, waved the spoon threateningly; the prominent vein on his forehead throbbed, and we joked he was on the way to a stroke before desert. Julie and his brother-in-law, Perry, could not stand that we waiters hung out in the kitchen waiting for the main line to open, while our guests presumably were left without our attention—as if our busboys patrolling for us were not sufficient. When, in the course of the season-long civil war of bosses and waiters, Julie and Perry managed to scare us out of the kitchen, we resorted to leaving our trays standing silent sentinel to hold our places for when the main line opened. Then we merely kept popping in to see when the race was really on, at which point we'd take our positions where the trays stood. When this outrageous tactic got to Julie, he outlawed tray placing, and we were back to the original status of putting our bodies on line, chatting and joking, listening to Julie's and Perry's nonstop harangues to at least stand straight and not slouch over the counter.

Some of our best efforts at pleasing the guests ran up against the bosses' attempts to control us. For instance, to keep the guests happy by serving them quickly, we tried to put lots of mains on our trays. Four dishes with metal (meat meals) or plastic (dairy meals) covers fit on a tray. The acceptable limit was three stacks of plates, allowing for only twelve mains. This often meant splitting up tables, which often had eight or ten guests; guests couldn't stand to see others at their table eat while they might have to wait ten more minutes to get theirs. A fourth stack of plates would give you two tables worth of guests in many instances. But bosses and stewards often prevented that practice for fear we would drop the whole tray, no matter how experienced and strong we were. One strategy was to have your busboy next to you, hand him some mains and then meet up with him between the kitchen and the dining room to add the mains to the stack. Often enough this backfired—when we were caught, the owner would halt us, yell, and take away the top stack.

Even if you got out early with mains, some guests would invariably gripe, "How come the other tables (in your station) always get served first?" Standing in our shoes, wearing our cummerbunds, we perceived the guests as always complaining. Picture the Passover Seder as recounted by a man of seventy: "One person said, 'I don't want this matzoh, I want Manischewitz egg matzoh!' Another says, 'I want Horowitz Margareten!' Another one says, 'I want Streit's! I want Streit's!' So the guy [waiter] quit on the floor!"

We viewed the guests as *altecackers* (literally, old shits) who wanted to eat all they could (rates included all meals). We mocked their accents and ridiculed their habits. To them, we were adorable college kids. They always wanted to engage us about where we lived and went to school, our career choices, and our sweethearts. In response, waiters tried to fool the guests: "I remember taking orders for things like steak, which they wanted medium rare; everybody I gave mediums. That was a trick my mother told me, 'Just get everyone mediums and no one ever says anything,' and they didn't."

We did try to be pleasant, both because we were trained to be and because our tips depended on it. As one waiter recalled, "I would throw in two Jewish phrases, which made people feel comfortable." But sometimes, people got so much on your nerves that you couldn't hold in your emotions. One troublesome guest told me there was too much water in the teacup, no matter how much I measured the amount. Unable to please her, I poured some water out in my busbox, and she still complained, so I poured half of the water right onto the floor in front of her. Another guest insisted on only a half-cup of coffee, and whenever I brought it, it was always too much. So I went to the cup bin and got a broken cup and poured a bit of coffee into the depression in the piece and gave it to her. Another example comes from an owner's son who recounted a story about a guest who disliked herring so much he demanded that the waiter put it at the far end of the table, as distant as possible away from him, instead of serving it family-style. So difficult was this guest that someone tied a herring to the pull-chain on the light in his room, which scared him enormously when he entered one dark night.

Strategically, the best thing to do was to "train" your guests. You didn't want them to send you back and forth to the kitchen for little side dishes of sour cream and then bananas. So you told them that it would be "easier" to ask for everything at once. To preclude their choosing from too many possible selections, you brought out what you thought would be the preferred soup and simply started dishing it out. If they wanted the other choice, you told them that it meant waiting until you could get back to the kitchen, after you served the rest of the table (who *were* behaving by accepting *your* choice). Similarly, it was common practice at breakfast to stockpile an assortment of plates of lox, pickled herring, stewed prunes, and grapefruits. When a guest requested something, you could retrieve it quickly, both saving a trip and impressing them with your speed. This approach to waiting tables was termed "speculating;" bosses and stewards (who ran the kitchen) hated it because food might get messed up from being piled up in your sidestand. Worse, if you didn't get orders for the speculated food, you might conveniently ditch it in the busbox rather than returning it to the kitchen where you'd get yelled at for speculating.

Another big sin was "scarfing," eating guest food, especially at your sidestand. Everyone did this, so it was mainly a matter of circumspection. At breakfast, while waiting for guests to amble in, you could move a chair beside your sidestand, hidden from the view of the maitre d', and eat in peace, even if briefly. If time was short, you just stooped down and gobbled up a whole honeydew slice in a big gliding-mouthed swallow. Scarfing was also possible on the way from the kitchen to the dining room, when you passed through hallways and anterooms containing toasters, egg-boiling machines, breadboxes, and bathrooms. We scarfed because the staff food was so bad, though I'm sure we would have done it even if that was not the case. They served us leftovers of food that we'd have rejected even if fresh—such as *flanken,* boiled short ribs of beef whose grey color made you think of putrefaction. Of her memory of waitressing in the Mountains, Vivian Gornick writes, "The mountains were always one long siege of vitamin deprivation. No one ever wanted to feed the help; the agony on an owner's face if his eye fell on a busboy drinking orange juice or eating a lamb chop was palpable." In the memory of another ex-waiter: "I was a skinny kid and came home fifteen pounds lighter. We were always hungry, and we would grab whatever we could in the walk-in refrigerator. When they sent you in for something, you'd take whatever you could find. In the dining room, you'd grab some extra desert and [go] to a corner, someone covered for you, and you ate it."

At the Karmel, the owners grew tired of having the kitchen crowded with staff picking up their own meals one hour before the guest meal. You can understand that two dozen waiters and busboys, four bellhops, two lifeguards, the chauffeur, and assorted others hovering at the range could get messy. So the next season started with a staff waiter, Willie, serving us all in a tightly packed anteroom to the kitchen. Willie was a veteran waiter, old and hobbled, who could no longer make the fast pace of the main dining room, so he was stuck with this sad job. We felt bad for him and meant no particular disrespect, but one day after a whole week of leftover chicken, dried out potato pancakes, and other such food that we found truly inedible, we decided we wanted real meat. One waiter began spontaneously, and in a moment a chorus rose from the whole group:

"Beef, Willy! Beef!" Our chant continued till the owners came running in from assorted locations, fearful that we would embarrass them in front of the guests. I think we got maybe one decent meal out of this the next day.

If you worked the "teenage station," you could get one kid at each table to take orders, and you could even dish out food for everyone to pass around. Busboys could get a whole table's dishes collected and stacked without lifting a finger until the pile reached the end of the table nearest the busbox. Teenagers mostly did not like soup and appetizers, so serving was quicker. Teenagers also enjoyed helping you set up tables after the meal. On the romance end, "working teenage" meant you usually got the first opportunity to meet new arrivals on Friday night, and to make a date for afterward. This, plus the ease of uncomplaining guests, made it worth the lower tips you got from the teens' parents.

Our tasks seemed always to expand. Besides cleaning and setting our tables after meals, we had to wash our own silverware. This was done in a fairly sloppy way. During the meal, silver was put in a slot in the sidestand and fell into a galvanized bucket of soapy water. At the end of the meal, we took the bucket to the sinks off to the side of the kitchen, poured out that water, added new soap and hot water, twisted this heavy load about ten times, rinsed it twice, and returned with it to the dining room—often with some burned skin and a sweaty face from the ferociously hot steam following an already hot meal. There we dumped the steaming silver—with occasional food pieces—onto a tablecloth already too soiled to keep on the table, bundled four corners together, and rubbed the whole assemblage till it was dry. For ten dollars a week, at some hotels, you could get your busboy to take over this task. We also had to wash our own goblets since the bosses feared the glasswasher would break them. Bosses also feared busboys' carelessness and yelled at us if we tried to unload this duty.

We all had "side jobs" as well: refilling all the salt and pepper shakers weekly, wiping off ketchup bottles, delivering hundreds of dishes from the dish room to the chef or the baker, cutting bread in the industrial-size slicer before the meal, storing sliced bread under damp cloth napkins afterward, sorting the soiled linen for the laundry truck. There was so much laundry that several staffers had this task. It was so boring that we often had spoon fights, throwing silverware across the room at each other—I still have a forehead scar from one of these episodes. About every three weeks we would have to spend an extra couple of hours between lunch and dinner burnishing the silverware. This miserable task involved waiting our turn to place our silverware in a revolving round chamber filled with a viscous, gloppy soap and thousands of BBs; it made a terrible sound as it removed egg stains, scratches, and tarnish and shined the silverware. You lost your whole afternoon. I recently visited the Aladdin Hotel in Woodbourne, where an old burnishing machine, without its brass top, serves as a flower planter in front of the main entrance. Another time-consumer was the periodic but major task of buffing the floors with a heavy power buffer. This required putting all the chairs in the dining room up on the table tops, hence being unable to set up for the next meal. By the time the buffing was done and the tables were set, little time remained for rest—another afternoon lost. At least this was very occasional at the hotels where I worked—some hotels had busboys mopping and buffing floors every day.

Like many elements of Catskill life, dining room staff relations had something of a cutthroat attitude. Waiters would steal silverware from each other's drawers, goblets from each other's trays, and even food from sidestands. It was often necessary to make sure that either you or your busboy was always present at the station to protect the sidestand from marauders. Inexperienced waiters would find more seasoned ones cutting in front of them on the line in the kitchen. One of the worst offenses was stealing toast. We had to make our own toast in large revolving machines, which held ten rows of four slices each. The best way to save time was to throw toast in on the way from the dining room to the kitchen, pick up egg orders, and fetch the toast to add to the eggs on the way back. Lots of toast was stolen in that interim, and the excuse was always, "Hey, I put that in before. Someone else took yours." The exact same thing held for boiled eggs, which we also had to make ourselves. A large vat of boiling water had a number of egg machines hovering over it. You placed your eggs in an egg-machine basket and pulled the chain down, lowering the egg machine into the vat, according to a marker indicating the number of minutes for that type of egg. When the time was up, the chain returned the basket to its original position. Eggs were stolen less frequently than toast, but only because waiters couldn't tell how well the eggs were done by merely shaking them.

Sydney Offit's 1959 novel, *He Had It Made*, offers a good glimpse into dining room rivalries, and along the way provides the best account of dining room and kitchen life that has yet been written. Offit's lead character, Al Brodie, appears as a hustling opportunist who not only takes on his waiter colleagues, but also hustles the whole hotel. Al weasels his way into a waiter's job at the start of the season, even though the Sesame Hotel (the fictional equivalent of the Aladdin in Woodbourne) has already hired its full staff, and this means an already hired waiter is demoted to the children's dining room. Later in the novel, Al sucker punches his chief rival, who has challenged him to a fight after a month of taunting Al. After landing the bullying antagonist in the hospital, Brodie quickly seduces a counselor, whom he later spurns. When the maitre d', Audrey, is despondent over a fight with the chef, Al sleeps with her in order to get a better station. But as the novel progresses, he becomes more attached to the hotel. He is concerned that the owners' daughter, Marsha, hates it and doesn't want to take it over from her aging parents. While we are never convinced that his romance with the daughter is more than an opportunistic ploy to marry into the business, Al Brodie does seem to care about the resort and its people. Offit paints Al Brodie as an ambivalent character, much like other Catskill characters, real and fictional, that I have met. Since so many people are hustling, Brodie's hustling is not unexpected, and perhaps the Catskill magic rubs off on him, too.

We played around a lot in the dining room, before and after meals. We did animal imitations and performed impromptu skits satirizing the chef, maitre d', and owners. We called make-believe harness races. We roughhoused with each other. A busboy recalled:

> We had contests after everyone left the dining room to see who could carry the heaviest tray. You would pack it all around on the tray and then see who could carry it into the kitchen without dropping it. I was carrying one of these heavy trays into the kitchen when the owner walked in and said to me, "If you drop a dish, you're fired. Even if you don't, you're putting on the amateur show on Wednesday."

Counselors

Most counselors were teenage girls, though the teenagers' counselors were often young men. For many parents, having their daughter work as a counselor was more palatable than other jobs. They would be supervised by a head counselor, typically a schoolteacher. Because they would be around children and their parents a lot, they would apparently be away from the temptations of the fast life of the dining room staff, bellhops, lifeguards, chauffeurs, and others. This was a silly assumption, since counselors represented the major source of female companions for the staff, apart from the young guests. More so than other jobs, counselors might even work at the same hotel their parents stayed at, simultaneously. A counselor at the Olympic in South Fallsburg in 1967 was particularly incensed by the fact that counselors had a curfew, something no other staff member was subject to. He attempted to organize the other counselors on the issue of the curfew—and got fired.

Counselors worked a long day, even though the labor was not as grueling as in the dining room. They had to endure three meals a day with rowdy children in the children's dining room. Their workday began at 7:00 A.M. and finished at 8:00 P.M., with snatches of time off before and sometimes after dinner. Three days a week, counselors did night patrol till midnight, making rounds of rooms to check on sleeping children while their parents were at the show, the track, or playing cards. This task was the worst burden for counselors, tying them even more to the hotel. It was a common sight to see female counselors making their night patrol rounds in the company of their dining room boyfriends, though head counselors were quick to snoop on this, lest there be making out while "on duty."

There was one rung lower than counselor—nursemaid. Nursemaids were girls too young to be counselors but who took care of children two and under who couldn't go to day camp. One such worker told me she only made twenty-five dollars in tips over the course of a summer in the mid-1960s. Another woman worked as a counselor only one season, at age fourteen. Seeing some parents tip five dollars for the whole summer, she quickly came to believe that the Mountains were loaded against women staff: "The guys in the dining room made a lot of money and the counselors made *bupkes*." She wanted to avoid that in the future: "My mother and brother always wanted to go to the Mountains, but my father and I didn't. I'd fail a course in order to stay in the city and go to summer school and take care of my father."

Staff Quarters

While money was spent on refurbishing guest rooms and facilities, nothing was spent on staff quarters. I heard from an ex-counselor his opinion that "If any code existed, I don't care if it was Hammurabi's code, it had to be in violation." In almost all the places I worked in, dining room staff, bellhops, camp counselors, lifeguards, chauffeurs, handymen, and dishwashers all slept in unheated pine-board shacks on stilts. If you were lucky, three people might share an eight-by-eleven-foot room with one dresser, maybe a sink. Otherwise you might be in a large room with six or more beds. As a waiter at the Stevensville, I slept in a huge dormitory room with forty young men, sharing twenty bunk beds, and I never felt more like I was in a barracks.

Bedding was so soft, it molded to your body and drooped almost to the floor. At Paul's, toilets and showers were at one end of the staff building, and you had to go outside and walk along the porch to get to them, even in the cool weather of Passover and Rosh Hashanah. Where knots in the pine had fallen out, there were holes to look into the next room, and it was necessary to stuff paper in them. Being used to this, I was shocked to work at the Brickman's and find my accommodations to be a neat two-person room in a well-kept eight-room bungalow that was no longer suitable for guests who had gotten used to fancier rooms with private baths. This was the kind of room that would still house guests in a hotel half that size.

Most staff quarters were at a distance from the main buildings, preferably on ridges behind the central hotel area, hidden by trees from the guests' sight. At Paul's, the lower range of a medium-size hotel, the staff quarters were a size-able hike, so that if you forgot a cummerbund it was a long uphill trek to get it. "Bimmies"—dishwashers, potwashers, vegetable men, handymen, and other maintenance staff—usually had their own building, in even worse shape than accommodations of the dining room staff. Day camp counselors, mostly young women, were often housed separately, sometimes in rooms attached to the casino or in the attic of a guest building—they were more in need of protection than the waitstaff. Chambermaids, too, sometimes had a separate building since they would not mix well with the dining room staff and bellhops. Within the minisociety of the hotel overall, there was a secondary minisociety of the staff quarters—three or four buildings that were more or less our own community.

Smaller hotels might have only one large building for all the staff, except bimmies. At the Seven Gables, this building was built on stilts onto the rising hillside just past the main part of the hotel, though quite visible. As a six-to-ten-year-old child climbing the staff building's high staircase, of perhaps twenty stairs, I felt I was entering the wonderfully special world of the teenagers and young twenties who lived in what seemed a perpetual party atmosphere.

Other hotels put staff in buildings housing the casino, where there was con-stant noise. Late afternoon rehearsals for the night's entertainment made naps impossible, and early sleepers had to tolerate the show still going on at night. Some hotels housed us in basement and attic levels of guest buildings. These might be slightly more comfortable than the distant shacks, but they limited the noise and partying you could have. This was the case at the Karmel, and the bosses were in our hallways every day, in the basement of a guest building just a hundred feet from the back door of the kitchen, telling us to be quiet since there were guests upstairs. The farther away from the rest of the hotel, the more independent we were. This was especially helpful when we were housing and feeding friends who were either visiting from the city or in between jobs in the

Mountains. Owners were aware that this freeloading occurred, and it really got to them since they knew we would smuggle food to our friends. In hotels where owners roamed through the staff quarters, we would make sure our visitors were out and away by the time everyone rose for work. I remember a few occasions when owners caught freeloaders and threatened to charge room and board to the staff person who put them up. There were also lots of inter-hotel conjugal visits. One Rosh Hashanah, I drove over every evening from the Karmel in Loch Sheldrake to Kutsher's in Monticello to spend the night with my girlfriend, a counselor. These visits rarely meant smuggled food, since the person sleeping over had a regular source of meals, but it meant a loss of control to the hotel, more a matter of principle.

Many Catskill dining room veterans remembered the famous towel or hanky tied on the door, signifying that people were inside making out and that roommates should keep away. That was not always the most comfortable or safest method. One waiter described how to get a better trysting place: "I would be friendly with one of the bellhops or [staffers] at the front desk and ask them which rooms were empty. If there was an empty room, I remember giving them free drinks at the bar if they would give me the key to the room. There was a lot of that type of bartering. Whatever you did, you helped out your coworkers. They helped you in return."

The Staff at Play

For the money, we worked long hours. We got up at 7:00 to serve breakfast. With luck you could be done by 10:00 or 10:15 if your guests finished trekking in early enough. Then back at 12:00 for lunch, and out again at 2:00 or 2:30. Free until 6:00 for supper. Time enough to go cruising other hotels or the streets of Liberty or Monticello in search of girls. Maybe just hang out poolside, play basketball, baseball, tennis. The advantage of smaller hotels was that you could use all of the guest facilities; many larger hotels segregated the staff. By hustling, it was possible to get out of the dining room by 8:30 at night. Almost everyone was after some fun. Sunday night was often poker, since we had just gotten the week's tips. Once a week, at Paul's Hotel, we hoarded food from the kitchen and rowed across the lake for late-night cookouts. But the best of times were at Monticello Raceway, at local pubs, and at rock shows at some of the larger medium-size hotels, like the Eldorado in South Fallsburgh where you could hear groups like the Four Seasons. A waitress at the Homowack in Spring Glen recounted how the dining room staff would celebrate the end of the season by going glider flying in Wurtsboro.

The best tavern I ever patronized was Kilcoin's in Swan Lake, just down the hill from town. Al McCoy, owner and bartender, was a jolly man and a great card trickster. To see Allie's tricks, the unspoken rule was that you had to sit at the bar and drink liquor, not draft. Draft beer, sitting at the table, was fifteen cents for a small glass, a quarter for a mug pulled from a freezer and then filled with the coldest beer anywhere in the world (New York's drinking age was then eighteen, and poorly enforced). Kilcoin's was pure roadhouse—hard wood benches, jukebox, coin-op pool table, and no decor save brewery clocks with electric bubbling froth. I worked several years in Paul's Hotel in Swan Lake and had ample time to visit Kilcoin's. During most nights of the year I worked at SGS Bungalows, and another year at the Commodore Hotel, when I finished work at midnight in the coffee shop, I'd drive down for an hour of sanity. Even the years I worked far from Swan Lake, I was drawn back to this spot.

My friends from the Cherry Hill Hotel band got a great job at the Raleigh's smaller bar, where they could specialize in mainstream and Latin jazz, instead of endless repetitions of Catskill war-horses ("Hello Dolly," "Havenu Sholem Aleichem," "Sunrise Sunset"). This was one of the few places where you could hear good jazz—apart from jam sessions held after the shows were over, when hotel owners allowed it.

Monticello Raceway was a major fun spot. "The Track" drew everyone— locals, staff, and guests. It was impossible for dining room staff to get there at post-time, but a mad dash could get you in by the second or third race if you worked close enough to Monticello. When we got tired of rushing and frustrated by losing money, we often opted for the free admission to the last two races. The Track exerted a pervasive effect. Guests often requested fast service with all the courses delivered at once, so they could make the daily double. At one place I worked, a busboy, Nathan, would grab the dining room mike and announce make-believe races during set-up time, only to be shut up by the maitre d', lest guests in the lobby hear it.

Some people were uncomfortable with the insular nature of the hotel. Especially in small hotels, there might be too few staff to provide variety. One of the reasons that staff were so often carousing throughout the Mountains at night was just to get away from the tightness of the surroundings that shaped their lives. One sociologist I know, who got his start in Catskill dining rooms, applied his theoretical tools to describe the closed-in feeling that you could get: "In effect the hotel was almost like a total institution in that we were working and spending our entire days, seven days a week, ten weeks a summer, at the hotel."

The Catskills were full of thousands of other workers our age, and that contributed to a party-like atmosphere. You could go anywhere—laundromat, restaurant, bar, sidewalk fruit stand—and you'd find compatriots with whom to compare working notes, make new friends, line up dates, and learn of job openings if you wanted to make a switch. Most—probably 90–95 percent—of these young workers were Jewish, up until the middle 1970s. This was logical, since the milieu was so Jewish that the guests would best be understood by Jewish staff. Also, many staffers got their jobs through family connections or via relatives who were guests. It was always noticeable who was gentile, but Jewish staff did not generally exclude others from social interaction. One hotel I worked in had some Polish waiters and busboys from Carbondale, nearby in Pennsylvania, and it was actually refreshing to have some people who were dissimilar from the rest of us. In another hotel, during Passover, one gentile bellhop didn't know what to call the rabbi's wife when he served her in the tea room, so he addressed her as "Mrs. Rabbi" until we corrected him.

The Shlock House

What waiters and busboys really feared the most was working in a *shlock* house. How can I describe a shlock house? In Yiddish, shlock means junk, but the colloquial usage refers to something of poor quality, especially if it has pretensions. In the Catskills, what many people termed a shlock house was a run-down hotel, which, if full, held maybe 75–150 guests. Above all, the schlock house was disorganized and crude. It had no real facilities beyond a pool, handball court (often with many cracks in the pavement), perhaps a decayed tennis court, and sometimes a hoop and backboard on crumbly pavement. Entertainment in some of the very small hotels might be quite circumscribed—some didn't even have a band and hence couldn't present singers. Not all small hotels were shlock houses. Some were run very well and tastefully, without the disorganization and cheapness of a shlock house.

You'd know a shlock house just by seeing it. One night some of us went down the road to pick up a friend for a night out. We had finished serving dinner, showered, changed, and gotten to the shlock house, and they were still serving! Everything was out of control, waiters and busboys aimlessly running about, helplessly behind. At any other hotel, outsiders like us would be thrown out of a dining room for entering in the middle of a meal. Here, there was no one to notice, no authority or direction. Often, food in a true shlock house was served "family style," with large bowls and platters in the center of the table. You wanted bananas and sour cream at lunch, your waiter brought bananas and you added the sour cream from the big *schissel* (serving bowl). At night, the waiter served your chicken and you added vegetables from a common plate. One saladman proudly told how he started working at a hotel that served family style, and gradually weaned them to the more modern, less shlocky, a la carte service.

Why would you wind up working in a shlock house? Maybe your parents knew an owner to give you your first job. Sometimes you could make just as good money as elsewhere, with lower tips but more guests. Perhaps you screwed up badly in a job, and there were no other jobs around. Maybe you just never got good enough to work anywhere else—I knew such guys. A high school friend from Florida wound up in a shlock house playing his trumpet, but with no real band to play it with. Many talent agencies put together pick-up bands, but they at least rehearsed them once to see that they could play. Not so in my friend's case. The opening night of the season, I came to visit him after I finished serving supper. Howard showed up, along with a piano player and a drummer. None had ever seen the others before and try as they might they could not play for the waiting guests. There were these three musicians basically pretending to play music for people who were fated to stay in shlock houses where they got this kind of treatment. Howard asked for help—he knew I played piano in the lounge at the Karmel after finishing a day waiting tables. But I declined—this situation was beyond salvage. It was the essence of the shlock house.

What might have been a small, but somewhat fancy hotel in the 1940s and 1950s could become a shlock house by virtue of neglect, or even by failure to expand. The small and smaller medium-size hotels where some of us worked were sometimes just a category above the schlock house. These were what we called "2–250 houses," hotels holding between 200 and 250 guests. Guys we knew in larger places even told us *we* were working in shlock houses. Shlock was always a measure of superiority over the next lowest rung on the ladder, whether it was working in the Catskills or was one's choice of clothing or furniture.

CHAPTER 7

What an Experience!

Waiting tables and doing other jobs in the Mountains was hard work, and we had plenty of conflicts with owners, guests, chefs, and maitre d's. Even in revisiting the Catskills, veteran staffers could see the negative side. For example, a counselor who returned years later, at the age of forty, with her parents to a large hotel for Thanksgiving found it a "bizarre experience." Black waiters were dressed in Pilgrim costumes, which she found demeaning. As to the entertainment: "It was all a series of has-beens or never-beens. Here's so-and-so who was in *Man of LaMancha* in 1960, and he would come out and sing 'Impossible Dream.' Everybody would be saying, 'Oy, listen to him!' and I would be on the floor laughing, thinking this is horrendous."

But that was only part of the picture. Overall, working in the Catskills was a positive experience. Jerry Jacobs, who waited tables for eight summers, believed that he learned good work habits in the Catskills:

You had to have a strategy for serving thirty to forty people in a short period of time. You could get overloaded with special requests and get completely dizzy and not know where you were. You had to know how to get things out of the kitchen. You had to know how to get through difficult situations, like when the kitchen would run out of a popular dish. You could easily get waylaid looking for a fresh slice of onion or some other garnish that was misplaced in the pantry. My wife has remarked about how my brother and I are pretty unflappable in the face of crisis, and we definitely got that from growing up in the hotel.

Similarly, another waiter remembered:

You never really considered the hard work. It was a job that you did. You dealt with people. Probably the best education that I ever received was waiting on people. You were then dealing with the various personalities. You knew the people who looked down on you; the people who took a liking to you; who would want to fix you up with their granddaughter; you were a college man. You got to become a psychologist in order to get the biggest tip. That's the kind of experience that you can't quantify.

For one waiter: Mountain labor "was a very maturing experience. After that I felt comfortable with older people. My friends were older. I went out with older women. Being away from home, taking care of myself—you know, you didn't leave home at that time." This might be important. These people couldn't afford camp, so the kids had no summer recreational experience. They didn't leave home till marriage, so this did give them a boost in life. As a waiter in the 1940s said, his average one hundred dollars a week was "phenomenal," and in particular, "it was far more than my dad used to bring home." One energetic man recalls:

> Between everything I had going—the bellhop work, the little extras, the chauffeuring, and everything else—there was a time when I was making $300 a week. Undeclared of course. At any rate, there were just tremendous opportunities. We hustled and did what we could to make a buck. That put me through school, got me some nice cars. I was able to put a little bit of it away. I was also able to do things for my family. At the time, my older brother was just starting out, so I'd try to come up with a few dollars to support him. I gave an allowance to my younger brother. I also helped out with my family and their struggles. Financially it was paramount. That job was everything to me.

Of the 1950s, one waiter recalled, "I struggled, was financially hungry, and [I] remember my fellow waiters as first-generation Americans just as hungry as I—hungry to succeed in school, anxious to please, and very financially needy." Where else could you make this kind of money as a teenager? Even spending freely on entertainment, I returned home in September with at least $1,000 of my own money. For a teenager in the early- to mid-1960s, that was a lot. I bought all my own clothes in high school and even a car. When I was in college, the bundle of summer money meant that I rarely worked during the school year, leaving me free for studying, dating, and antiwar activities (of course, when I worked, it was either as a bartender at Dodger's in downtown Brooklyn or waiting banquets at Goldman's, a Catskill-style resort in West Orange, New Jersey).

Years later, those who complained while they worked the Mountains would look back with a more balanced vantage point, such as this waiter: "I consider it a badge of honor, something akin to surviving an earthquake, making it through a great and bloody war. And yet I wouldn't have missed it for the world. Forty-eight years later, I'm still drawn periodically back to a place I was once happy to have escaped. Wherever I roam, I come across people who once worked the Borscht Belt. Like old veterans we sit around and tell our war stories." Reuben Wallenrod's novelistic voice records the feeling of typical staffers a few days shy of the Labor Day season ending: "All these days in Brookville will be seen in retrospect as one long warm day flooded with light, and the long and tiring hours of work will be interspersed in memory with some sparks of joy and youthful pranks."

Chapter 8

Guests

"The food? I essed and I essed"

Coming mainly from New York City, Long Island, and New Jersey, Catskill guests ranged from working class to upper-middle class, and they had a wide range of hotels to choose from. Sometimes there was a class mix within one hotel, though not at the extremes. In the small- and medium-size places my parents and I worked, workers, small businessmen, and lesser professionals predominated; doctors and lawyers were rare. People with more money might stay a month or even the whole season (July 4th to Labor Day), with husbands coming up only for weekends. Those with less money might stay a shorter time: "My father was a furrier. If he had a good season, we'd go for two weeks. If he didn't, we'd go for one week." From another furrier family came this story about how to pay for the vacation: Several of the fathers were partners in the fur trade. When they did well enough and graduated from a kuchalayn to Brickman's, they stayed for the summer. Jack Fuchs, one of the fathers, came up on weekends with the newest classy fur piece. His wife wore it Saturday night, the women ooed and ahed, and he sold that piece, saying to his family, "Good, another week at the hotel paid for." Sarah Sandberg tells a very similar story about her family's fur business in *Mama Made Minks,* but the family I spoke to were sure they had never heard of Sandberg or her book.

Some people could only afford to go on vacation in the Catskills when their organization had a conference and they got very low rates or when the organization paid their way. For a family of modest income, even a weekend at those rates required saving up. One family had little enough money that they stayed at a bungalow for only one week; there were few bungalow colonies that allowed that. As one unskilled laborer's daughter recalls, "Sometimes it wasn't certain until the Friday before we left that there would be enough money. Throughout the year I was told that the cost of the week at Ben-Ann's was why I couldn't have piano lessons."

Amazingly, a great number of working-class Jews could afford some sort of Catskill vacation. In the old country, Jews' festivity centered around Sabbath, holidays, marriages, and children's births. In America, Jews found a looser set of social norms, including freedom for men and women to socialize together in public. This allowed for more public entertainment, including vacations. As Andrew Heinze put it, the vacation was part of the "symbolic consumption" of American Jews—goods and entertainment that were previously unavailable to these largely immigrant people were now accessible to most of them. This represented an acculturation to American life—the immigrant was no longer a greenhorn but a citizen of the New World. Thus, Heinze continues, "the vacation came closer than any other custom to fulfilling the notion of the earthly paradise that Jews carried to America." As a result, "by the 1890s, a summer vacation had begun to be a normal expectation for Jewish wage earners." In 1906, the *Morgen Zhurnal* published articles with titles such as "One Goes because Everyone Goes" (in which the paper discussed the embarrassment of a woman who could not join her friends in the Mountains). By this time already, a Catskill vacation was common for many wage workers, not merely for business owners and professionals. Michael Gold, writing in 1926, spoke of a "revolution on the Lower East Side" in the last decade, in which the labor movement provided enough financial and political support to working-class Jews that they could "cast off the sad, self-pitying, melancholy helplessness of the Ghetto. . . . Their revolution has taught them to be their own saviors. Among other things, they now take vacations."

The cost might be a stretch, but many New Yorkers made the Catskill vacation the highlight of their year. An ex-waiter, now sixty-seven years old, recounted the story of "Sammy, who used to come for a week or two every year. Sammy was very flashy; he used to wear bright blue sports coats and doeskin shirts. He'd attract all the ladies. He'd flash his bankroll. He was a loud kind of guy. Very pleasant though. Always going on dates. Requesting tables with single women. Then I went to school in downtown Brooklyn. One day I'm walking by one of these little candy and cigarette stands, and there selling stuff is Sammy. It dawned on me that this poor guy was saving all year to spend a couple of weeks in the Catskills and the crazy thing is that the women that he met and tried to romance were probably in the same position. They probably worked in a garment factory, saved up all year to go up there to meet a guy like Sammy."

In the 1930s, a small hotel's rate would be twenty-two dollars a week, and half that for a child. Some hotels even provided transportation to and from New York City included in the rate. The Flagler, one of the top places in that era, got thirty-five dollars. As late as the mid-1940s, one woman, earning $30.00 a week, went to Grossinger's for $39.50, sharing with two others. She recounts a cheaper alternative: "Something else I did as a young woman. We used to hire the hack, go up on Saturday just before lunch and get there just after lunch, spend the whole day and the next day until dinner and that was a full day. That cost eleven dollars. Eleven dollars, you spent two days." Top accommodations could go higher, of course. Overall, the Catskills were affordable for people without much money. As a travel agent recounted, "For the first time, you had a luxury vacation offered to a working-class population. The clientele included secretaries, taxi drivers, clerks—mostly nonprofessionals. It was a respectable place for people to meet. The real story is what this industry did for the poor man."

Some of these guests drove a hard bargain when they sought a hotel:

There were people who shopped. This would make a terrific movie. They would shop it at the moment of purchase. They would come up with a car and their children and all their luggage looking for a place. They would drive up, and you would think you had them. No. They had you. You had the empty rooms and if you didn't fill them, they'd be empty. It was a buyer's market. . . . I would show the room, and I knew the economics were so marginal that it was extraordinary that people could negotiate you down. . . . We'd be showing a room, climbing up the stairs and be lowering the price. One hundred dollars a couple, maybe the two children [at] twenty-five dollars a piece. You would try to get a little more. The room was the sale. Most of the rooms had adjoining baths or [their own] baths. We walked into the room with a double bed and a crib, with a bureau—there isn't a lot of room. That's the premise. That's why it's so cheap. . . .

The great line was walking into the room with a gentleman born in Eastern Europe, working in the garment district. This was his big two-week vacation.

They walk in the room and ask, "So tell me, what are you getting for a room like this?"

I'd say, "Well sir, $150."

"They're giving you $150 for this room? I want to wish you good luck."

We have the intro, the price on the table, and I'm saying (I don't want him to leave), "Sir could you give me an idea of what you think this is worth?"

"I'm not here to play games. It's your room; you want $150; I wish you good luck." He turns and starts to walk out. His wife is in the car with the children.

[I'd] say, "Would you be interested in a cottage. If you give me an idea of how much you want to spend, I could give you a room."

"You're the merchant here."

"Would you be interested in a room that's a little less?"

"We'll take a quick look."

You bargain. You had to beg the guy to come and sign.

A Refreshing Vacation

While not everyone enjoyed the outdoors as much as they enjoyed the dining room, the beauty of the Catskills was a draw. As this small businessman's fond memories reveal:

The biggest thing to me was it was country, and I'm sure you have heard people say that, and you know that's what it's called. Nobody said we are going to the "Catskills" this summer; we were going to "the country." So, until I moved to Connecticut in 1979, the only place that I knew of that had trees and grass were the Catskills. . . . The two biggest memories that I have are the grass and trees number one; and number two—fresh air. Because you could see almost immediately the difference, especially at night. You could breathe the air. You could look up and see stars; I never saw stars when living in the Bronx. I lived my whole life in an apartment building, never had a house, and so I didn't have a lawn, I didn't have a backyard. The Catskills was my backyard. . . . Most of the places that we went to had a lake, and that's one of my fondest memories of the Catskills is just being around a lake. And [I] remember rowing a lot with my father and my sister and mother, although a lot of times just my father and I, just going out to the middle of the lake with the boat, and it was real fun, and there used to be a lot of frogs, and I used to run around all over the place, spending half a day catching frogs and looking at frogs, putting them in jars and then letting them go. Well, unfortunately, it's become an affliction, and you don't see any here, but I have frogs in strategic places all over this house and all over my desk at work. I must have ten frogs on my desk at work—not real frogs, porcelain frogs. When I go to different places, I travel a lot for my work, and whenever I'm in a different city [I collect them]. I have a frog from Texas with a ten-gallon hat, and stuff like that. A lot of that stems from the fact that I really liked them [while] growing up in the Catskills, cause you don't see too many in the Bronx.

For some guests, the sports facilities were more important than the countryside. Such people couldn't help but notice the sedentary nature of others:

We got up early in the morning. My husband was a golfer and he was on the course before the greenskeeper was out. From there we went to the swimming pool. From the swimming pool, we got our ice skates and went to the skating rink. We were going constantly. We realized that going past the pool there was a fairly big room where people were playing cards and mah-jongg. Whether you passed at nine in the morning or ten at night, the same people were sitting at the same table playing the same game. We used to say, "What did they bother coming up here for?"

Morningside Lake covered ninety acres and was stocked with fish. A descendent of the Morningside's owners remembers that fishing was a major attraction for guests when the hotel started in 1907: "Surprisingly, a lot of these Jews in New York who were tailors and furriers and whatever loved to fish. Where they learned to fish, I don't know. But they used to come up to go fishing. My grandmother would cook the fish they caught."

The Catskills provided athletic exposure that would be unavailable or rare back in the city:

We went to the Brickman's [in the 1940s]. I didn't know how to swim. The first day we are there, we go down to the pool, and I don't know how to swim. I go back to my room crying. I was nine or ten. My father says, "Sonny what's the matter?" "Well Daddy, everyone's swimming and I don't know how to swim. " My father in his direct manner says, "Come with me." He takes me by the hand, marches me down to the pool, motions for the lifeguard to come over and says, "Phil, this is my boy, Sonny. You teach him how to swim this summer." He says, "Okay." That made a tremendous impact on me. Phil was tall and athletic, a clean liver. He taught me to swim, and I made the swimming team in high school. I swim now every day I can.

Sports were important, especially at the larger hotels that could provide facilities and attract star athletes, either as staff or as visitors, for training or exhibitions. Many hotels and colonies alike featured daily softball games, which many people remembered as "baseball." At the Flagler, in the mid-1940s, "the rabbi was one of the best players we had, and he used to slide from first into second with the yarmulke flying. That was priceless when you saw that."

Sex and Romance

Matchmaking, often with a professional *shadchen* (matchmaker), was part of Jewish culture in the Old World and even in the New. Why would the Catskills not be full of this? Professional shadchens were scarce, but hotel owners, social directors, and guests served in that role. Even if there was no one officially looking to make the match, people came looking for it. Romance—with or without sex—was one reason people came to the Mountains. They wanted to meet the right person. A young woman, or her parents, sought a student on his way to being a professional. The student sought a woman whose family might have money to help him through medical or law school. Romancing between guests and staff thus crossed income levels, but the class differences were minimal when one looked ten years down the road. Even in the orthodox Lebowitz's Pine View Hotel in South Fallsburg, one young worker remembers that orthodox waiters and orthodox guests made matches. Comedian Joey Adams joked that "for those whose life-long ambition was matrimony, Mountaindale, Monticello, and South Fallsburgh proved the greatest Garden of Eden since Eve propositioned Adam."

Many people I spoke with either met their own spouses in the Mountains or knew others who did so: "And that romance—[points to a couple at her apartment complex] see the older couple—she met her husband in Grossinger's, and it was one of the best romances that I know of. " If it worked once, it could work again: "I met both of my husbands there."

Staff and guests alike had different memories about sex and romance in the Catskills. Some took pains to separate the two: "I don't know about romance, but sex!" Another similarly exclaimed, "It was a place of great sex. I wouldn't say it was a place of great romance. I think there is a mystique about living and working up there. You were really roughing it up there, living in these shacks that they put you up in. . . . It's a weird existence being up there in the summertime, living in one of these shacks. It really is roughing it—a pigsty. There is something about having sex in a pigsty that is exciting." For these men, there was a wild life of sexuality, though it didn't mean the traditional searching for a mate that was the staple of Catskill lore. Women responded more cautiously: "I loved the country, but I didn't like the folks who thought anyone who worked there was fast."

Writers make much of the owners pushing male staff to romance the women guests, though my experience was that this was accepted more than demanded. Several waiters recalled that they were required to socialize with the guests, even at a fairly sizeable hotel such as the New Roxy, which could hold 700. But it was not so widespread as the legend makes out. Of course, even without that pressure, affairs would start. A musician reported that: "Our tenor sax man almost had a one night stand with a married woman whose husband was up there. One night, he and his ladylove went into the darkened casino and they both fell on the cymbals and drums. The percussive noise awakened everybody—and they took off like frightened rabbits." A different tenor player, who married a guest in the early 1930s while working at the Loch Sheldrake Rest, told me that "it was dangerous to leave wives alone," since they might get involved with a staff member. Even youngsters knew what was going on; a guest who vacationed at the Kiamesha Country Club in the late 1920s claimed: "As children, we were aware of the Monday to Thursday night actions of many women, which changed on Friday, Saturday, and Sunday."

A waiter who worked in the 1950s and 1960s spoke of the "barracudas," women whose husbands were away during the week and who sat at the bar waiting to be picked up by young staff. But while I heard many stories about women alone at the resorts, only one person raised the problem of men alone: "I had one cousin who had a wife and child up at the bungalows, and during the week he had a girlfriend in the city." Given the morality of the era, male infidelity was a more likely occurrence. Perhaps the frequent tales and jokes about women's affairs were the projection of male infidelity onto their wives away in the country. At any rate, the women in the hotels were being watched by others, so their transgressions were more visible than their husbands' transgressions in the city. And, of course, to the extent that hotel owners and social machers pushed young male staff to accompany the female guests, it is interesting that the 'blame' should fall entirely on the women.

In any case, the hypersexual mythology caused much trepidation: "My wife always wanted to go up as a waitress, and my father-in-law said, 'I'd never send my daughter to one of those places.'" Herman Wouk's protagonist Marjorie Morningstar gets the same response from her parents. Their solution to her strong desire to work in the Catskills is to arrange for her uncle to work in the same hotel. Even success in a matchmaking situation left people in awkward situations, as per this waitress who returned later as a guest with her parents: "Sometimes I'm embarrassed to tell people that I met a spouse at the Concord. Some people, when they think of hotels, they think that they are real pick-up places."

As is often the case with sexuality, exaggeration is easy. In the opinion of one male counselor, "Whether there was a lot more sex going on, I don't know. But there was certainly a lot more ambitions about sex. I suspect that there was a lot more going on. It was getting people together in life when they were first inclined to have some serious sex. I think it all came together with a very sexually charged atmosphere." In the words of another Mountain veteran, "People forget that if you take a community of three hundred, [then] fifteen people having relationships overwhelms. If you, the observer, are unfamiliar with it, it's startling."

I think this steward from the 1940s had a pretty accurate perspective on the sexuality of people in the Mountains:

Well, at twenty years old, I was a young tike—you're not going to cloister yourself in your room. Things happened up there; people had a different frame of mind up there in this setting. It was all to have fun, good time, vacation, dancing, entertainment; that was it. There were many people that met other girls. Many times marriages broke up because of the Catskills, but basically it was quite a harmless life, even whatever people say—that [a] woman used to come up there and used to fool around while her husband was in the city. It may have happened, you know, but it wasn't the norm up there.

The ambivalence about free sexuality is well put by Stefan Kanfer in his history of the Catskills: "It is significant that in the late thirties, a time of suppressed personal liberty, so much of the sexual character of the Catskills was so furtive. The air was charged with double entendres, the games and exercises aimed to titillate, but there was always a great ambivalence about letting go." We see this in Herman Wouk's *Marjorie Morningstar,* when Noel tells Marjorie, "The wonder is not that there's so much sex at South Wind, but that there's so little of it. Most of these people get nothing more in the way of sex than a few fumbled kisses and hugs, and the handful who do go farther with it skulk and crawl in the dark as though they were committing a crime." Wouk continues in narration: "If South Wind was Sodom, it seemed to be a cheerful, outdoors sort of Sodom, where tennis, golf, steak roasts, and rhumbas had replaced the more classic and scandalous debaucheries. Marjorie did notice a lot of necking in canoes and on the moonlit porch outside the social hall, but there was nothing startling in that. Perhaps terrible sins were being committed on the grounds; but as far as her eyes could pierce there was nothing really wrong at South Wind." Yet when Marjorie and Noel Airman become a couple (still without making love), she receives everyone's confidences about who is sleeping with whom.

Some hotels had a reputation for being loose. The White Roe was a classic singles place early in the Catskills' twentieth century. Sha-Wan-Ga Lodge was joked about as "Schwenga Lodge," from the Yiddish for pregnant. So, too, Tamarack Lodge was viewed as a hot spot. At the very small Maple Court, near Tamarack: "If a proprietor's daughter wore short shorts or a too-revealing bra-top, the ultimate insult was, 'You look like a Tamarack boarder.'" These places contributed largely to the legend of Mountain revels.

I don't think there was more sex in the Catskills than at other resort areas—but this was the first time these people went to resort areas! Hence it was easy to build up the aura of sex. Catskill sexuality probably attained the notoriety it did because there were clever comedians who made it into a legend through an overly sexualized humor, and writers who wished to romanticize the Mountains in all ways possible—what better device than sex and romance? Coming-of-age novels and films that centered on Jewish culture would obviously make magic out of the Catskills, for that was indeed the only place that Jewish people could get away from the routine restrictions of life.

Catskill Cuisine

Catskill cuisine was the ultimate trademark of the Mountains. People loved to eat mammoth meals full of Jewish favorites—what one hotel owner's son terms "a celebration of abundance." This started from the domestic production and the *haimish* [homey] atmosphere of the original farmers' boarding houses, such as Brickmans, whose owner Murray Posner said:

> You didn't come to a hotel. You didn't come to a resort. You came to our house. You came to our family. And [we] treated you as part of the family. And it didn't matter if you wanted another potato, because we were growing them here. We grew the corn. We made the cheese. We made our own butter. And the cows were giving us milk twice a day. We could make all the butter and sour cream and milk and sweet cream and everything you needed. So we served with a full hand because that's what people came up here for.

The kitchen, pantry (salad counter), and bakery turned out a wondrous assortment: brisket, chicken fricassee, kasha varnishkes, blintzes, kishke, noodle kugel, stuffed cabbage, carrot tsimmes, gefilte fish, pickled herring, pickled lox (a dish that some people remember as being found only in the Catskills), apple strudel, rugulach, danish, cheesecake, and the quintessential chicken soup—with fresh dill floating on top and matzoh balls or kreplach bobbing under the surface. Recalled one woman, "In the days that I went there, you had to gain weight. That was a sign you were enjoying yourself. You came back and said, I gained five pounds. Now, it's a tragedy." Another guest was so enthusiastic in remembering the food that he ran down an entire menu in rapid fire:

> The food, I could talk an hour about the food. The food was so great, breakfasts were phenomenal. Whatever wasn't on the menu you could order, for instance, kippers weren't on the menu. You could order them and they'd make them for you. Some of the guests used to get up for a golfing breakfast. They'd eat a breakfast and then they would come back and eat another breakfast; they'd eat two breakfasts. The lunches were outstanding—there was usually cold California tomato juice, grapefruit juice, prune juice—you'd start off with a juice. Then they had a choice of fresh vegetable soup, red beet borscht with a boiled potato or cold schav. For your entree there was baked filet of Boston sole, baked or boiled potato perogi with sour cream, mock-seafood luncheon plate Cantonese style, baked vegetable cutlets with a French sauce, Duxelles, golden blueberry pancakes with hot blueberry sauce, a bouquet of fresh garden vegetables with a potato. Vegetarian chopped-

liver salad garmigiere, chopped hard-boiled egg salad supreme, minced albacore white meat tuna fish salad, California fruit salad plate with cottage cheese, heavy sour cream with strawberries, blueberries and sliced bananas, peaches, cottage cheese or diced vegetables. The vegetables for this meal were potatoes au gratin or diced Harvard beets. For dessert there was chocolate eclairs, banana pound cake, chocolate pudding, danish cinnamon buns, Chinese almond cookies, fruit flavored Jell-O. Not on the menu, which guests ordered, were ice cream or dietetic ice cream or a fresh fruit cup. Beverages were coffee, milk, buttermilk, chocolate milk, Sanka, or tea. Some guests were not satisfied with one entree, they would order two entrees. They would actually eat two entrees. These are the world's greatest eaters.

Great eaters, perhaps, but not healthy ones. As one man mentioned, "I still remember someone at our table asking for a small pitcher of liquefied chicken fat so he could add it to the chopped liver and other delicacies." A unique alternative to this cuisine was the Konviser's Vegetarian Hotel in Woodridge, operating from 1920 till as late as 1987. As one member of the last generation of owners noted, they "catered to health-minded people, serving natural, whole, unrefined foods, with no meat, fish, or fowl." The menu allowed for much specialization since they "catered to all diets—saltless, fatless, wheatless, sugarless."

There was much pleasure, but also greed. A goodly number of guests tried to take advantage of the owners, typically by eating as much as they could on the "American Plan," with three meals included. They came from a tradition of actually or potentially not having enough, whether in Eastern Europe or in New York; in the Catskills they could order all they wanted, even if they didn't finish the serving. They talked about this incessantly, and comedians used it for endless gags. One guest recalled, "In the afternoon, sometimes you'd take a nap. Get tired, you know. Tired of eating!" Tania Grossinger remembers one Yom Kippur at "The G," when the day-long fast was broken at sundown. A supposedly brief, but actually full-course dairy meal was served around 6:30, followed by an especially abundant meat meal at 8:30. Tania asked a guest how they could eat so much in such a short time and was told, "If I can't find the room, I'll make room. After all, I've paid for three meals and even though I can't make up for breakfast, I'm going to get my money's worth." Eileen Pollack's novel of hotel life makes the same point: "They had paid a flat sum, which earned them the rights to all they could eat, three meals a day. Most of them tried to wolf down enough to recoup their investment, and, if they could, to accumulate interest." At "midnight suppers," guests would swarm over the staff, grabbing hors d'oeuvres from trays before they got to the serving area. When I worked at Paul's, we exited from the rear of the kitchen to go down a service road to the nightclub, and we had to have someone be on lookout duty to tell us when it was clear to make the run. Otherwise, the attractively arranged and garnished displays of food would have had a scavenged-through look.

Many hotels prided themselves on being able to deliver many special requests. Guests could not help notice this: "The hostess would be running out with a little plate like this, and the people, 'What do you got there, what do you got.' 'Dietetic spinach for somebody.' 'I want some, too.'" Even the children's dining room could provide a source of jealousy, as this baker recalled:

> I made a hullabaloo one time. I made frogs for the kids. These are cupcakes with butter cream, and I would use butter cream and cover it with chocolate and then I would cut a slit with a knife and pink icing butter cream would be the tongue. And I'd put eyes on it and it would look beautiful. I would make this for the kids. I think I had three or four of these left over, and one of the guests saw it in the kid's dining room and he wanted one in the main dining room. I said, "I can't give it to you." So he got Mrs. Komito and she came in. And I said, "I'm sorry, I can't give it to you. You'll start a whole hullabaloo in the dining room." I said [to Mrs. Komito], "If he'll eat it here, he can have all four. But he's not going to carry it into the dining room." Well, the wind-up was he didn't get it, and she was *plotzing*, the owner—"How do you do this to a customer?" It got OK after that. I said, "You don't do that. You don't take this out [because] everybody is going to want it, and what am I going to give them?"

A more restrained guest related, "I was upset when people made *chazers* [pigs] of themselves, eating until they couldn't move." In *Mama Made Minks*, Sarah Sandberg tells of the food taken back to the rooms as well: "My plates seemed bewitched. As quickly as I emptied them, they seemed magically to replenish themselves. . . . Not only did the family stow away at table banquets that resembled the last meal of a condemned prisoner, but whatever might be left over mother would wrap in a napkin, stash away in the huge purse she carried for this purpose, and nonchalantly bear off to her room, 'in case we should get hungry for a snack in-between.' You could find almost anything in mother's room—ranging from Bing cherries to half a chicken."

Such behavior carried over to the children's dining room as well. One woman recalled how "mothers often stood behind their little ones making sure they ate at least as much as they did at home." In the memory of one owner:

I was in the kitchen. I heard a scream and then quiet. I says what the hell is that. I go into the children's dining room. The mother has the child on the table. When he screamed, she shoved the food down his mouth; he had to be quiet until he swallowed it. I said, "Your child could choke to death." She said, "You mind your business and I'll mind mine. He's got to eat. I'm making him eat." Another time one of the mothers was feeding her child sweet cream. When the other mothers saw, they all did. All the children were throwing up afterwards.

Another owner's child remembers a set of images from the children's dining room that truly conjures up the chaos:

Imagine the children's dining room, with one large table and one hundred children, almost an equal number of mothers, and one waiter without any busboy. Also, imagine the mothers forcing food down each kid's throat, and the kids throwing it up just as rapidly as the mothers were forcing it down. Imagine the mothers ordering another main dish because their kids did not like the one that was served, and the mothers saying to the kids in Yiddish, *"Ess, ess—Papa schickt checks"* ("Eat, eat, Papa is paying the bill"). Imagine the noise and yelling of the kids and their mothers. Imagine the horrendous filth on the floor and on the tables after the children had eaten that the children's waiter had to clean up three times a day. Imagine all this for a one-dollar-per-kid-per-week tip. Even though the children's waiter made money, I think he deserved a medal in addition.

If people hadn't eaten enough, there was a "tearoom" around nine o'clock when tea, coffee, and cookies were served. These were originally for hotels without a coffee shop, but the people were used to them and they remained. One hotel tried to end the "free" tearoom when they built a "pay" coffee shop, and the guests wrote a successful petition. At another hotel: "After the second season, I think, they did away with the tearoom so the concession wouldn't lose out. So what would the people do? They would take extra cake from the dining room, carry it down to the concession, just order coffee, and eat the cake from the dining room."

On the food front, some owners got back as well as they could—water was added to milk to make skim milk; belly lox was soaked in water to make it taste like the less salty nova.

Guest Behavior

It would be unfair to brand the typical guest as an overeater, a complainer, a demander. Guests covered a wide range of behaviors, but the ones that stand out were the difficult ones. Further, the small community structure and the small business economics of the average Catskill hotel made it easy for guests and bosses to lock horns as if they were at a Lower East Side pushcart.

Alice Gutter remembered how guests bargained at her parents' small Maple Court Hotel in Dairyland, between Greenfield Park and Woodbourne. One woman confronted her father, "Mr. Nass, if I pay you forty-five dollars a week, I won't have enough money to tip the busboy and chambermaid. How about if I give you forty dollars?" Even third cousins, Gutter recalled, expected special reduced family rates. Some people came up before the season to strike early bargains for a month or summer-long rate. While this may seem crass, it was little more than an extension of the bargaining mentality that dictated market relationships in the pushcart and small-retail businesses that framed this early culture. But the habit continues—as I visited with Carrie Komito in 1997 across the front desk at the Aladdin, one guest came up to bargain over five dollars, at a time when the weekly rate was far higher than the forty dollars mentioned above.

Sunday checkout was a hectic and anxious time at most small resorts. One owner's child recalled:

My grandmother and the waiters were very conspicuous [on Sundays]. My grandmother was there to say goodbye, but also to scan certain bags for hotel blankets and linens. The waiters were there to collect their tips. If they were passed over (stiffed), which rarely occurred, they became enraged and could barely wait for the guest to leave before cursing them out. I think the presence of my grandmother restrained them from violence.

We sometimes referred to demanding guests as *bahaymishe menschen,* literally animal people (and even more precisely, cow people), meaning stupid, ignorant, vulgar. The term is an interesting twist on *haimishe mensch,* a worthy, wholesome person. To those of us working in the hotels, guests seemed unappreciative and demanding. For many young staff, the guests represented Jewish culture in general, which was unfortunate since the staff (most dining room staff were Jewish at that period) received a very circumscribed view of their heritage.

As the Mountains grew old, so did the guests. Jerry Jacobs recalls that:

During the 1960s, the clientele changed from families to an older group, and this presented a new set of challenges. Some would wake up before six in the morning and would be waiting in the lobby with a list of complaints before my dad could even run out to buy the newspapers. He always tried to have a joke ready to brighten up the mood. Then there were special diets. By the time the hotel closed, it seemed like nearly all the guests were on salt-free or sugar-free diets. The hotels were famous for serving Jewish specialties, but by the 1980s we served more prunes and buttermilk than lox or herring.

Some proprietors came right back at their difficult guests, as this hotel child recollects:

One time at his boarding house, a female guest, a chronic complainer, accosted Zada Megel in the yard with some complaint. He told her she was driving him to his death and he pulled out a bottle of iodine from his pocket with the skull and crossbones prominently displayed on the label, which he drank and fell to the ground, feigning death. Of course, he had replaced the iodine with tea, but needless to say, she never bothered him again.

Such conflicts were common, but often took place in a context of shared living in a folksy settlement. Catskill resorts were, to a large extent, *shtetl* (small village) cultures mediated by the journey to the New World.

A Sense of Community

One thing that was overwhelming was the extent to which people felt the Catskills provided them with a *community.* Mountain resorts prototypically began as rooming houses, and the transformation into hotels never eradicated the familial culture. People developed loyalties to hotels where they knew staff, owners, and fellow guests and were treated in kin-like fashion. Over and over again, I interviewed people who spoke of the places they had stayed with a tender familiarity. They were placed in a miniature society where relationships were amplified by closeness, and where they got to create additional components of their microsociety. Betsy Blackmar describes how people returned each year to resorts as part of the "rhythm of their own family lives." In the words of the Excelsior's owners, "Our clientele were quite loyal. Many families, and constellations of families, returned year after year. A core group spent a month or the whole summer at the Excelsior." The owner of the Grand Mountain claimed that 70 percent of the guests left deposits that season for the next. Children progressed from infants to day campers to junior counselors to counselors or dining room staff over the years. A fairly typical scenario is depicted in this reminiscence: "The first year I went away—I was fourteen—to the Plaza Hotel. When I was fifteen, they gave me a job because I didn't want to sit around doing nothing all summer. I was an elevator operator. They paid me twenty dollars a week. I still stayed with my parents in a room." Having the guests' family work in the hotel could provide more loyalty and discipline: "I had my first busboy stint at Ridge Mountain, where my grandfather was a frequent guest. He once had to admonish me for pouring spilled coffee from the saucer back into the cup."

Most small hotels used a few guests as "solicitors" who enticed their friends and relatives (what they called their "following") to stay at the hotel, in exchange for a discount on their own vacations. Soliciting was another element of the small-time, friendship-based economy of the lesser resorts. For some medium-size hotels, solicitors were not always regular guests, but might be professionals who were "associated with" the hotel. Similarly, a number of hotels had representatives in Florida to recruit guests. This solicitation, along with the general tendency to go where your friends went, resulted in some hotels having clumps of people from a particular neighborhood or fraternal organization, thus adding to the personal connectedness of many smaller hotels. Guests remembered this familiarity:

> I would say at any given time, we knew at least 20 percent of the guests. It was very *haimish* [friendly and homelike]. And Lilly and Charlie Brown [owners of Brown's Hotel] made you feel at home. This is one of the reasons why we went there, they made you feel wanted. You weren't a number, you were a friend.

❧

It was like a second home almost. Same people every year.

Such arrangements produced strange notions of loyalty. The Frommers tell a story of Fred Gasthalter, owner of the Paramount, who overbooked his hotel. A couple of long-term guests showed up and there was no room for them. When they got angry at the owner, he replied, "Why be indignant? You should be happy to see me getting so much business." At the same time, guests felt their friendship with the bosses gave them the authority to intrude on hotel operations. They also felt that this closeness entitled them to demand more. Not only did guests feel that a businessman was shortchanging them, but also that a kinsman was treating them poorly. This relationship got more complicated when you took into account that owners often hired their guests' relatives.

In addition to neighborhood groupings, there were workplace and political groupings as well. At the Maple Court, for example, a group of garment workers came every year when their shop closed between seasons. The Fur Workers' Union had their own resort in White Lake. Eileen Pollack's novel includes a group of communist guests: "Comrade Beck only paid twelve-fifty a week for his stay at the Eden, a rate guaranteed to each of the Communists by Grandpa Abe because he had once been in charge of a sweatshop at which they led a failed strike." As well, "the Eden had been a haven for Holocaust survivors since my grandfather placed an ad in the *Forward* that all Displaced Persons could stay there half-price." Staff, too, brought along people from their communities— whether neighborhoods, colleges, or fraternities. Some hotels would be known as hotbeds of one particular fraternity.

For those who went to bungalow colonies, the interrelationships were more central, for several reasons. First, every single one of them was there for two months with the same people, and they had to develop social groupings and interaction styles. Second, apart from any monetary reasons, they were people who tended to like being thrown together with others. Finally, they simply had to share resources—like food shopping trips to town, borrowing cups of sugar or coffee, arranging the softball game, watching each other's children at the pool while the others cleaned house.

Hotels and bungalow colonies were both minisocieties, but the colony more resembled an old country experience: "It was almost like an extension of the shtetl, to a degree, you know what I mean? With everybody being together, a lot of conversation, you always had somebody to talk to." No wonder this woman remarked: "Even the loudspeaker had an accent."

Friendships developed in the resorts, which endured for many years. Recalling years of vacationing at the Majestic, a woman remarked that:

It was like one big happy family. You got to know each other. Everybody made plans during the winter. We had a clique of people—they were all invited to my son's bar mitzvah. We still see some of them. That's where you made some very fast friends. In the bungalow colony, my husband met a group of friends, and they formed a men's club called the Ramapo Boys. They started to meet at a place in the city every third Wednesday. Unfortunately some of the gentlemen have passed on, but ones that are in Florida we see when we go down there. These are friendships that have remained through the many years.

In the hotel or bungalow colony community, people were in a microcosm of society, playing out parts as in any larger society. They were discovering who they were, both their heritage and their present-day directions. They were landsmen in a resort world. Does this mean that they all liked each other then, or would do so if thrown together today? Of course not! Communities are not paradises, as we know from our own experience. A community is composed of many elements, and we have mixed feelings and ambivalent relationships with those in our various communities of neighborhood, school, work, and religion.

One waiter I interviewed retains memories of truly disliking the guests he served, yet he feels attached to the memories of what the Catskills meant to him on a broader scale. As I think and write about my own memories here, I cannot suspend the critical feelings I had toward the owners and toward the people I served in the dining room. Those were real feelings even if situated in a certain time in my life, even though I can now look back with a different appreciation of this whole world. We are all thrown together in these communities and for better or worse that is our life. Now, with distance and hindsight, we can better understand the complexity of life and the many ambivalent feelings we felt in the Catskills. We can perhaps feel more sympathetic to the complaints and desires of the guests, the foibles of the owners, the competition from our coworkers, knowing that all those things were part of the necessary hustling in this set of communities.

The very Jewishness of the Catskills provided a particular sense of community. In this matter, there was an interesting difference I found between the

New York and the New England visitors and workers. Boston, Providence, and Connecticut people were not used to an intense Jewish community with such a strong atmosphere of Yiddishkeit and in fact did not go to the Catskills for that reason. They went because they heard there was a nice, inexpensive place to go, one that did not feature the anti-Semitism they often saw in some New England resort areas, such as New Hampshire's White Mountains. The head of one large Boston-area travel agency addressed this:

> I would say that every summer I would send to the Catskills perhaps a volume in excess of $100,000 worth of business. Not that they came in and said they wanted to go to the Catskills, but we suggested it to them and some people liked it. We created for the Catskills a Boston clientele. We sent maybe 250 or 300 people. We didn't send people there who wanted to go there because of Yiddishkeit. No. They wanted a place that wasn't too far, that was all-inclusive, that served good food, that had entertainment.

I was surprised to find many native New Englanders who vacationed in the Catskills. Fewer went as workers, though. As one man said, "In most respects it wasn't a common occurrence to go up to the Catskills. But I knew some other families that went up. But not a big deal like in New York, people going up every weekend, on singles weekend." For him, "I think it was a good socialization experience for me, a good growth experience just in terms of living with other people and getting along with different types of people. I was totally naive to the New York way of life. In fact, there was such foods that I had never heard of before I went there, like the *bialies* and the egg creams and things like that. That's indigenous to New York, not Boston. But it was a great experience."

Mel Simons, a Boston-bred entertainer, worked many years as a social director at Brickman's. "Basically," he said, "people in Boston only knew three resorts. Those three resorts, I'm sure you know what I am going to say, are Concord, Grossinger's, and the Nevele. People were not aware of these other lovely resorts. Eventually a lot of Bostonians came to Brickman's. He [the owner] would put my name right in the ad, 'Boston's own Mel Simons, Master of Ceremonies.' And I had a lot of friends and acquaintances, people that I worked for in Boston, and they came."

New Yorkers made much more of the special Jewishness of the Catskills, though often only in hindsight. One person, for example, told me that the Yiddishkeit was important in retrospect: "Now, as an adult, when I look back at it. But then, I didn't even think of that. Everybody on my road was Jewish. I came from Brooklyn where everybody was Jewish. It was just there." Even if people did not think that they came up especially for the Jewish experience, they were enmeshed in that milieu and would remember it later.

Dinner at the Nevele Hotel in Ellenville, 1961. *(Photo from Rhoda Herscovitch.)*

Dining room at the Laurels Hotel in Sackett Lake.
(Copyright 1998 Bill Bard Associates, Inc., Monticello, New York.)

Record cover from *The La Plata Sextette Swings at the Raleigh Hotel*, Seeco Records. Latin music was popular in the Catskills in the 1950s and 1960s, and the liner notes state, "This album has a twofold purpose—firstly, wonderful for listening and dancing—secondly, a memento of an exciting vacation at the Raleigh Hotel." Among the tunes are "Raleigh Riff" and "Mishugina Mambo."

Today's Events

"PROF." ALAN TRESSER, Director of Activities
DAN BARNES, Director of Athletics

MONDAY - APRIL 20, 1981

```
 8:00 AM   TO 10:00 AM  MAIN DINING ROOM OPEN FOR BREAKFAST
 8:30 AM   GOLF COURSE & DRIVING RANGE OPEN - MEET OUR PRO WERNER TEICHMAN
 8:45 AM   MORNING SERVICES IN THE EAST ROOM
 9:00 AM   INDOOR TENNIS COURTS OPEN  MEET OUR PRO KEN BAXTER
10:00 AM   ALL OUTDOOR COURTS OPEN - PADDLEBALL - BASKETBALL - BASEBALL -
           SHUFFLEBOARD - BOCCI - HORSE SHOES - TENNIS & VOLLEYBALL -
           SEE DAN BARNES FOR ALL EQUIPMENT
10:00 AM   INDOOR ICE SKATING RINK OPEN
10:00 AM   INDOOR POOL - HEALTH CLUBS - MINI GYM - SUN LAMPS - SAUNA &
           STEAM ROOMS OPEN - MASSAGES AVAILABLE
10:00 AM   INDOOR MINIATURE GOLF COURSE & DRIVING RANGE OPEN
12:00 NOON     LAUGH YOUR WAY TO BETTER HEALTH WITH AEROBIC DANCING & YOGA
               STRETCHES. FANTASY ROOM
 1:00 PM   LUNCH
 2:00 PM   INDOOR MINIATURE GOLF COURSE & DRIVING RANGE OPEN
 2:00 PM   PING PONG & SHUFFLEBOARD TOURNAMENT - TROPHIES
 2:30 PM   SYMPOSIUM - ISRAEL VS. MIDDLE EAST - WITH ARCHIE KINBERG -
           EXECUTIVE SECRETARY NEW YORK STATE ZEONIST ORGANIZATION
           IN THE FANTASY ROOM
 2:30 PM   INDOOR ICE SKATING RINK OPEN UNTIL 5:00 PM
 3:30 PM   FREE BINGO FOR PRIZES IN THE HARLEQUIN LOUNGE
 6:30 PM   EVENING SERVICES IN THE EAST ROOM SYNAGOGUE WITH REV. JACK ERLICH
           AND CANTOR MORT FREEMAN
 7:30 PM   DINING ROOM OPEN
 8:00 PM   INDOOR MINIATURE GOLF COURSE & DRIVING RANGE OPEN
 9:00 PM   DANCING IN THE HARLEQUIN LOUNGE WITH THE BARRY LYNN TRIO
10:15 PM   SHOW TIME IN THE FANTASY ROOM WITH M.C. ALLEN TRESSER
               STARRING
           *** MARTY BRILL  ***  DENA CLAIR  ***
```

HOTEL FACILITIES

```
MAIN HOUSE      PING PONG & SHUFFLEBOARD - INDOOR POOL - INDOOR GAME ROOM -
                MINI GYM - SUN LAMPS - TENNIS COURTS
LOWER LOBBY     MASSAGES AVAILABLE - ORIENTAL GIFT SHOP - COFFEE SHOP -
                BEAUTY SALON - NARCISSUS MENS & WOMENS CLOTHING SHOP
```

Daily activities listing from the Fallsview in Ellenville, showing a wide range of sports, lectures, religious services, and other events.

The band at the Kiamesha Inn in 1940: Julie Jussim, Harry Frank, Irving Marder, Gus Roney, Murray Sperber, and Gene Thaler. *(Photo from Harry Frank.)*

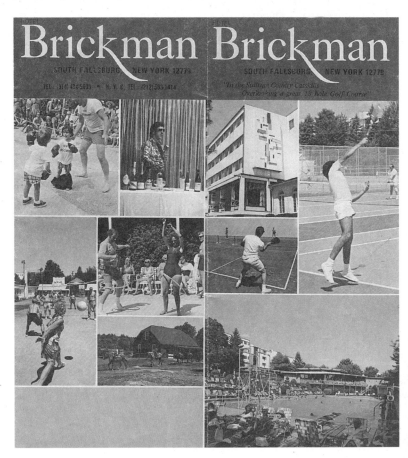

Brochure from Brickman's. *(Courtesy of Steingart Associates.)*

Leslie Uggams performing at Brickman's.
(Photo from Bebe Toor.)

Robert Alda, father of Alan Alda, performing at Brickman's. *(Photo from Bebe Toor.)*

Barry Sisters performing at Brickman's.
(Photo from Bebe Toor.)

Jack Wakefield performing at Brickman's.
(Photo from Bebe Toor.)

Ontario and Western Railroad's "Summer Homes among the Mountains," an annual publication that served as a major source of publicity for Catskills resorts in the early decades of the century.

The band at the Fur Worker's Lodge in White Lake in the early 1950s: Henry Foner on tenor saxophone, Jack Foner on drums, and Allan Tresser on violin; Tresser is still in the Catskills working as the social director of the Fallsview. *(Photo from Henry Foner.)*

The Commodore Hotel in Swan Lake in the 1930s.

Men's beauty contest at the Granite Hotel in Kerhonkson, 1962.
(Photo from Harriet Lennard.)

Seven Gables Hotel in Greenfield Park in the 1930s. My family and I spent six years working there, 1955–1960.

Dining room at Fallsview.
(Copyright 1998 Bill Bard Associates, Inc., Monticello, New York.)

Simple recreation at a Kuchalein in 1945—the seesaw is made from an old water heater.

Stevensville Lake Hotel postcard.
(Copyright 1998 Bill Bard Associates, Inc., Monticello, New York.)

Fountain Hill House in Ellenville.

Brochure from the Morningside Hotel, Hurleyville, probably 1940s.
(From Stan Golembe.)

Rate card from the Heiden Hotel in South Fallsburg, 1960s.

Large grouping of hotel and bungalow billboards at Exit 107 on Route 17. Clusters like this were common throughout the Catskills. *(Compliments of Al Kross.)*

Outdoor theater at Sha-Wan-Ga Lodge, High View.

Small guest cottage at Sunny Oaks Hotel, Woodridge, home of the History of the Catskills conferences. *(Photo by the author.)*

Rate card from the Sha-Wan-Ga Lodge, High View, 1939.

Kaplan's Delicatessen, Monticello. Perhaps the best-known restaurant in the Catskills, it has been closed for some time now. *(Photo by the author.)*

Band members at the Saxson Hotel, Monticello, 1937. From left to right: Henry Foner, Moe Foner, Jules Novick, unknown. The Foners and their musician colleagues often chose hotels based on the quality of their tennis courts. *(Photo from Henry Foner.)*

Passover at Grossinger's, 1950. Martha Mendelsohn and her father. *(Photo from Martha Mendelsohn.)*

Rachel Robinson, wife of Jackie Robinson, with girls at Grossinger's, 1952. *(Photo from Martha Mendelsohn.)*

Hotel Brickman pool, 1950s. *(Photo from Bebe Toor.)*

Children at day camp and guests on lawn, from brochure with various scenes at the Aladdin Hotel, Woodbourne. *(Copyright 1998 Bill Bard Associates, Inc., Monticello, New York.)*

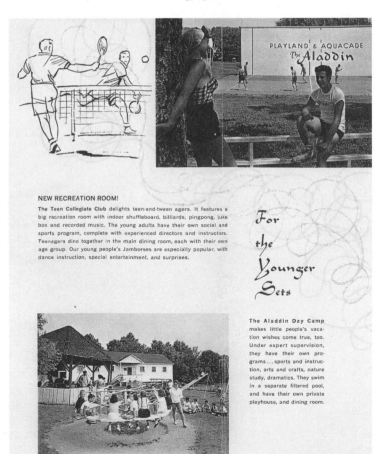

NEW RECREATION ROOM!

The **Teen Collegiate Club** delights teen-and-tween agers. It features a big recreation room with indoor shuffleboard, billiards, pingpong, juke box and recorded music. The young adults have their own social and sports program, complete with experienced directors and instructors. Teenagers dine together in the main dining room, each with their own age group. Our young people's Jamborees are especially popular, with dance instruction, special entertainment, and surprises.

For the Younger Sets

The **Aladdin Day Camp** makes little people's vacation wishes come true, too. Under expert supervision, they have their own programs...sports and instruction, arts and crafts, nature study, dramatics. They swim in a separate filtered pool, and have their own private playhouse, and dining room.

Brochure from Aladdin Hotel, Woodbourne. *(Copyright 1998 Bill Bard Associates, Inc., Monticello, New York.)*

An assortment of business cards from various hotels.

Chapter 9

Resort Religion and Yiddishkeit

*"The world to me was basically Jewish, in terms of friendship
patterns I had. To be in the Catskills was part of that world."*

I wrote in an earlier chapter about how the farmers built a solid infrastructure of synagogues, which then made it easier for urban Jews to feel comfortable in the Catskills. Hotel owners, as I mentioned, also spoke of their involvement in building *shuls*. I heard an example of this from a woman who worked in the Grossinger's office, where she met her husband, who worked as a caddy and bellhop. Her family owned a dairy store in Youngsville and took in a few boarders:

> Of course the town was so small, there was no shul. Since we were the largest family [eight children] and perhaps one of the more orthodox, my mother (may she rest in peace) saw to it that we had a Torah in the house and she would make sure there were services for the big holidays. [For] the holidays [occurring] soon after Labor Day, the hotels would open their doors to the Jewish community, a very generous gesture. The one general store, owned by Sam Heller, always donated the herrings, etc., while the rest of us baked the challahs, cakes, and other goodies.

The Jaffes, a well-known farming family, had two Torahs in their house for services, as well, for ten years, until the Glen Wild shul was built. They still treasure the shul's huge ledger-size minute book, which they keep in their house.

There was no doubt about the Jewishness of the Catskills—these Mountains were full of Jews, and some towns, such as Woodridge, were predominantly Jewish. Into the 1950s, some shuls still took minutes in Yiddish. Many never had rabbis, yet hardworking congregations maintained their Sabbath and holiday services. The Jewishness of the area was strong enough to permit the presence of many ultratraditionalist Jews, even though they were not tied to the resort industry. In my memory, there were always ultraorthodox and Hasidic places, though far less than at present. More modern Jews often spoke of these ultraorthodox Jews as *"beardlach,"* people with beards.

Resort Religion

The Catskills were more important in terms of Yiddishkeit than in terms of religion. Nevertheless, the Catskills were a place where the rudiments of Judaism were at least talked about and practiced in some way. In her discussion of "gestural Judaism," Jenna Weissman Joselit says that American Jewish ritual is characterized by intermittence, selectivity, voluntarism, and the centrality of sentiment. People fashioned festivals and rituals to suit their new American needs. This is different from the traditional Judaism that leaves less room for choice. The Catskills played a large role in shaping "secular religion." For example, even into the last lively Catskill years of the 1970s, observance of *kashruth* (kosher laws concerning food) was typical in most Catskill resorts. By that time, many young people had little or no experience of kashruth in their own families and only learned of it by working or staying in the Catskills. So, too, for the quasi-observance of *Shabbos* (the Sabbath). Both kashruth and Shabbos observance were truncated, partialized, and selective, shaping a new, modern, and easy-to-grasp Judaism. In the absence of a ritualistic Jewish home life, I learned in the Mountains a tremendous amount about Judaism that I would otherwise not have known.

For Jews of two generations ago, eating kosher food was often habit even if not ritually meaningful. Many of their parents were more vigorously kosher, and that required their own homes to be kosher so that parents would eat there. And for the many Jews who did not keep kosher, the Mountains gave them an opportunity to experience dietary laws even if they did not do so at home. Because many guests expected kosher food, virtually all the hotels served it. The Ridge Mountain Hotel, in the 1920s, even had its own *schochet*, the ritual slaughterer. The separate silverware for meat (*fleishedich*) and milk (*milchedich*) meals had different patterns, but often got mixed together before we re-sorted them. Walk-in refrigerators typically held both meat and dairy on the same shelves. The effort seemed more important than the outcome. At the time, it seemed that there was something disingenuous about the whole model, and we in the dining room expressed many doubts about it. I realize that for many observant people there are clear demarcations about what constitutes acceptable action, but when we worked there that was less understandable. If you could not work on Shabbos, was it not hypocritical to serve boiled eggs when fried eggs and pancakes were forbidden? The waiters still performed the labor—the rationale was that we dropped the eggs into water that had been continuously boiling since before the sun set on Friday night.

An owner's son recalls the "kosher cops," the religious inspectors who investigated the kitchen's kashruth compliance and who could fine the hotel for violations:

> I've never seen my mother so scared as when the kosher cops descended. They worked in a highly coordinated team—one would appear simultaneously at each door of the kitchen, a third would head straight for the garbage can to make sure that we hadn't tried to cover our tracks by throwing away ham, while the fourth would head into the walk-in refrigerator to measure the distance between dairy and meat sections. I recall thinking that these inspectors inspired more fear than love of religion.

By virtue of being kosher, the food had certain drawbacks. Steaks were only rib steak, much tougher than sirloin (which comes from the forbidden hindquarter location in the cow). There could be no cream sauces on meat or chicken. In the years I waited tables, margarine and nondairy creamer were often avoided at meat meals, even though it was clearly not a violation of kosher laws; this always rankled me. We often joked about the very few Jewish resorts that attracted clientele based largely on featuring nonkosher cuisine—billboards for the Nemerson in South Fallsburg showed photos boasting of their shrimp in lobster sauce. I worked there once and couldn't stop scarfing the food.

At all but the most avowedly secular of the Jewish hotels, Shabbos was welcomed at Friday evening dinner with challah, wine, and the *bruchas* (blessings) over them. It was completely second nature for me to greet my guests with a hearty "Good Shabbos." For the waiters and busboys, the blessings entailed an important responsibility—we had to make sure that all the wine glasses were empty before they reached the glasswasher; otherwise he would drink the left-overs and get frighteningly drunk, unable even to finish washing the dinner glasses. Regular services, usually held in the card room, were optional and sparsely attended, except in orthodox hotels (a distinctly small number of Catskill resorts, places which closed their gates on Shabbos so that cars could not enter or leave).

While not orthodox, Grossinger's was observant and, until 1948, had no entertainment on Friday night. Seeking to stay competitive by offering shows on Friday night, the hotel consulted its rabbis and came up with a solution: Each Friday, the owners would conduct a *shtar m'chirah,* a ritual sale to other owners, so that the Grossinger family did not feel they were violating Shabbos injunctions.

For guests, the Catskills was also a place to go for Passover (in April) and Rosh Hashanah (in September), but this tradition developed later on. Indeed, a long-time Catskill guest recalled that in the 1940s her father conducted the Seder be-cause: "In those years, it was not ordinary to go away for Yom Tov [holiday]. Yom Tov was home with the family. So when we used to go up to Pesha's (The Majestic), we were maybe twenty to twenty-five people. There was no question that an outsider should be hired to conduct the Seder. In those years, it had to be someone in the nucleus of the family." Once hotels began to routinely open for Passover and Rosh Hashanah, guests had no intention of attending local syn-agogues; they expected and got makeshift synagogues on the premises.

Passover in the Catskills made sense, since guests could avoid the heavy work of making their homes free of *chometz* (foods not kosher for Passover) for those eight days. Not that the hotel did such a good job of making the kitchen kosher for Passover—we ignored residual breadcrumbs in the tablecloth-covered bread slicer.

If you went to the Mountains for Passover, you didn't have to worry about which friends or relatives might be slighted if you didn't invite them to your home Seder. I even heard from a modern orthodox man how his family went to the Catskills for Passover, but took an extra room to hold their own Seder in, since the hotel's Seder wasn't satisfactory. A longtime Grossinger's Passover guest remembers a teacher asking how her family got ready for Passover. She responded, "My mommy writes out a check to Grossinger's." A Catskill Seder was an hours-long event conducted by a hired rabbi or cantor reading the Hag-gadah; medium and large hotels added a choir. There was time enough for the dining room staff to go outside and hang around or to play cards in the staff dining room. We were never happy about staff food, but at Passover it was too much to bear. Once, working at the Karmel, a bunch of us were so starved for "regular" food that we left the staff meal and hopped in the car for a two-mile ride to Herbie's in Loch Sheldrake, famous for roast pork on garlic bread.

But apparently even religious people could have fun at a Catskill Seder in an orthodox hotel:

> My family-in-law has a "custom" of reciting the Four Questions in every language they can, whether real or made-up, and the custom extended to making up entire new versions of the old song/ritual. One cousin had made up a "rap" version a number of years back; not to be outdone, I made up a reggae version, complete with Jamaican accent. The other guests heard and saw what we were doing the first night, and the word spread throughout the whole place so by the second night, they crowded around our table when the Four Questions time came around. It was a lot of fun. It also dispelled a lot of negative opinions my in-laws had about the black-hat [very orthodox] crowd.

Rosh Hashanah made less sense in the Catskills. One would expect this rather solemn holiday to be more appropriately spent around neighbors or fellow congregates. But there were sometimes good reasons for going away for the High Holidays: "The first time I went away for Rosh Hashanah was when my children were out of the house and not accessible to come for Yom Tov [holiday]. I said to my husband, 'We're going to be alone for Yom Tov.' He said, 'Like hell we will, we'll go to the country.'" What you might gain—only at the fancier hotels—was a talented cantor such as Jan Peerce or Robert Merrill. But mostly it was a pretty routine, even bureaucratic, observance. The gravity of the New Year ritual seemed out of place with the playground atmosphere of summer resorts. Rabbi Israel Margolies of Manhattan questioned, "How can you expect to have a solemn religious service in a converted nightclub, where the whole congregation was dancing the Watusi the night before?" Rabbi Benjamin Kreitman of Brooklyn worried that Catskill observances "reduce religion to the level of entertainment." Grossinger's resident Rabbi Harry Stone had a more resort-based impression in his complaint about the difficulty of getting a *minyan* together for prayers: "Even those who pray back home have too many distractions around here. How can God compete with a golf course?"

Still, for observant Jews, holidays in the Mountains were as legitimate as the burgeoning "Jewish centers" that were replacing synagogues throughout Long Island and New Jersey. For nonobservant Jews, the Catskill milieu exposed them to kosher practices and liturgical traditions they might otherwise miss. In this way, the Catskills contributed to the continuation of Judaism. As Jenna Weissman Joselit put it, "summer resort Judaism" was not an abandonment of religion, but rather an adaptation of religion. She notes that many hotels went out of their way to emphasize on brochures and signs how "strict" their dietary laws were.

Another contribution to Jewish tradition was the large number of Jewish children's camps that dotted the Catskills. Non-religious camps included Yiddish-speaking secular places, Hebrew-speaking Zionist camps, and labor Zionist camps. The religious camps ranged from the conservative Judaism of Camp Machnaim to the modern orthodox Camp Hi-Li (Hebrew Institute of Long Island), to the strictly orthodox Camp Emunah. Today, there are a good number of Jewish camps, though they are Hasidic or ultraorthodox.

Orthodox Hotels

At the orthodox hotels, the dining room staff were almost all yeshiva boys and girls. The few who were not yeshiva students were nonpracticing children of orthodox parents. As in other hotels, people sometimes had second jobs—while waiting at the Pioneer, one young man served as a private Chumash (Torah) teacher for a guest family. Because there were so few orthodox hotels, jobs were at a premium; one veteran waiter said, "It was like getting into Harvard," and "I was very proud of working there. . . . I was lucky to be part of that club." For this modern orthodox man, "To us, it was the orthodox Mountains, not just the Jewish Mountains. . . . It was like one big family. . . . We would feel at home. . . . The guests and the staff came from the same cloth." They did, however, look down on the Hasidim, who were not as populous in the 1960s and earlier as they are now.

Orthodox hotels had varying degrees of religiosity. The Pine View's clientele was the most modern orthodox and the most Americanized clientele. Conservative Jews stayed there as well, and conservative rabbis were among the speakers. On Friday night, they had speakers on religion and related topics—otherwise they had entertainment like any other hotel. Many of the Pine View guests were affiliated with the Young Israel organization, which used to be more modern. In the last three decades, it turned to the right and, among other things, now forbids dancing. The Pioneer, the largest and most elegant of the orthodox hotels, held eight hundred guests, who were more recent immigrants, mainly Hungarian, of the Agudah type. They had major acts like Jackie Mason and even ran singles weekends. The *Jewish Press* newspaper was headquartered there. At the Pioneer, staff were not required to attend the minyan, but they stored their tefillin in the dining room linen closet and held their own services in the dining room while the guests prayed in the shul. At Passover, since the staff couldn't sit with the guests, they held their own Seder in a separate room while the main Seder was conducted. The Lake House, still operating, was visited by mainly German Jews; it was the strictest and even required staff to attend daily prayer services.

Recent changes in the Mountains are reflected in the growth of more religious hotels. Orthodox owners bought the Homowack in 1980 and the Tamarack in 1995. In 1995, an even more orthodox owner bought the orthodox Homowack. In the 1990s, the son of one of the Pioneer's owners started operating a glatt kosher kitchen and dining room at the Concord to attract orthodox guests who might otherwise find the Concord's regular kosher observances to be insufficient.

Yiddishkeit

Yiddishkeit has many meanings. Hasidic believers at present use the term and think of Yiddishkeit as the sum of their religious and cultural practices, circumscribed by a traditionalist set of beliefs. Less observant Jews would see it as both religious and cultural, though not dogmatically religious. Secular Jews and Yiddishists would see Yiddishkeit as essentially the cultural and nonreligious milieu of the Jewish legacy. There are obviously many other versions in between these polarities. In the Mountains, Jews of many degrees of tradition found an environment that was immersed in Jewish experiences.

Yiddish speaking was a central component of Yiddishkeit. The transnational language of Eastern European Jews was a daily tongue for many in the New World. Especially in the pre-World War II era, and even into the 1950s, Yiddish was likely to be spoken not just for jokes, but as a major component of ordinary communication. As one hotel owner's son remembered, "Half the people in the hotel association spoke Yiddish at meetings." And from this assistant steward, a survivor of the Holocaust who worked at the Flagler in the 1940s:

> I spoke Yiddish when I was hired. Somehow Mr. Silverman, [who] was the steward, spoke to me only in Yiddish. I think that is why he sent me down to [work in] the laundry. But, at one point in time, I must have answered him in English, and that's when he woke up and said, "You

speak English?" and I said, "Why not?" So apparently his experience was only with . . . new Americans that came to this country, that they couldn't speak English. His experience. So it helped me later on because I got a better job.

People now in their forties and fifties can remember the difficulty of not speaking, or at least understanding, Yiddish:

> It was really frustrating for kids to be in the nightclub because the punch lines of the jokes were always in Yiddish. And so you'd have to sit through these very long stories, and then they would come to the punch line of the joke and they would give it in Yiddish, and I'd never understand what it was, and everyone would laugh uproariously and bang on the tables with these sticks with little balls on the end.

Not surprisingly, many people also remembered Yiddish as the language their parents spoke when they didn't want children to hear the conversation.

For quite a number, however, this widespread Yiddish speaking provided a learning laboratory, as with the waiter who said, "I learned some of the Yiddish that I know just through osmosis from hearing people speak Yiddish a lot in the Catskills." But this common parlance in Yiddish was part of a passing era. An MC of many years recalled that "at the sing-a-long, when I first started, boy, they would yell out Yiddish songs, Hebrew songs, I'd do them all. And then my boss said, no more Hebrew, no more Yiddish. The only time I did Hebrew and Yiddish [after that] was Rosh Hashanah and Passover. No more Yiddish songs during the summer."

Yiddishist culture—the preservation of Yiddish as a language of both culture and ordinary communication—had a home in the Catskills as well. The Grine Felder (Green Fields) literary colony in Woodridge was a major center of Yiddish writers, including Isaac Bashevis Singer. Merging both socialist and Yiddishist traditions, Grine Felder had bungalows named Emma Goldman, Karl Marx, and Mendele Sforim. Singer's stay in a Mountaindale kuchalayn in 1937 and his visits to Grine Felder played a major role in his transition to becoming a major American writer. His short story set in the Catskills, "The Yearning Heifer," immortalizes the traditional small farmer putting up New York City boarders.

A majority of the people I interviewed took it for granted that they were spending time in an undeniably Jewish atmosphere. "Somehow being Jewish was so much a part of the atmosphere that it almost wasn't worth commenting on," noted a then-counselor, later a Jewish educator. A waiter whose father was a garment worker, that prototypical Jewish working-class occupation, had this worldview: "The world to me was basically Jewish, in terms of friendship patterns I had. To be in the Catskills was part of that world. Since I knew no other, it was a little taken for granted. In retrospect, thinking about it, it's unique. A resort community that was almost exclusively Jewish was a unique type of setting. But for me at the time it was something that I never reflected upon. It was something that I just accepted as being the norm."

For others, the aura of the Catskills' Jewishness was more specifically desirable. A secretary, married to a cab driver, recalled, "I still think like Friday night, with the meal and the candles. . . . I felt when we were planning the trip, oh, we're going to have Jewish this and Jewish that. I do like to be in Jewish environments." From a Connecticut vacationer, I heard: "It's really sad that those places are gone. I think it's a loss to Jewish culture. Where else are a group of Jewish people going to get together and feel comfortable and play cards and mah-jongg and have political discussion and can feel as relaxed that they could say anything they wanted to a fellow Jew that they would not say if there were a gentile sitting there? That's sad."

Most significantly, when they reflected on the Catskill experience years later, the people I interviewed understood that it was a formative Jewish experience. A woman told me that she believed that her bungalow life helped to perpetuate a vanishing culture: "I looked forward to going to Ben-Ann's [bungalow colony]. In retrospect, I understand it to be a sort of hotbed of lowbrow, working-class, secular Jewish culture. I think a lot of the adults who went there had grown up in Brownsville but had since moved and were scattered in other parts of Brooklyn and Queens. I think Ben-Ann's was a place where they could commune with their past."

Assimilation, Acculturation, and Modernity

They may have been communing with their past, but Jews faced a culture clash between the old and the new. The whole question of assimilation took on a special meaning in the Catskills, since the vacation experience was precisely a way that Jews could become more like other Americans who took vacations. A good number thought that they could escape anti-Semitism and become more successful and American if they gave up much of their Jewishness. So, even in the very-Jewish Catskills, some chose the more assimilationist route. Abraham Cahan's protagonist David Levinsky makes fun of Talmudists and scholarly look-ing men who are, by his definition, ugly. He is, though, also quite ambivalent about the significance of Yiddish literature. But Levinsky shows his underlying character when he gets to choose American culture: While staying at the Rigi Kulm House, perhaps the most stirring experience for him is the patriotism of singing the "Star Spangled Banner" and "My Country, 'Tis of Thee," which at the same time is the only way that the tumult of the dining room chatter is brought under control; it is also an affirmation of being in a country safe for Jews. Herman Wouk's Marjorie Morganstern takes the name Morningstar, and his Noel Ehrman changes his name to Airman. Instead of *klezmer* music and Jewish vaudeville, the South Wind resort puts on Broadway knockoffs and pseudo-Mexican fiestas (though even the fiesta has some Yiddish touches).

Despite such assimilationist directions, the Catskills remained for a long time very Jewish in all manners. For most, the Jewishness of the milieu was per-vasive, and hence being more Americanized did not mean that they lost touch with their legacy. Quite the opposite, the extensive Jewish culture was present in cuisine, Yiddish, accents, and the quintessential Jewish humor that so often poked fun at everything Jewish. Comics regaled their audiences with tales of overeating, slothfulness, intrusive Jewish mothers, and retrograde old-country customs. Thus, at the same time that Jewish culture thrived, very strong Jew-ishness was easy to disparage. And so, I think it is much more appropriate to see the Catskill experience not as assimilation, but as acculturation. American Jews learned many rudiments of New World culture, but they kept a tremen-dous amount of Yiddishkeit in which to frame the new elements. As Gerald Sorin notes in his book *Tradition Transformed,* acculturation, rather than as-similation, best fits the Jewish experience in America in all its aspects.

Since the early 1970s, of course, the entire area has declined so dramatically that it is no longer the premier vacation spot for Jews. With most of the resorts long closed or recycled, it becomes easy to point to the fact that the few re-maining places have downplayed their Jewishness, especially in light of the clientele, which often includes Christian organizations.

New and Old Religion in the Catskills

The Siddha Yoga ashram is built on the ruins of three large South Fallsburg ho-tels—Gilbert's, Brickman's, and The Windsor, lavish and elegant beyond their original style. Statues of Hindu gods turn up as you walk through the cropped gardens where devotees pause and pray, leaving offerings of coconuts, pineapples, and other foods. Swami Chidvilasananda, known to the faithful as Gurumayi, leads her followers in chants and meditation in pavilions of glass walls and heated marble floors. Rings of concentric dancing circles, separated by grass, are under construction. Mammoth boulders have been carted in to surround a newly built hillock upon which a new sanctuary will be constructed. Here it is all talking, meditating, walking—no tennis, golf, swimming, or handball. Devotees must put in some small stint working in the ashram, so that ordering a snack at the restaurant may mean listening to the counter person's mantra. The place is so large that constantly moving shuttle buses ferry people from one section to another. The clientele is quite well-dressed in the middle of the day, in clothing that would be more like hotel evening dress. Everyone is polite, mellow, and many seem quite spaced out—not at all the classic Catskill clientele and staff.

Also in South Fallsburg is the Shivananda Sharam Yoga Ranch, a smaller center. In an ironic twist, the director, Swami Sankaranda, was born to a Jewish family in South Africa in 1950. The Swami believes the Jewish Catskills were too materialistic and that the spiritual and vegetarian life of his believers is appropriate: "Maybe we've come back to cleanse these mountains from the material world." The Tennanah Lake Lodge is now the Foundation for a Course in Miracles.

In the space of a mile, you go from New Age ashram to Eastern European *shtetl* (small village) culture at Yeshiva Gedolah Zichron Moshe, on the site of the Laurel Park Hotel. At first glance, the main building appears deserted, wood covering the windows, and paint long worn off the facade. But it is a forty-family, year-round institution of ultraorthodox Jews running an accredited elementary and secondary education program, and even offering bachelor's degrees. The building inspector has prohibited the use of the dilapidated upper floor, while somehow tolerating the ground floor. So, the yeshiva has simply boarded up windows to prevent their falling as the building collapses further. No one cares at all about the aesthetics. Entering the Beis Midrash (House of Study), some fifty boys and men study Talmud in pairs, some standing, others sitting. Dressed in black and white, many in traditional long black coats, with *tsitsis* (fringes) hanging from their waists, these students mumble, gesticulate, nod, and exclaim their way through the lessons. People have given up most of their worldly wealth and concerns to live a very religious life. Women bear many children, since birth control is forbidden and large families are seen as a blessing. People care neither about the appearance of the ramshackle buildings nor their own dress.

As thousands make their way up to the bungalows they now dominate, they stop and pray the late afternoon Mincha service. At first, this occurred at the shoulder of the New York State Thruway, a dangerous undertaking. Highway authorities then set aside a marked "Mincha area" at a regular rest stop, where as many as two hundred worshippers are found at once. One participant offered, "In my opinion, if the Messiah is going to come, it is going to be right here on the Thruway."

One estimate gives a year-round ultraorthodox/Hasidic population of 20,000, swelling to 50,000 in the summer. That figure comes from the Hotzoloh, the orthodox and Hasidic volunteer ambulance service, which counts five hundred camps, colonies, and retreats, though this seems high to me. Ultraorthodox Jews and Hasidim have taken over many bungalow colonies, most in complete disrepair. Some of the larger Hasidic congregations in Williamsburg have established their own bungalow colonies. Their pools are surrounded with mesh so the men cannot see the women bathing. The roadways are lined with males, from young boys to old men, dressed in traditional garb, many of them just hanging out, many sitting at tables outdoors with prayer books in hand, sometimes conversing over cellular telephones. When asked, they have no sense of what was the previous name of the bungalow colony in which they are now living, no sense of history. The Hasidim of Yeshiva Viznitz only recently bought the Gibber Hotel at Kiamesha Lake, and when I saw them in 1994 they were starting their first repairs. Already this group runs the Yeshiva Viznitz for Girls on the site of the Nemerson Hotel. Even when hauling full sheets of plywood in the August heat, they keep on their full-length wool frock coats.

These ultraorthodox Jews have come almost in mass in the last ten years, so the flavor of the Catskills, if anything, is theirs. When Woodridge received a huge influx of Hasidim, they told Mortman's bakery that they wouldn't shop there unless it closed on Saturdays. The proprietors agreed, glad for both the business and for a day off after decades in the hard grind of work. The business card for the Woodridge Taxi Company notes it has both "Men and Women Drivers" to provide the same-sex propriety required by this population. In many of the small towns, Hasidim run some or most of the stores, which are often branches of stores from Williamsburg and other Hasidic areas. As George Kranzler notes in his book *Hasidic Williamsburg:* "They have garages, medical services, even a center where teams of *dayanim,* judges, and *poskim,* rabbinical ritual authorities, meet regularly as announced in advance in the weekly *Der Yid.*" Woodbourne, never with more than a dozen stores, is now mainly glatt kosher bakeries, food stores, religious book stores, and restaurants offering knishes and falafel. As one local native told me, "They took over the whole town of Wood-bourne." After sundown Saturday night, when Shabbos ends, Woodbourne's main street begins to pulse with hundreds of religious people filling the small town center with hardly room for cars to pass. Talking, eating, and buying religious books and articles, they remain until two or three in the morning.

There were always some Hasidim and ultraorthodox on the scene, but you didn't see that many of them. Like previous generations of Jews, they cluster because they need each other to have a critical mass to maintain their traditions. Why didn't they come before? Conservative, reform, and modern-orthodox Jews coming in earlier periods were people who had finally made enough money so they could have vacations of whatever sort, from the inexpensive bungalows to the most luxurious hotels. During this time, the Hasidim and the ultraorthodox were perhaps not wealthy enough to even do that. Perhaps they may have even felt that the irreligion or the adapted religion of the mainstream Jews was anathema to their concept of Judaism, and therefore it held no attraction for them. Perhaps there is something of taking over almost the carcass of an old culture, an ability to move in where nothing is left and rebuild it. There is now literally no place in Sullivan County that one can go without seeing large numbers of ultraorthodox and Hasidic Jews.

So the ultraorthodox are recycling the Catskills. They will not likely become more mobile, or be attracted to Europe and the Caribbean. These are not people who go for holidays of complete pleasure; they are not completely tourists or travelers. The males are in their study hall most of the days. One bungalow colony manager notes that "studying is one thing you never take a vacation from." They are simply people who need to cluster in very orthodox communities. By going back to the old bungalow colonies, they are in a sense reverting to the original Catskills. Yet it is unlikely that they will create a culture of interest to a larger community, as mainstream Jews did in earlier periods. They are there precisely to be secluded. Mainstream Jews brought humor and cooking, vacations with style and romance. They brought a sense of upward mobility, of a place to work and make enough money to go on to be the first generation in college. None of this holds for the Hasidim and ultraorthodox. While there are some wealthy merchants, this is not overall a rich clientele. When they work, many of them work at the most marginal jobs—teaching and selling things to each other, living off very small amounts of money. The Catskills have a very special attraction even for this group—as legend tells it, the Lubavitcher Rebbe Menachem Schneerson never left New York, except once to go to Gan Yisroel near White Lake.

In the boom era, many Jews disparaged these orthodox, old-world co-religionists, but that bias is harder to maintain today. A previous resident, who returns to visit his family who have lived in the Mountains for generations, recalls:

> Personally, I used to feel very uncomfortable being around Hasidic Jews. Now I don't feel uncomfortable at all, much less uncomfortable. So when we go home (to South Fallsburg in the Catskills), I can tell my mother to go and buy kosher food at these places, you know.

Despite the common Hasidic insularity and their opposition to other Jewish culture, their presence has been somewhat of a help. A life-long farmer commented on their spread: "I think it's good. They look down on our kind of Jews. [But] if not for them, you'd have rabbits running around. There would be nothing. The young [non-Hasidic] Jews don't come here anymore. They go to Aruba. The package deals are terrific."

The Hasidim even produce their own playfulness:

> There's a wonderful amusement park run by Hasidic Jews (in Fallsburg). It opens on a Saturday night, after Shabbos [Sabbath] is over, and it's open for the rest of the week until Friday. And it's really great, you know. You see families there, older men with beards, you know, children with *payis* [curled sideburns worn by orthodox males] and it's great, I enjoy myself. I mean, you can see them on bumper cars.

From his study of the Hasidic resurgence in Williamsburg, George Kranzler argues that "this is one of the 'by-products' of the Hasidic revival of Williamsburg—they have saved the 'Jewish Mountains' from total ruin." This is true only in the sense that a large number of Jews have taken up summer residence once again. But it is not accurate if we mean that they are preserving the overall traditions of the Catskills. Tummlers, comics, and singers will not grace stages in the yeshivas and Hasidic bungalows. Romance will not flow freely in the Mountains. And above all, Jews will not keep cultural traditions while integrating more into American society because the orthodox/Hasidic culture in the Mountains is one of preserving a form of ultratraditionalist shtetl culture, supposedly unchanged for centuries.

Chapter 10

Decline, Present, and Future

"I'm ninety-two. I'm still running.
I think all my guests tell me that the reason I stay alive
is because I'm running the hotel."

Decline

People were always worried about the decline of the Catskills. The very title of Reuben Wallenrod's 1957 novel *Dusk in the Catskills* makes that point, even though Wallenrod was talking about the last years of World War II. So, too, does his epigraph from Jeremiah 6,4: "Woe unto us! For the day declineth, For the shadows of the evening are stretched out." Wallenrod's novel starts with the sad and lonely time following the summer season and progresses through the interim, then an entire resort season, finishing the next fall. Despite measures of joy and good fortune, hotel owner Leo Halper mourns the comfort he indulges in while the Nazis ravage Europe. He laments the hectic, more impersonal style of a hotel that grew from a more familial boarding house. He mourns the passing of an old friend who has stayed with him through all those years. Despite his accountant's post–Labor Day praise of a profitable summer, Leo cannot keep his mind off the creditors.

In Martin Boris's 1980 book, *Woodridge 1946,* there is also the fear that the Catskills were already in decline just after the war (though this might have been easier to assert in a 1980 publication date):

Our Place [the luncheonette], the town, the whole Borscht Belt, would last another five years, tops. Once the airlines got wise and brought the fares down, people would discover a whole world out there. GIs returning home, like knights from the Crusades, would tell tales of the wondrous places they'd been to. And the offspring of the present vacationers were a new breed: children of post-Depression America, they were the first generation not worried about saving money. Restless, hard to please, quick to bore, and certain never to return to what had satisfied the three generations before. It was just a matter of time.

Many resort owners clung to hope as late as 1975, when the Hotel Association reported 10,700 hotel rooms and 1,350 other rooms available. But this was the last turning point. By the 1970s and 1980s, people easily noticed the changes. Smaller hotels went out of business quicker, and by the 1980s the decline was evident in the closing of well-established hotels, such as Grossinger's, Brickman's, and Gilbert's: "We used to go to Brickman's for the holidays. When we found they were closed, we were devastated. Each time we got attached to a place, they would close." Grossinger's, with a capacity of 1,800 guests served by 500 staffers, was sold in 1985 and closed in February of 1986. The new owners made a publicity stunt of imploding the nightclub in front of a huge crowd of people, which included past entertainers, an act that most Catskill veterans experienced as a clear slap in the face.

It is not possible to pinpoint a single reason for the decline of the Jewish Catskills. There are many causes, and they are often intertwined: changes in family structure and gender roles, a loosening of family and religious ties, increased geographic and economic mobility, the aging of the older population of Catskill guests, changes in vacation habits and resort structure, a decline in anti-Semitism, the particularities of the Catskill resorts and their ownership and management, the rejection of traditional Yiddishkeit forms, changing food preferences, and the economic downturn beginning in 1973.

Changes in family structure were important. By the 1960s, women were entering the workforce in large numbers. This knocked out the tradition of summer vacations where the mother and children could be away for all or a large chunk of the summer. The growth of feminism, combined with outside labor, meant that women disliked being so 'on' in their vacations, especially in bungalow colonies where they had to cook and clean all the time. Even if women did not have jobs, it became less appealing to stay in hotels where they were often taking care of their children by themselves except on the weekend.

As family ties loosened, people did not seek resorts that had a familial character, one of the central elements of the Catskill hotels. Intermarriage might have contributed to the decline. Jews who married before 1924 almost always married other Jews—98.3 percent did so. Intermarriage rates increased over the next three decades, but only slightly, so that in marriages between 1955 and 1959, 93.4 percent still married Jews. The dramatic change started in the 1960s and moved rapidly. Jews marrying between 1960 and 1964 married other Jews 88 percent of the time, almost doubling the intermarriage rate from 6.6 percent to 11.6 percent. Still, in total, 89 percent of Jews married before 1965 married other Jews. For those married between 1965 and 1974, the figure plummeted to 69 percent; for marriages between 1975 and 1984 it dropped further to 49 percent, and for marriages between 1985 and 1990 to 43 percent. Conversionary marriages (where the non-Jewish spouse converts to Judaism) have declined, and this is most pronounced in younger intermarriages. It was hard to be in the very Jewish Catskill environment with a gentile spouse. This is just one manifestation of the effects of intermarriage on the whole of Jewish culture. Though you can practice religion separately, you wouldn't be likely to go separately to the Catskills. The higher divorce rate also made it harder for single parents to go to family resorts in the Mountains. While the Jewish divorce rate is lower than that of other religions (for 1972–1980, 12 percent of all Jews were ever divorced, compared to 17 percent of Catholics and 24 percent of Protestants), their divorce rate is still more than twice the 5.1 percent rate found in the 1971 National Jewish Population Survey. Even the traditional matchmaking function of the Catskills could be obtained elsewhere. Singles bars, dating services, and even ethnically and religiously sponsored singles clubs became available in the city for meeting potential spouses.

Geographic mobility made it more likely that people would live far away from relatives, and therefore not go to a "local" resort area. Jews were not only moving to New Jersey and Westchester, but to California and Florida. Where in 1960, 45.8 percent of American Jews lived in New York State, by 1990 only 30.8 percent did. In those decades, California's Jewish population went from 9.6 percent to 15.4 percent, and Florida from 2.0 percent to 9.5 percent. Many "snowbirds" already had a lengthy, easy, vacation-like period in Florida and had neither the need nor perhaps the means to go to the Catskills.

Jews no longer worked so predominantly in the seasonal industries that had slack summer periods. For many jobs, the summer was too busy a time to take off. Nor were Jews concentrated in certain industries, such as the garment and fur sectors, that would lead them to seek vacations together. When Jews made it up the economic ladder, many associated the Catskills with their poor past and hence rejected the area. By the 1970s, the same Jewish youth who used to need Catskill earnings for college might already have made enough money to support their own children through college. Once Jews stopped working the Mountain dining rooms, they were less likely to become guests.

The aging of the population was central. Immigrants of the 1910s and 1920s might have gone to the Mountains from that time into the 1960s. That was all the vacation they were used to. When they began to grow too infirm to vacation, and when they died, that traditional group of Mountain-identified people shrank rapidly. Younger people might have tried the Catskills, but they were not as tied to it and could easily move to other vacation spots. What a good number of people saw as the very style of the resorts—gross overeating, ethnic entertainment, self-deprecating humor—was embarrassing to many young Jews.

Even old people didn't want to be around other old people: "When my mother (who passed away a year and a half ago at the age of ninety-eight) [was] at the age of ninety-five, I suggested that she go someplace. She told me that she didn't want to go where there is old people. How many times can you go to a hotel and see people with walkers and in wheelchairs, God bless them, and want to go back?"

Vacation choices changed as well. In the late 1940s and into the 1950s, one person proclaimed, "Jews didn't go back to Europe, because they had run away from there." By the 1960s and 1970s, this had changed—it was the next generation who had never been there, who wanted to see it. Much of this was due to their children visiting Europe as teenagers and young adults, a common practice starting in the 1960s. There were more highways for travel, especially after the interstate system got under way. The growth of recreational vehicles and camping offered cheaper alternatives to resorts. With increased income, especially in families with two wage earners, second homes became a preferred alternative. The traditional two-week vacation for many was replaced by two or three shorter vacations. Airline travel, a rarity for the average person even in the early 1960s, spread rapidly, offering more points of the globe in a shorter time. With air conditioning so prevalent, there was no drastic need to escape the city heat.

A more businesslike tourism industry led to the development of more exotic vacation areas in places previously unheard of. At the same time, resorts became more homogenized. The hotels in Hawaii, the Caribbean, Florida, and the Carolina Sea Islands all began to look quite similar. In this overall homogenization of culture—what George Ritzer calls the "McDonaldization" of society—people found endless distractions and predictable rooms; they were no longer driven to resorts that had a special identity. Murray Posner, shortly before his Hotel Brickman closed, mused that "I used to think I'm competing with the hotel down the road. I'm competing with every resort in the world."

Anti-Semitism had once made it impossible for Jews to vacation apart from their own. As this declined, they realized other choices existed. As well, an owner noted, "the seasonal families really came to a lesser degree in the mid-1950's when the metropolitan New York area country clubs permitted Jews as members, and with the creation of new country clubs by Jewish people."

Even if the old resorts wanted to try to keep up with the modern vacationers, there were too many obstacles. Many of the hotels were based on in-law or sibling partnerships and extended family workforces. The particular kind of owner partnerships that were precisely necessary to run these small- to medium-size hotels were hard to re-create. They were part of an Old World or new immigrant culture that faded away into the more modern economy. Small- and medium-size hotels couldn't keep up with larger ones that were expanding with the express intent of capturing the convention business. An owner of a major resort recalled, "There was a great deal of interaction between guests and owners. That created a problem when we hired general managers that were not a member of the family. Guests refused to have these people solve their problems and insisted on a family member."

On top of all these other factors, in 1973, the American economy entered a two-decade downturn. Although small sectors did very well in this period, real income declined for large numbers of people in the lower end of the income pyramid. Changes in the job structure hurt many middle-class people, including small business owners, professionals, and managers. So, vacations were not as affordable to the whole range of people that used to go to the Catskills. Hotel owners also faced drastic increases in building and maintenance costs, making it difficult to keep up their resorts.

For three or four decades, Catskill resort owners were remarkably adaptable. The typical progressions, from farm to kuchalayn to boarding house to hotel, or from small to large hotel, were carried out with minimal financing but with incredibly creative approaches and the unceasing hard work of extended families. But the changes I mentioned above were too much in combination. Why didn't hotel owners make transitions to other kinds of businesses? The Zalkin's Hotel flattened their decrepit buildings and started a campground. At the Aladdin, Carrie Komito figured out an interesting way to adapt after her husband died in the early 1970s:

> When he passed away, I started to pick up on bungalows wherever they were for sale. I made this bungalow colony here. Who could build them? I moved them over and air-conditioned, heated, carpeted them. I rented

them to Floridians. I gave them linen and maid service. China, silver, air-conditioning, heating, entertainment every night. . . . I have 70–80 bungalows. They are all air-conditioned, heated, carpeted. I cater to Floridians because they are the ones who come up north. . . . The thing about Floridians, when it rained, New Yorkers used to run home—the Floridians can't run. The main buildings, for the last couple of years, I haven't been using because senior citizens can't climb stairs.

But, generally, the hotel owners were not talented businesspeople with a smart sense for making transitions. Rather, they were experienced only in running family-type resorts that depended on certain people from a particular milieu.

The physical plant of the average hotel was too old and tired to be maintained, much less modernized. A good number of the buildings were a half-century old, with antiquated systems. Even the largest places, with more modern buildings, began to look frayed. Nor was it possible to continue the exploitative labor practices that long allowed the Catskills to operate with "bimmy" labor. The state labor board came around increasingly in the 1960s, checking on working conditions and making it harder to exploit the lowest rungs of the workforce. There were other problems with the resort labor force. One owner, who sold out as late as 1987, recalled that "what happened was that in the '80s the labor situation got so difficult. The alcoholics were now drug addicts. It was frightening." On top of that, Jewish teenagers and young adults no longer wanted to take the jobs they traditionally held. Hotels had to recruit dining room staff from as far away as Ireland. Judaism in American was very innovative and many of the traditions easily fell into disuse. Kosher cooking, a specialty of the Catskills, was no longer in such demand with younger people. Many Jews no longer felt the need to have even the toned-down ritual observances offered in the hotels. Yiddishkeit became less central as well. By the 1960s, Yiddish was rarely spoken by American Jews, and so the traditional Yiddish-speaking or Yiddish-tinged resort atmosphere was no longer necessary. The cooking and humor associated with Jewish culture lost much of its appeal. The particular protection of a *landsman* culture [based on fellow residents from the shtetls, a commonality that held together synagogues, social, and fraternal organizations] was no longer required. Jews could travel very widely without fear of anti-Semitism and without the need to be expressly Jewish as they vacationed.

Food habits changed as well. Besides turning away from traditional tastes, modern Jews turned away from the meat- and fat-laden meals, and from the large amount of food consumed in the Catskills. Americanized Jewish palates became interested in a variety of international cuisine, as well as more inventive domestic ones.

And lest many or all of these were not impediments, visitors would come to the current Catskills and see widespread ruins and an enormous amount of Hasidim, making the whole tenor of the place less conducive to a playful holiday. But the ruins should remind us of the past, as owner Cissie Blumberg asserts: "Today when you pass a closed, decaying resort, know that in the sagging gray timbers and weed-choked pool are buried the dreams, expectations, and prodigious labor of a family. The faded signs and crumbling entrance gates are a mute memorial to the Herculean efforts of real people who struggled and eventually lost."

The Catskills at Present

Starting in the 1970s, the Catskills clearly shifted its character. In the 1970s, business conventions, special ethnic weekends, church organizations, singles weekends, and sports sessions were more frequently offered by Catskill hotels. By 1974, the Nevele's publicity chief estimated that over 60 percent of large hotels' business came from conventions. By the 1980s, just twelve large hotels survived. In that decade, the maitre d' at the Pines convinced his World War II unit group, 99 percent gentile, to have their annual convention in the mountains at the Pines. He tried to explain what kosher food is, and finally just said that it is very clean food. Whether the explanation worked or not, the vets enjoyed it and returned another year. The ex-maitre d' made this general point about the Mountains' new clientele of the 1960s: "Gentiles realized they would not starve with kosher food." Other hotels, however, such as the Nevele, left the dietary fold and started serving nonkosher food to bolster business.

Today, the Catskills bear little resemblance to the way they were in their heyday. Not only does the Concord, the largest ever of the Catskill hotels, now have ethnic weekends of every stripe but also Spring Break for college students who dance to grunge bands and stage-dive as in a mosh pit. In the 1990s, about half that number of hotels remained, and as I write my book I await the news of another hotel closing—the Granite shut its doors in the summer of 1997. Hotels survived with different approaches than in the old Borscht Belt days. A 1996 blues festival at the Concord drew five hundred people to hear fifty bands playing music, quite distant from the typical entertainment. Sunny Oaks, in Woodridge, caters to folk dancers, holistic healing groups, and other alternative clientele.

At Kutsher's, the Homowack, and the Concord, Latino waiters serve the old Jewish dishes. So many Brazilians, mostly from the town of Governador Valdadares, work at the Nevele and Fallsview hotels that the Fallsview's owner, Charles Slutsky, built a soccer field and supplied uniforms for a high-level soccer league, which also includes teams from the Granite, Concord, Pines, Pine Grove, Kutsher's, and Homowack. The story of their recruitment sounds a bit like the old days: A woman working at a Manhattan employment agency ate lunch frequently in a Brazilian restaurant on West 46th Street, where she saw many new immigrants looking for work, so she began sending them to the Nevele. Racially and ethnically, the Catskills look very different today. By 1990, blacks comprised 23.9 percent of Monticello's population, 21.5 percent of South Fallsburg, 12.5 percent of Liberty, and 12.5 percent of Ellenville; Hispanics made up 15.9 percent of Monticello, 12.1 percent of South Fallsburg, 9.4 percent of Liberty, 23.6 percent of Ellenville, and 12.6 percent of Livingston Manor. An Asian influence has appeared as well. In 1993, Soung Kiy Min, a Korean-born Japanese businessman, bought the famed Grossinger's, which had been closed since 1986, operating it as essentially a golf club with only forty-two rooms open and few hotel facilities. In speaking of the "sushi belt," Tania Grossinger wrote: "Forget the sumptuous eight-course kosher meals of yore. Instead of herring prepared three ways—kippered, schmaltz, and matjes—the menu features trout prepared three ways—sushi, sashimi, and tempura. Miso soup has replaced borscht, and bacon is served with bagels at breakfast." Hak Men Kim bought the Golden Swan on Swan Lake. Ye Shik Choi turned a bungalow colony into the Bethel Mission Village for Bible study. Recent Russian immigrants began to go to the Mountains, though they are not necessarily all Jews. Some Russian community groups rent entire bungalow colonies and allocate them to members. A two-week rental goes for only $400. But overall, Hasidim dominate the bungalow colonies. The manager of one, where bungalows rent for $1,200 a summer, believes that the Russians and Koreans will become more upwardly mobile and forsake the Catskills, but that the Hasidim will remain. He notes that "the Hasidim have no choice. You can't take ten children and go off to Europe." Drug rehab centers and communities for children and adults with special needs found cheap land and buildings in the decaying hotels: The Delmar in Loch Sheldrake became Redirections for nine years, from 1987 to 1996 (Redirections closed, and the hotel is sitting empty right now), Green Acres (previously the New Roxy) in Loch Sheldrake is New Hope Community for retarded adults, and Paul's in Swan Lake, where I worked for two years, is Daytop Village; the Youngs Gap in Parksville is Logos, the Murray Hill in South Fallsburg is Dynamite Youth Center, the New Brighton in Parksville is the Hebrew Academy for Special Children, and the Furst is a rehab center. Various ashrams and meditation centers have also sprung up, including the Transcendental Meditation Center on the site of the old Waldemere, and the huge Siddha Yoga Center that I talked about in earlier chapters. Loch Sheldrake's Hotel Leroy became Sullivan County Community College, and the nearby Hotel Evans was recycled for college dorms. The Fallsburg Mansion in South Fallsburg was converted to public housing. South Fallsburg's Ambassador Hotel became Catskills Playland, an amusement park geared to Hasidim and other ultraorthodox people. The Flagler, a grand hotel of the early years, is now the Crystal Run School for retarded adults.

Another alternative was housing developments. The Evans closed, circa 1975, and two couples bought it, razed the hotel buildings, refurbished the nightclub, pools, and tennis courts, and built 200 homes in their Vacation Village. Joel Gamel and his partners bought Brown's Hotel in Loch Sheldrake in 1995 at auction for $1.5 million and started the 422-unit Grandview Palace condominiums. One hundred eighty rooms in old, decrepit buildings were torn down, but the main house remains, keeping its familiar shape. Most units are studios and one-bedrooms, converted from hotel rooms with kitchenettes; smaller ones lack a full stove, offering only convection ovens and microwaves, but selling for $21,900 to $23,900. Some larger condominiums range from $25,900 up to $89,900 for a 900-square-foot two-room suite. And Kutsher's, still operating as a hotel, added Hidden Ridge condos on its property.

By the summer of 1996, large surviving hotels were feeling the crunch and hoping for either legalized gambling or a Native American casino on the grounds of Monticello Raceway. The Concord owed $5.6 million in back taxes; Grossinger's (even under its new, limited golf club format) owed $219,752; the Nevele owed $728,451; and the Pines owed $746,000. The Granite filed for Chapter 11 bankruptcy in 1996 and closed in 1997. In the spring of 1997, the venerable Concord, largest of the large hotels, filed for bankruptcy, though it is continuing to operate. Its owners faulted New York State's failure to pass a special gambling bill that would have allowed casinos in certain areas, with a clear favoritism toward the Catskills. Owners, with their classic resilience, still hope to continue the Catskill legacy, as Mark Kutsher of Kutsher's notes: "We're celebrating our ninetieth anniversary this year. This resort has survived world wars and depressions. We'll get through this, too." Other hopes lie in the 1997 purchase by media magnate Alan Gerry of Yasgur's farm and much surrounding property. He hopes to make the Woodstock concert site into a Woodstock theme park, which residents believe will create many jobs and boost tourism. Yet in the midst of the Catskills' decline, a handful of small places continue to operate. Why would someone hang on, even in the face of a very decent purchase offer? I think the answer is that Mountain

Rats get it into their blood. The Aladdin's Carrie Komito, long in the business as a second generation of hotel operators, recalled: "We had a big tree in front of the main house. When I came here it was a sapling. I said if I ever see that tree grow . . . It's the biggest tree here now. In my youth it sheltered me, and I protect it now." And so, "I'm ninety-two. I'm still running. I think all my guests tell me that the reason I stay alive is because I'm running the hotel."

As one old kuchalayn dweller recounted upon a one-day drive to Loch Sheldrake after many years, "It used to be like Times Square in Manhattan. It was open twenty-four hours a day. Same thing with Monticello. It never closed. You know, people used to first get into town at 3:00, 4:00 in the morning, and restaurants and everything was open. It was entirely . . . just to have fun, and now at 6:00 at night everything is locked up tight with iron curtains on." An ex-steward recalls: "It was a couple of years ago I went to the Nevele for a few days and there was nothing like it used to be. The food was different; the type of entertainment was different. It hasn't got the flavor of what it used to be." And an ex-waiter, now a lawyer, similarly noted: "I went back as a guest two or three years ago. It's totally different. Your viewpoint is different. The hotels are not as Jewish as they used to be. The food doesn't have that flavor." Comparable comments came from so many people I interviewed.

When I go to the Catskills these days, I spend lots of time driving main roads and side roads. In addition to my sadness at the loss of this vital Catskill culture, I feel disoriented because I can't identify many of the abandoned and collapsed hotels. My memory plays tricks on me—I convince myself that a certain hotel was on the opposite side of the road than its hulk or current recycled version is. And I constantly say to myself: "It can't all have just disappeared and died like this."

Eileen Pollack's novel *Paradise, New York* laments the decayed area around her narrator's hometown: "Fifty resorts had once decorated the branches of Paradise. Now they clung to the back roads like cracked, fading baubles." She continues, "Most of the resorts had simply been abandoned. The main houses stood, but the stucco had peeled from beneath the windows and these looked like haunted eyes. Handball backboards poked up from overgrown fields, warped plywood tombstones inscribed in flaking paint with the names of the dead."

Pollack's portrayal, when I read it in 1995, hit me with great force. Her take on the current ruins is so much like mine. Just as her protagonist returned to try and salvage her family's hotel, I returned to find my family hotel and to salvage family memories.

An old, small hotel, now used as a private house, Mountaindale.

The Bradstan Hotel, the current incarnation of Brown's Hotel Royal, is a very elegant small hotel with beautifully appointed rooms and a robust nightclub life. The extensive rehabilitation by the new owners of the Bradstan won a Sullivan County architecture award. Some smaller buildings, already crumbling, were torn down. The two rooms on either side of the porch, visible in the postcard of the Brown's Royal on the book cover, also fell into disrepair and are gone.

(All photos in this section by the author.)

Lake House Hotel, Woodridge, an orthodox resort.

Yeshiva Gedolah-Zichron Moshe, South Fallsburg, on the site of the Laurel Park Hotel.

South Fallsburg today, full of orthodox Jewish stores.

Zucker's Glen Wild Hotel, Glen Wild, an orthodox hotel.

New Hope Community, a residence for retarded adults on the site of the Green Acres Hotel, Loch Sheldrake.

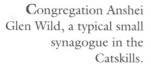

Sign to a *mikvah* (ritual bath), an important element of orthodox life, Woodridge.

Congregation Anshei Glen Wild, a typical small synagogue in the Catskills.

(Above, l.) **A**ctivity board at the Aladdin, Woodbourne.

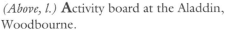

(Above, r.) **A**n orthodox bungalow colony in Thompsonville that atypically notes its previous name.

Postcard of Sunny Oaks Hotel, Woodridge, home of the History of the Catskills conferences, now in its fourth generation of family ownership.

"The Annex" at the Aladdin, Woodridge.

Carrie Komito, still running her Aladdin Hotel at age ninety-two.

Sol and Dorothy Eagle, old family friends. Sol worked for years as a saladman, and Dorothy followed her parents in operating the Pine View Hotel in Loch Sheldrake.

Nat and Evelyn Leibowitz ran Leibowitz's Pine View in Fallsburg, an orthodox hotel (different than the Pine View in Loch Sheldrake), until the state prison took it by eminent domain. Until 1997, the Lebowitz's ran reservations at the Homowack, a resort that only became orthodox under new ownership in the 1970s.

An abandoned hand-
ball court, a common
ruin in the Catskills.

The Heiden Hotel in
South Fallsburg was
temporarily refurbished
for the filming of *Sweet
Lorraine,* but it now
stands abandoned.

Abandoned chicken coops, a legacy of the once vibrant agricultural life. Sullivan County was for a while
the leading egg-producing county in New York State.

The pool at Laurels Country Club on Sackett Lake. Endless pools dot the country-side and, as at the Laurels, nothing else remains.

Birchwood Lodge, Greenfield Park.

White Lake Mansion, White Lake, used till the mid-1990s for extra rooms for a bungalow colony across the road.

"The bungalow," a six-room building at the Seven Gables. Besides the day camp house, it is the only structure still standing.

Trees growing over the foundation stones of "The Main House" at the Seven Gables.

Chapter 11

What Made It So Special?

"The Catskills will always be the wonderful Catskills. I don't think anybody who has ever been here can think about it without having a good feeling."

For years, I told myself that my parents died from hard work in these hills. My father's fatal stroke occurred as he worked his little concession at Chait's in 1972. My mother lasted longer, but her body was wracked from too many years on her feet behind the range. Up until 1978, she cooked at Chait's. When she could no longer take it working the whole summer, she commuted on weekends, while the owner managed to prepare midweek meals for the small number of guests (much of that was based on food my mother had prepared during the weekend for later use). After my father's death in 1972, my mother lived with Ray Williams, who worked with her as a second chef, and who teamed up with her to run a very small catering business in Cambridge. Without sharing the drive and the labor with Ray, I am sure my mother could not have continued as long as she did. It was a grueling effort, with long drives for her, but she was a Mountain Rat and couldn't stop.

I missed Woodstock, while working a few miles away in Swan Lake. I missed the protests at the 1968 Democratic Convention in Chicago, while serving food in Loch Sheldrake. What would happen if I did something I wanted, instead of working in the Mountains? One year, I told my father I really wanted to go to the music festival in Newport, Rhode Island, with my girlfriend, and then come up to work after that. The result—my car engine blew up on the Connecticut

Turnpike on the way back. When I called to tell my father that I would be delayed, he told me that the gas on the coffee urn had exploded in his face earlier that day. Luckily the burns were pretty minor, and more good fortune brought a quick hitch from some fast-driving people my age, but I did feel like I was being punished for shirking a couple of days of Catskill coffee shop labor.

How, then, could I appreciate the Catskill legacy, much less enjoy it there? That, sadly, is the nature of being a Mountain Rat. You really were trapped in this little system, a world that gave you the good and the bad, that encapsulated the whole gamut of life. For me, this accounts for the long period in which I put the Catskills out of my system. Now, doing what I am doing in this project, I have to work hard on myself to examine all the aspects of this complicated life of ours. So, coming from the hardships that the Catskills often meant for me, my appreciation of the Mountains is a signal of the importance of their place in my world and the world of my people.

At the first History of the Catskills conference, in 1995, I felt like it was a spiritual homecoming, so much so that in my talk on "Rekindling Yiddishkeit in the Catskills," I recited the Shehekiyanu, a prayer said at many festivals, to give thanks for reaching the point to which we have come:

Boruch Atau Adonoi, Elohenu Melech ha'olam, Shehekiyanu, vekeemanu, veheegeeyanu, lazman hazeh.

(Blessed art Thou, O Lord our God, King of the universe, who has kept us alive and has sustained us and enabled us to reach this season.)

At the second conference, I continued that tradition, linking it to my appreciation of Jack Kugelmass' *The Miracle of Intervale Avenue: The Story of a Jewish Congregation in the South Bronx,* which I had recently read. Kugelmass, an active participant observer of that synagogue for five years, provides us with a tender view of this last shul in the ruins of the South Bronx, a religious and social center for mainly older people who remained in the neighborhood largely to preserve the run-down shul. Some are quite untraditional—Black American Jews, Ethiopian Jews, a slightly retarded elderly man, others with various quirky ways. Non-Jews pop in to ask Moishe Sacks, the lay leader (there is no rabbi), to recite blessings for them or for their sick relatives; others hang out there for the company. In a basically orthodox shul, Moishe Sacks finds creative ways to assemble minyans of fewer than ten and to adapt Judaism to the needs of the congregation. I cannot adequately describe the clever resilience of the people, nor do justice to the good-heartedness of some of the members. But there is one thing that stands out for me: When an English film company did a documentary on the Intervale Jewish Center, Kugelmass, the anthropologist, traveled to London for the premier. He asked the shul's leader, Moishe Sacks, what he should say.

Sacks offered this: "I'll tell you what you can say. Tell them we should all thank God that we have lived to see this day."

"You mean I should say the prayer Shekhiyanu?" Kugelmass queries.

"Yes, say Shekhiyanu," Sacks affirms.

This rang powerfully for me, bringing up the same feelings of gratefulness for reaching the second conference of remembrance. And I said the Shehekiyanu again, since it seemed continually appropriate.

On the opening night of the first Catskills conference, I participated in a Shabbos (Sabbath) service, something I would not have done in my past history as a hotel worker. Indeed, it felt like a totally appropriate way to start the conference.

Part of the homecoming aspect is the handling of memory. Since we held the Catskills conference on Labor Day weekend, shortly before Rosh Hashanah, the Jewish New Year, in one of my talks I focused on the fact that the holiday has several names. One name is Yom Hazikaron, the Day of Remembering. This often is taken to mean remembering the events of the year, in order to take account of ourselves. But I believe it includes all remembering—the remembering of a long tradition of a people. For Jews, our common memory holds us together, despite war, persecution, and diaspora. Cast throughout the world, often fleeing without their possessions, Jews had to make memory matter. As the renowned Yiddish author I. L. Peretz wrote, "A people without a memory is like an individual with amnesia."

A Personal Specialness

In the last four years, as I have interviewed Catskill veterans, tapped my own memories, written about the Catskills, organized the Catskills Institute, run conferences, lectured on the subject, and taught a Catskill course at Brown University, I have so often thought: Why did I not think of this before, this idea of keeping alive this history? Why did I not save the menus and postcards? Why did I not take more photos? Why did I not commit to memory the rows upon rows of hotels and bungalow colonies that I passed every day? Why did I not learn Yiddish? Why did I not appreciate the food and the music and comedy as much then as now? It hurts to not have lived that life more fully, to not have remembered when the remembering was good. This is not, however, my personal failing alone. No, it is something that many of us did to some extent, and now we are trying to redeem ourselves. Many people told me that they now understand the significance of the Catskills as a major cultural phenomenon, though at the time they were too enmeshed in it—and often ashamed of it—to know that.

I think of the wonderful revival of klezmer music in the past decade. Now klezmer concerts are held all the time. Many younger musicians are learning these old traditions, and music stores have whole sections of klezmer music. The great classical violinist Itzhak Perlman records albums with top klezmer players, as does the famed country mandolinist David Grisman. Granted, these modern groups are sometimes more innovative than many older Catskill entertainers and house bands, though ultimately they are playing the same music I heard thirty to forty years ago—"Beltz, Mein Shtetle Belz," "Rumania," "Schain Vi Di Livone," and a host of untitled *freilachs, shers,* and *bulgars.* But it so often sounded trite and corny then. I was like other youngsters in preferring rock or jazz to Yiddish music. Yet the roots of this music struck deep inside and waited for the recent klezmer revival to unlock my love for this music. Now it feels just right, as I have come to appreciate still another part of my legacy.

The Yiddish language was the same way—too much of the old country. Unlocking the memory, though, can be profound. My friend took a Yiddish class at the Workmen's Circle in Brookline, Massachusetts, around 1985, and it so awakened his spirit that he recruited a few friends with young children, and they revived the Workmen's Circle's I. L. Peretz Shule, a school dormant for years. My children began attending this shule, which grew quickly to overflow the building, as some 110 children now attend from kindergarten into their teen years. I had the wonderful fortune in 1994 and 1995 to teach, along with another parent, my son's class of ten seventh graders who, in our secular Jewish tradition, have a collective bar/bat mitzvah. This is a rekindling, similar to the way that we kindle candles to welcome Shabbos or holidays. It is a way back in, or deeper in, to places in our hearts and spirits that we may have shied away from.

Why, though, do we so often retreat from Jewish culture and religion in the first place? I think a lot of Jewish cultural experience is like this—younger generations seek a more modern identity, cast off the old ways, and even dump on them. Judaism is not a purely private religion. Jews for centuries were visibly different from their neighbors. Even in this modern era, Jews have two special languages—Hebrew for prayer and, for many, Yiddish for conversation. Observant Jews have a large number of holidays to observe, a weekly Shabbos holiday, and a special set of dietary laws. Hence they are very visible. For those less observant or nonobservant, the noticeable appearance of more orthodox Jews, even if only the wearing of a yarmulke, has often been an embarrassment. Thus, it has been common to see American Jews rejecting much of their legacy. In a society with so much less open anti-Semitism than that which Jews suffered for centuries in Europe and elsewhere, there is actually a "free choice" to reject Jewish identity, a choice less available in more rigid societies.

We return for one reason or another, however, and we recapture some of the legacy, but there is still too much gone past already. So often we hear how the Holocaust caused Jews to renew their Jewishness, yet by then so much of the legacy was destroyed. In terms of the Catskills, for the most part, we are unable to return to the places we knew: The old markers and signposts have disappeared; we can hardly find the postcards and menus. Now we have to nourish the memories, write commentaries, and pass the tradition on. We may also be able to locate some of the mementos and artifacts, but too much of the larger physical evidence is gone. Still, Jews have always found ways to remember, to keep alive the history and traditions, and that is what my Catskill excursion does.

For some I spoke with, thinking about the Catskills brought out evocative images. Remembering a childhood in the 1920s, one man told me: "I recall, very vividly, certain panoramic views from our hotel room when I was put to bed every evening. I would gaze out the window, in the darkness of the starry night, and observe the passenger trains, in miniature, traveling miles away, around the mountainside, between the Ferndale and Liberty stations; the locomotive belching smoke and the lights reflected through the passenger car windows." For another who began vacationing in that era: "I have been back to the Catskills many times in recent years—at $97 a day—but to me the word 'Catskills' still means the road to Hurleyville on a bright clear morning, the whistle of the train as it approached the station, the star-studded sky at night, and the water pump, smelling of oil, at the back of the hotel that meant we could have water to drink just as we did at home."

Return and Revival

I am continually struck by the common themes of return and revival in novels and films about the Catskills, as well as in the interviews I have conducted and letters I receive. Eileen Pollack's novel centers on her main character's attempt to keep alive the family hotel, for various interrelated reasons:

He set the table for tea. Then, as we sat drinking, I told him my plans, everything from reviving Yiddish theater and music to proving to the world that kosher cuisine needn't be bland. "In a few years," I told him, "the Eden will be the only place left where a person can see what the Catskills were like."

But on the other hand, Pollack's character was very much on a personal quest: "I didn't want to be the savior of *yiddishkayt* or even of the Borscht Belt. I wanted to be the little girl in the red polka-dot swimsuit who even now was preparing to jump in the pool." The hotel was her identity:

> There were so many clubs for Jews it was hard to feel distinction for be-
> ing a Jew. Yet, standing at that fair, it occurred to me that I was the
> only student whose family owned an authentic Borscht Belt hotel. I
> would be nothing without the Eden. If my parents really sold it, as they
> had been threatening to do, I would have no kingdom to reign.

In Harvey Jacobs's 1975 *Summer on a Mountain of Spices,* the final chapter takes place three decades later than its earlier 1940s action but is titled "Minutes Later." Harry Craft, teenage concessionaire of the Willow Spring Hotel, learns his uncle Shlomo, one of the partner-owners, has died. Harry is sure his uncle's "marinated ghost" (Shlomo ran the salad counter and was known for his many pickled dishes) "would stand near the Washington Bridge and bum a ride up to the Willow Spring, where it belonged." And hence, "In the morning he announced that instead of going to the funeral the family would head down the New York Thruway to Monticello," since it would be a more appropriate way to send off his dear uncle.

Terry Kay's 1994 *Shadow Song* gives us a Southern gentile, Bobo Murphy, whose one 1950s summer in the northern Catskills, near Fleishmanns, made such a profound impact on his life that he returns each summer to visit. His main contact is with an elderly, eccentric Jew who has taught him many lessons of life and is a father figure. When Avrum Feldman dies, Bobo stays longer than usual and finds his soul's roots in the Catskills—through Avrum's memory, through his friends the hotel owners, and through the teenage sweetheart of decades ago that he finally marries.

In the feature film *Sweet Lorraine,* there is a tender portrait of a granddaughter who never saw the Catskills. She arrived from the Southwest for the experience of working a summer, and then sought to keep her grandmother from selling out to the Hasidim. Just a summer of the Mountains lifestyle got her addicted. *The Rise and Fall of the Borscht Belt,* a documentary, shows old Mountain guests who have now bought summer homes near their old stomping grounds. They reminiscence about the lively times of the past and even re-create them in informal lawn entertainment.

In my interviews, I found people who drove up for a revisit, often long after they had last been in the Mountains. A man who attended the Dror socialists' Zionist camp in the early to mid 1970s took friends from Vermont for a visit in the early 1990s, just out of a longing to see the place again. A forty-seven-year-old man, who grew up in Liberty and who worked in the Catskills as did his father, recounted, "Last year [1995], when my father passed away, my older brother and I decided to take a drive around the county one day after the funeral. . . . Very little was left of the 'glory days.'" Other respondents remarked on how they, too, felt a need to recover the Catskill experience, even if they didn't like it in the original.

Death brought Eileen Pollack back to Liberty, when her ninety-nine-year-old grandmother passed away:

> My sister and I started noticing all of the other gravestones of people we knew—my grandfather, our friends' parents and grandparents. The names on the gravestones read like the handball courts of all the hotels around Liberty. We tried to put a pebble on each to show we'd been there to pay our respects, but we finally realized we couldn't put so many pebbles on so many stones. I picked up a handful of pebbles and tossed them up in the air and hoped that covered everyone.

Some folks considered buying the old properties. Marty Portnoy went back in later years to his parents' Seven Gables Hotel, long since burned. He was unable to stay long since "there were too many ghosts." But some years after that, his niece suggested he buy the property if it was available. He entertained that idea, but when it became apparent that other family members were not going to help with the work of it, he dropped the idea.

A fifty-eight-year-old man who had not vacationed in the Mountains since 1950 returned in 1985 to look at old places—Camp Wonderlake (a kuchalayn) and Camp White Lake (a bungalow colony). One was gone, save a chimney and some bricks. The other, Wonderlake, was standing uninhabited, with the main building's roof caved in: "I had fantasies of buying it and reopening it, as a museum or something." The museum fantasy is a rich one. In my lengthy drives around the Mountains, I keep looking at ruins of hotels and thinking, "Which one would be salvageable for a museum, if we could get the funds?" In 1996, I came upon a small hotel still operating, with a number of buildings that captured the essence of typical small resorts. I eagerly informed my Catskills Institute colleagues about this place being the ideal hotel to rescue for a museum. (I won't say the name, for fear of scaring the owners!)

We can see the powerful impulse to return in these words, written to me by a sixty-five-year-old man:

> I drive with a fractured orange-reddish brick sitting atop a box for sundry objects, which rests astride the transmission hump of my auto. It is from the foundation of the long since demolished Congress Hotel in Monticello. The Congress Hotel was the first Catskill hotel at which I ever stayed, the year 1947. In 1984, while attending a state conference at the Nevele Hotel, I decided to ride over to see the Congress, not having been back since 1950, when my parents decided to upgrade as it were and spend two weeks at the Windsor Hotel in South Fallsburg. I suppose because of my wonderful memories of the Congress, it never occurred to me that this place of joy could cease to exist. As I drove up the road, I felt a rush of memories and nostalgia that brought tears to my eyes, only to be abruptly startled by the vacant space with pieces of the hotel's foundation strewn about, recalling as I do now my feelings, if only fleeting, that this was all wrong, this could not be. I walked about the fields, reveling in my sweet sorrows, picked up the piece of brick, blew a kiss to the Congress Hotel, and started to leave, only to see another figure walking toward me. It turned out to be a gentleman, then in his late forties, who had been a waiter at the hotel for many summers, who was also drawn back by his memories, though our memories were of different times, mine preceding his by some years. We were, though, for a while, close, for we shared a special feeling for those summers and that place.

For others who do not keep a hotel brick in their car, there is still a tender contact with the Catskill earth:

> I still go back today because I have a daughter up there. I get a great feeling within myself of bringing back my family. My mother, my father. I visualize them there as I walk the grounds of the old Cherry Hill. Today it's a camp for children that are wayward. There are some houses

that are still there. To me it's sacred. I remember most everything that went on there as a kid. I had a good childhood. I guess when I go back there it's like Holy Land. Some people go to the cemetery to visit their parents. I get more of a good clean feeling when I'm up at this place. . . . I think it was beautiful years. I still get kicks out of just touching that ground. It's important to me.

The daughter of an Accord bungalow colony owner returns to the area frequently, since some relatives settled there: "My family owned Stein's Bungalows in Accord, New York. My childhood was magical. Even to this day, when my cousins and I view old movies of our Accord home, they manage to bring tears to our eyes." For her, like many others, driving the old roads brings up many feelings: "Every time we go to Ellenville, my husband and I laugh at a handball court on route 209 that gets lower and lower. I'm sure it will disappear completely very soon!"

For some people, the hotels they stayed in as children live on in other ways. Carrie Komito of the Aladdin Hotel recalls a recent experience:

When I came back from Florida on the plane, I was sitting next to a man. About halfway through, I told him that I ran the Aladdin Hotel. I thought he flipped. He said, "I went there as a child [in the 1950s]. My mother took me there. My mother's father brought me up there." He took out a card and said, "Look my business is called Aladdin Services." It's amazing. He said he's coming up [to visit] during the summer.

It may very well be that such encounters are what keep Carrie Komito going, running her hotel after six decades in the business. A place that has been so integral to one's life is hard to give up.

People deeply want to keep alive the Catskill past. At the first annual conference, I was astonished when people came up bringing offerings of materials—a short story on kuchalayns, postcards of old resorts, a handful of photos of a parents' hotel from the 1920s, newspaper clippings of Catskill history. Others just told stories of places they stayed. By the second conference, I began to expect these gifts. Over and over I have heard people there and elsewhere speak of the places they stayed with a tender familiarity. For so many people, these places were more familial than resort-like.

Presently, there are a few individuals who have assembled collections of postcards and memorabilia, including a British Jew who fell in love with the area on his first trip to the Mountains in the 1980s. He came back yearly and began collecting postcards and other memorabilia. The Catskills Institute has collected many items as well to establish a permanent archive. Many wonderful people have sent us menus, postcards, photos, activity schedules, brochures, rate cards, home movies, videotapes, audiotapes, stationery, mugs, and a host of recognition products from the hotels. My students come up after class, bringing mementos, such as the photo telescopes that were taken in dining rooms on Saturday night. These materials offer a window into the Catskill past. As I hold them, catalogue them and share them with museum exhibitions and Jewish organizations' fundraising efforts; they cascade us back through the decades.

As another way to keep alive the legacy, people are now having Catskill reunions. Since 1981, there have been *two* annual reunions in south Florida, one a general Sullivan County reunion and the other a reunion of Woodridge/Mountaindale veterans. Hotel-specific gatherings also take place—in 1997, there was a staff and guest reunion of Pioneer Hotel people, and a Kutsher's staff reunion weekend as well.

Responses to me based on newspaper articles about my research and the Catskills Institute affirmed even more this desire to keep alive the Mountain memories. One article in particular, by Martha Smith, was published in the *Providence Journal*. In syndication, it was reprinted in several other places, including the *Akron Beacon-Journal* and the *Miami Herald*. This article, especially the *Miami Herald* reprint, produced a tremendous response—108 letters and 22 calls. There were several interesting findings as a result. One is that many of these people had been in the Catskills very early on. A good number had stopped working or staying there over fifty years ago. Many were in their eighties. In their letters and calls, the majority told me about their memories but also added details about where they were now living (most in Florida, though some Floridians sent the article to friends elsewhere), their current job if they were still working, the clubs and organizations they were involved in, their families (especially their grandchildren). They were telling me the latest details of lives in which the Catskills had been an intrinsically important feature. It was as if they were rounding out their total life history by talking about Catskills' place in it that history.

There was also something like a parent's or grandparent's story-telling that wanted the ear of a child or a grandchild. I got teary reading a letter from a woman from a hotel-owning family who responded to the Martha Smith article: "Phil, you write that your mother has passed away and you cannot ask her specific information. If I can help with this, please use my memory. I bet she would be proud of what you are doing. I am."

Personal Identity, Jewishness, and the Larger Quest

So much of my being a Jew is tied up with living in the Catskill milieu. Many interesting and important things in my life happened there, largely by virtue of the fact that I was there for so long. These things could have happened anywhere, but there was something different about this context. Here's one example:

Leon Uris's *Exodus* was published in 1958, when my parents worked at the Seven Gables in Greenfield Park and I was a nine-year-old staff kid floating around the hotel. There was such a palpable excitement about the book that summer. A handful of people had copies, and everyone was waiting their turn to borrow it as they talked about it incessantly. This story of the birth of Israel became amplified by our summer world, all of us tied together by the bounds of this small hotel society, eager to read and talk about *Exodus*. I don't think I read the book until two or three years later, but I knew at the time what a significant event this book's publication was.

More generally, the Mountains provided a Jewish learning laboratory for me. My parents were culturally very Jewish, but not religious. For instance, it was my desire to have a bar mitzvah, not their interest or pressure. I got them to go to shul and to keep holidays, though that only lasted for the few years that I pushed it. They spoke enough Yiddish to get by, though they could not read it and were not learned in any classic Yiddish culture. Here, in the Catskills, I was surrounded by endless daily immersion in things Jewish. Challah and wine on Shabbos, small services in the tearoom, a bunch of burning candles, Yiddish music and humor, awareness of *kashruth* (kosher laws), the spoken language of Yiddish, the exposure to many people from Eastern Europe—all this was a school of Yiddishkeit. And as I said earlier, I often failed to appreciate it, but that is the way children are with any school. Certainly our winter life in Miami Beach and North Miami Beach provided a Jewish context, too (though for about eight years we lived in Fort Pierce, two hundred miles north of there, in a small town with perhaps a dozen Jewish families). Yet the Catskills was so self-contained, so pronouncedly Jewish, and so much connected to the Jewish life of New York, that it was the more dominant place for me to get my exposure to Jewish culture.

Others who have written about the Catskills find similarly that people did many of the things in the Catskills that they might do anywhere. But those experiences were made more colorful and memorable because of the milieu, the history, and the compact little world that was in so many ways a microcosm of a larger world.

A personal quest can yield meaningful knowledge that can be applied to larger circumstances. Just for one example: In the summer of 1995, while preparing for the first Catskills conference, I read Victor Perera's just-published book, *The Cross and the Pear Tree: A Sephardic Journey*. Perera examines his own family history and then goes back centuries as he traces many lines of his Sephardic relatives in Spain, Portugal, Holland, Israel, and America. In many ways, it is the power of his search for family roots that enables Perera to weave an exciting narrative of the Golden Age in Spain, the Inquisition, and the years since.

If many of us, looking just as individuals, search for our roots, the search can become larger than just individual efforts. I think of the ability of slave narratives to tell the tale of American slavery. I think of the incredible power of personal narratives to teach us about the Holocaust. These personal tales encapsulate a larger world; they facilitate our learning about the broad sweep of history around us. In sociology, my area of training, the voices of ordinary people have become so central in the last few decades. Whether looking at tragedies of world-historical proportions or at the mundane life in households, we have so much to learn from the oral histories and sociological interviews that elicit information on routine, daily life. When we can hear a number of such personal narratives, we can construct a larger picture.

I have found this individual/collective nature of the search for roots to be true in another arena, which I entered in 1996—Jewish genealogy. As a member of JewishGen, an online Jewish genealogy discussion list, I have participated in the give-and-take of searching for ancestors and missing relatives, and in using the enormous range of databases that JewishGen has put up on the Internet. Members post messages to seek help, offer hints, respond to queries, and just mull over the meanings of their efforts. All of this seemingly *individual* searching is in fact an immensely *collective* effort, for several reasons. One, people are helping each other, *kvelling* (expressing joy) over successes and mourning losses, linking people to families, locating old synagogues and cemetery plots. Two, they are helping preserve a Jewish world that was so largely destroyed by the Nazis. Jewish life was ruptured beyond belief, and the threads of family, city, and shtetl remembrance that seem to be individual efforts are truly part of keeping alive the memories of that era and what came before it. Three, they are building databases for future generations to use, to tell the story of their whole people. People engaged in Jewish genealogy, whether in this cyber-community or in one of the many local Jewish genealogical societies, are very aware of the larger meaning of their often tedious archival meandering.

Interestingly, a number of people post queries on JewishGen looking for relatives who owned hotels in the Catskills. I have been able to help by referring to the list of hotels that is appended to this book, as well as by using my personal knowledge. My best success so far was in helping a man find a never-known cousin, who happened to be the owner of a hotel my parents worked at. Even more recently, I helped someone else locate a relative by using my existing Catskill connections.

A Larger Specialness

Countless responses from owners and their families, guests, staff, and entertainers spoke to the indelible memories of this unique environment. Whatever happened in the Catskills seemed to be more precious and notable than if it occurred elsewhere. It was an overwhelmingly exciting place with action of all sorts. It was a refreshing experience for those in need of rest, a maturing experience for young workers learning the ropes of the world of work, a romantic experience for people of all sorts, a financial boost for a couple of generations. Catskill veterans deeply longed for a taste, a memory, a recollection of their times in the Catskills.

One way we can look at the specialness of the Catskills is to envision a living theater with multiple stages, upon which are played the gamut of social roles, relations, and entertainment. In picking up on this approach, Stefan Kanfer concludes:

> There has never been a domain like it in America: with performers who shaped the taste of a nation, men and women who affected the operations of film studios and the commercial theater; hustlers and gangsters, basketball stars and basketball fixers; waiters and busboys who were later to run hospitals and serve on appellate courts; and audiences who saw it all from the beginning.

Writer Joyce Wadler, who grew up in Fleischmanns, fondly remembers:

You ask me my memories of the Borscht Belt. I can tell you, again, the first thing is noise. Noise at canasta; noise in the dining room; noise (this is only theory) at the astonishment and joy of being alive. They dried the silverware in the kitchen by putting it in a pillowcase and shaking it, to give you an idea. The second thing—it cannot be repeated enough, and repetition is the signature of the worrisome Jewish soul— it was funny in the mountains. The bosses yelling at the help were funny. The busboys spitting in the soup were funny. The social directors chasing the weekday widows were funny. Morris the goddamn *butcher* was funny.

The Mountains were definitely a theatrical milieu where people could temporarily escape from the routine, as recounted by this man who spent many years as a social director:

It was like a Disneyworld for adults, everything was there for you, there was so much to do, there were so many activities, so much food to eat. It was a fantasy world in some instances, but not reality, and that's the best way I can say it. I would get back to reality on Labor Day. It was enough—as much as I loved it, as much as I enjoyed and looked forward to going there.

Many veterans and commentators have focused on the coming-of-age theme:

What I learned, I learned there. Whether it's sex, whether it's business, whether it's the wise guy-ness of that character charging [for free refreshments] in the tearoom, or the brutality of some of the guests, whether it's the jokes, the getting along, the fabulous Mountain earnings giving me the means to get an education and make it—to all of us who worked there as young people, going up to the Catskills was an awakening of unbelievable proportions.

Catskill culture was for many people their fundamental social realm. One musician recalls, "Growing up in the 1950s, I could name at least two hundred hotels in the Mountains the way kids could name baseball players and batting averages." This resonates with my own experience. Because my parents knew so many people in the Catskills, because my father worked at the employment agency, and because I often went with him to transport staffers, I saw and heard a lot about what was going on at many hotels. Collecting hotel stories and seeing hotels in operation was my childhood pastime. My most commonly recurring dream to date is getting dressed to wait tables, only to find my black bow tie missing and nowhere to buy or borrow one in time for the meal. The Catskills have taken up residence in my unconscious as a way to manifest some fundamental anxiety concerning being unprepared in life. I heard an ex-waiter address the same issue: "My ultimate nightmare in life is to have to work in hotels again. I go in the kitchen, and you have these people and they keep on growing. Every time I look, there are more people, and I have to go in the kitchen to get something like French fries. I go in there and I can't get it together. It is hopeless."

Whether conscious or unconscious, it is hard to get away from the Catskills. From birth to graduate school, the Mountains dominated my life. Then there was a period of being away, but now the Catskills have once again taken over my life. Since I began working on this book in 1992, I have been busy with the research, interviewing endless wonderful people, writing articles as well as the book, running the Catskills Institute and its conferences, collecting memorabilia, working on museum and other exhibitions, and even teaching a course at Brown University on the Catskill legacy. And, on top of that—talking to everyone about all of this. I guess that once the Mountain Rat material is in your blood, it never goes away, even if it hibernates for a while.

The Catskills were part of the social production of culture by American Jews, an enterprise that yielded a different milieu than the Jews were used to. That experience has something in common with the post-1945 movement of Jews to what Deborah Dash Moore calls the "golden cities" of Miami and Los Angeles. Jews left communities with long-established structures and created a new identity that was based more on individual searching for a new order than on rootedness in a prior community, "a Jewish identity derived less from tradition than from personal choice." In their "brashness and exuberance," they developed a new life in a less fettered context where leisure was far more integrated with work than Jews had previously experienced. In this quest, Jewish migration to the sun made them into what Moore terms "permanent tourists." The patrons of the Catskills were largely New Yorkers, still plugged into the more traditional urban ways. But they were, like Moore's "permanent tourists," fashioning a work-leisure combination unlike anything in their Eastern European legacy, and doing so in a setting quite unfettered relative to their urban homes. They were certainly brash and exuberant in their playfulness, and their resorts were often garish jumps into the future, as are the new Miami and Los Angeles buildings.

Looking through a larger sociological lens, the Catskills are a channel through which flowed the major currents of American Jewish culture. The Frommers write that the evolution of the Catskills "mirrored—even crystallized—a twofold process: the Americanization of the Jewish population on the one hand, and the impact of Jewish culture on America on the other." It was Americanization because the idea of vacationing was new for most Jews of the time. The Catskills imparted Jewish culture from the comedians who "delivered their particular view of life—with its pathos, irony, self-mockery, sarcasm, and vulgarity—that would, via radio, movies, and television, reach the nation at large. So was America informed about the Jewish mother, the insatiable Jewish appetite, the anxieties, foibles, and feats of the American Jew."

Beyond this conveyance of stereotypes and images, I view the Catskills as a central vehicle for Jews of Eastern European descent to become Americanized while keeping Jewish. Orienting themselves to the business and professional worlds of America, they needed to also play like Americans. In the resorts, people could do that, while keeping sufficient Yiddishkeit culture and ritual observance. Jewish children's camps, many of which were in the Catskills, offered a similar social function, providing an institution that, as Joselit writes, "melded two distinct imperatives, that of assimilation on the one hand and ethnic persistence on the other":

> Through its celebration of "Hebraic ideals with the American democratic milieu," the Jewish summer camp blended American notions of play and peer culture with *yidishkeyt,* Zionism, secular Judaism, and denominationalism. Experimenting with games, campfires, nature hikes, athletic tournaments, songfests and theatrical pageants—activities not commonly associated with Jewish culture—it demonstrated that "being Jewish could be fun and not a burden."

All ethnic/religious groups need symbol sets to demarcate their unique experience. The Jews needed a cultural location to symbolize their transformation: their growth into the middle class, their ability to replace some anxiety with relaxation, their particular brand of secularizing their religion while still preserving some religiosity in their secular life. New York City was the essential urban cultural location of American Jewry; could it be otherwise that the New York Jews' resort area would play such a role? The Catskills were so special because *everything* happened there. And the abrupt fall of the Borscht Belt like-wise is so dramatic because it represents the fear that much of our routinely accepted cultural symbolism can so readily be lost.

A clothing wholesaler, who got his first job in America in the Catskills when he escaped the Holocaust, bemoaned this loss: "It can never be repeated. I think it is gone forever. It was a time, it was a place, and these days are gone." A bellhop who is about my own age treasures the experience: "I would say it was one of the more special, electrifying times of my life. I can't imagine what it would have been like not to have done it. I've tried to explain it to people from other parts of the country or other parts of New York. If you didn't do it or didn't experience it, there is almost no way to explain."

Because it was once so thriving and vibrant, the current status of the Catskills is depressing. One woman stayed nine years in the 1950s at the then new Mintz's Bungalow Colony in White Lake: "About three years ago [1993], I went back to Mintz's to see it. It was so depressing. Tears came to my eyes when I drove up. This beautiful colony; clean, magnificent pool; beautiful casino. What I saw depressed me so. The day was 90 degrees. I saw these orthodox children with long sleeves, *pais,* with long dresses. The pool was no longer a pool. I drove away with tears, that's how badly I felt." Two other long-time residents spoke sadly of the present:

> I belong to Senior Citizens, and we meet in Woodridge every Monday, so on the way we have to pass where Zeiger's used to be. And you know, when I pass that hotel, it hurts me to see what happened to it.

> Well, you know, when I go from here to Liberty, it hurts me knowing that I knew all the hotels. There's nothing. Nothing.

One owner's child, who still returns every year or so, notes: "There were years when you'd see things looking kind of ramshackle and falling apart. But now it's gotten to the point where some of it's just completely overgrown and you don't see the old buildings any more. So, in a way, it's like nature taking over, and maybe it'll be pretty again some day."

Indeed, the drive through the Catskills is a desolate one, shocking to me upon a return after many years away. There may be little but ruins on the roads that once teemed with "hotel after hotel," but the Mountains planted its mark on American Jewish culture in powerful ways. That mark is fashioned from a roadway of music, humor, culinary abundance, romance, and ethnic recreation/re-creation. Truly these were the "Jewish Alps," soaring heights and rich traditions of the American Jewish experience.

One Last Reflection: A Child on White Lake

Driving from Florida to our summer labors in the Catskills represented the only vacation my family ever took. My parents would stop at a few tourist attractions on the way, perhaps taking an extra day instead of the normal two overnights. One year, we went far out of our way, to New Orleans and Chattanooga, taking perhaps two extra days. That was it! Our task in life was to work in the Mountains for other people's vacations. An only-child, riding the 1,300 miles from Florida to New York, I had a rich fantasy life. One fantasy only occurred on the way to New York, not on the return to Florida. We would find a bedraggled young girl on the highway, stop and pick her up, and find out that she was my long-lost sister. I had one other fantasy riff about my sister, a flight of fancy that took place in Miami Beach, when I was ten: One Saturday I would return home from Saturday morning movies, and my parents would introduce me to the long-lost sister who had just been found. I always thought that this was all wish fulfillment—I wanted to have a sibling, as do many only children, but had no idea I truly had one somewhere out in the world. My mother only informed me when I was a sophomore in college that I actually had a half-sister from my father's first marriage, born twenty-three years before me. My father had not seen his daughter, Marilyn, since she was around six, the time that he and his first wife separated. William Brown's first wife refused to let him or his brother see Marilyn after then. Not until after my mother died (some twenty-four years after her disclosure) did I put together the logical fact: I must have overhead conversations between my parents and perhaps between them and their friends and relatives about Marilyn, but only responded through fantasy life. When I began this book it was clear that it was about searching for family roots, but it took a while later to realize that it was a search for Marilyn as well. My cousin, Gloria, around the same age as Marilyn, found a photo of the two of them at around age six—the first time I ever saw a photo of my sister. Surely if I rediscovered my parents' hotel and the Mountains around it, I might also find Marilyn! Probably not, but a powerful fantasy once again.

In 1996, through hard work and fortuitous connections, I finally located Marilyn, but she had died four years earlier, just over two years after my mother's death, which itself had propelled me on my manifold odyssey. I never got to meet her, but I spoke with people who knew her from as long ago as high school, in the 1940s, and I got to know her husband, Paul, and her sons, daughter-in-laws, and grandchildren. Perhaps in some way I did find some part of Marilyn along one of those highways through the South. But had I known how to start looking earlier, I might have found her alive. Now, I am trying to find what is still alive of the Mountains, because my life resides within them.

Given my life-searching journey through Catskill history, it came as no surprise to me that my cousin Gloria, rummaging through family photos, found a wonderful group portrait. It was of my paternal grandparents, who had a fiftieth anniversary celebration in Fallsburg sometime in the late 1920s or early 1930s, with dozens of their children, grandchildren, and friends. Perhaps my father's visits to the Catskills with his parents formed the origins of a future Mountain Rat.

My sister Marilyn is in the group photo, too, along with my father. There is also a photo of Marilyn alone, with the classic hotel in the background. It is so fitting to me that one of the few photos that exist of her as a child is in the Catskills.

I have so often said to myself, "If only I had thought years ago to study the Catskills, because there would have been more hotels standing and more people to tell tales." Lacking good archives and other research, it is so hard to capture this incredible cultural environment. There is substance to my sociological desire to better graph this society, but I think perhaps that it is also very much about personal searching. At the Seven Gables, my first and longest-stayed hotel, I walked many times daily from our room in the "White House" to the back door of the kitchen/dining room building. On that path were two parallel water pipes, half emerged from the ground, that I always imagined were magical railroad tracks. I wanted to keep following them, but they separated and stopped resembling tracks just before my destination. Probably I didn't know what I was then searching for, but writing about the Catskills has put that into perspective: I was and still am searching for lost family—deceased parents, a never-known sister from my father's first marriage, other relatives—and for the glue that binds together the memories and elements of my life. Bits of it fall into place—for example, I now understand that my parents' denial that their lost hotel still stood was but one manifestation of their dominant style of denial in all aspects of their lives.

Coming back to the restored Brown's Hotel Royal, I could see myself as a child on the lake, and I realized that my early self still has a firm location. Returning to the Seven Gables, I immediately thought of it as a classic site of ruins. Now I at least know where the archeological dig is.

APPENDIX

Hotels of the Catskills

This hotel list is an ongoing project. Each newly found name is another treasure to add to the collective memory of the Catskill hotels. Ben Kaplan, a longtime Catskills resident, was for twelve years the executive director of the Sullivan County Resort Association, and for another ten years the head of Sullivan County's Office of Public Information. In 1991, he published a list of hotels in the *Sullivan County Democrat* newspaper, in four parts: July 26, July 30, August 2, and August 6. Many people responded with additional hotel names, adding to the historical record. Ben Kaplan provided me with the original published list and a typescript of the updated list. I am grateful to Ben Kaplan and to the *Sullivan County Democrat* for permission to print the whole list, updated and based on their initial research. I found many additional names of Ulster County hotels, which have been less well-documented and written about, from the 1956 edition of the Ulster County Resort Association, kindly located by John A. Umverzagt, and from the undated but clearly World War II-era "Ellenville, Town of Wawarsing on the Shawangunk Trail—A Vacationland Guide," kindly located by Gary Platt. I have located other hotel names from my research and interviews as well.

The list printed here includes 926 hotels; a very few of them may have been small boarding houses, but most appear to be regular hotels, even if very small. This number vastly exceeds the commonly heard estimate of 500 hotels, making even more significant the extent of hotels in the Catskill Mountains of Sullivan County and Ulster County. This list does not include the hotels of northern Ulster County and southern Greene County (the Tannersville/Fleischmanns/Phoenicia area). I have grouped Fallsburg and South Fallsburg together. For hotels listed in the Ulster County Resort Association and the Ellenville Vacationland Guide, I have grouped Leurenkill hotels in Ellenville, since Leurenkill was not commonly used as a town name, and have grouped Briggs Highway hotels in Greenfield Park for the same reason. It is common to find the same hotel name used in different towns. Sometimes there would be four hotels with the same name. The word "camp" does not refer to a children's camp, but to an adult resort. Readers who know of other hotels not listed here should inform me so that future listings in the Catskills Institute Archives will include them.

Accord
Chait's Hotel (later Su
 Casa, now Elat Chayim)
Kutay's Lodge

Barryville
Barryville Hotel

Beaver Brook
Beaver Brook House

Bethel
Emr's
Horseshoe Lake House
Liff Hotel
President Hotel

Black Lake
Brown's Lake View
Levine's

Bloomingburg
Coronet Lodge
Fair View House
Gowdey House
Maple Crest Farm
Mountain View Farm
Spring Farm
The Van Wyck

Bradley
Mrs. Edna Bonnell
De Lux House

Bridgeville
Hotel Kinne

Burlingham
Daneb's Woodland Manor

Callicoon
Callicoon Inn

Delaware House
Layman's
Olympia Hotel
Polster's Villa
Robisch
Soloway's
Valentine Mall
Villa Roma
Western Hotel

Callicoon Center
Hahn's
Hill's Summer Resort
Mootz Lone Pine
Tumble Inn

Cochecton
Erie Hotel

Cragsmoor
Cragsmoor Inn

Dairyland
Maple Court Hotel

DeBruce
Brookside Farm
DeBruce Club Inn
DeBruce Country Club
 (formerly Nangle's and
 Ararat)
The Homestead
St. Brendan's Hotel
Mountain View Farm

Divine Corners
Ganz
Neversink Inn
Riverside Hotel (now
 Foxcroft)
Schildkraut's House

Eldred
Tallwood Lodge

Ellenville
Arrowhead Lodge
Boxer's Hotel
Breeze Lawn Hotel
The Cathalia
Evergreen Manor
The Fallsview
Fountain Hill House
Griswold's Tourist Inn
Hastie's Mountain House
Kinberg's Castlewood Inn
Merryville Hotel
Mountain Spring Hotel
Nevele Country Club
Overlook Hotel
Rabinowitz's
Rande's Hotel
Rivera Country Club
Ritter's Sagamore Inn
Robin Hood Inn
Wayside Inn
West Orchard House

**Fallsburg/South
Fallsburg**
Alpine Hotel
Ambassador Hotel (now
 Catskills Playland
 amusement center)
Barlou Hotel (formerly
 Branlip Hotel)
Biltmore Hotel
Blue Eagle (formerly
 Hotel Wadler)
Brickman's (formerly
 Pleasant Valley Farm,
 now Syddha Yoga
 Ashram)
Cedar Hill Hotel

Claremore
Commodore Hotel
Didinsky's Villa
Elm Shade Hotel
Fain Lodge
Fallsburg Country Club
Fallsburg Mansion (now
    public housing)
Flagler Hotel (now Crystal
    Run School)
Flamingo Hotel
Hotel Furst
Gilbert's (now Syddha
    Yoga Ashram)
Grand View House
Heiden Hotel
Hoffman House
Irvington Hotel (formerly
    Hotel Glass)
Laurel Park Hotel (now
    Yeshiva Gedolah Zichron
    Moshe)
Leifert Hotel
Hotel LeRoy
Hotel Levitt (formerly
    New Prospect)
Lorraine Hotel
Majestic Hotel
Mayflower Hotel
Mohawk Hotel
Mountain View
Murray Hill Hotel (now
    Dynamite Youth Center)
Nassau
Nemerson Hotel (later
    DeVille, now Yeshiva
    Viznitz)
New White Rose Hotel
Oakland Hotel
Olympic
Pancrest Lodge
Peckler Hotel
Pine View Hotel
Pines Hotel (formerly
    Moneka Lodge)
Plaza Hotel
Premier Hotel

Raleigh Hotel (formerly
    Ratner's)
Regal
Riverdale Hotel
Riverside Hotel
River View Hotel
Rosaler House
Russell House
Sandler and Forman
Saxony (later Polonia)
Schenk's Paramount (now
    Camp Shalva)
Senate
Hotel Summit
Sunrise
Tree of Life Hotel
Turner Villa
Windsor Hotel (formerly
    The Lakeside, now
    Syddha Yoga Ashram)
Zeiger's (later El Dorado)

Ferndale
Avalon Hotel
Balfour Hotel
Blue Paradise
Brook Spring House
Brookside Inn
Bunger's
Bush House
Bushville Paradise
Capitol Mansion
Chelsea House
Crispell Farm
Crystal Lake House
Chesler's Hysana Lodge
Dan Bee Lodge
DeLuxe House
Eager Rose Garden
Empire Hotel
Fairmount Hotel
Ferndale Manor
Ferndale Mansion
Ferndale Palace
Greening House
Gregory's Mongaup
    House

Gross' American House
Hysana Lodge
Kanco Inn
Kubler's Hemlock Grove
    House
Lakeside Inn
Lakeview Farm House
Leader House
Leffler House
Leibush Goldberg's
Marko Palace
New Majestic
Orchard House
Overlook House
Pine View House
Plaza
Pollack's Hotel
Queen Mountain House
Royal House
Roxy Inn
Seiken Lake House
Shady Grove Hotel
Shelbourne Hotel and
    Country Club
Stier's
Susser's
Spring Wood
Terrace Hotel
Upper Ferndale Mansion
Yarish House
Walnut Mountain House

Forestburgh
Forestburgh Inn
Inn at Lake Joseph
Kleb's
Klein's Halfway House
Leininger's
McCormick's Sunset Farm
Martin Miller's
Theimer's
Humphrey Toomey
    House

Fremont
Gamrak
Mountain Laurel Farm

Fremont Center
Central Hotel

Fosterdale
Recreation Farm

Glen Spey
Bel Air Resort

Glen Wild
Central House
Empress Hotel
Glenmore
Hotel Frederick
Jaffe House
Rosenblatt's
Zucker's Glen Wild
    Country Club (formerly
    Grand Mountain)

Greenfield Park
Ackerman Hotel
Beerkill Lodge
Birchwood Lodge
Bookbinder's Hotel
Cherry Hill Hotel
Claremont Hotel
Cromwell Hotel
Echo Lodge
Epstein's Villa
Grand Hotel
Grand Mountain Hotel
Greenwood Inn (now
    Camp Bnos Beltz for
    Girls)
Harry Kaplan House
Hasbrouck House
Highland Hotel
Jockey Country Club
Kerness House
Krevat Hotel
Luxor Manor
Maple Leaf Inn
Maple Mountain House
Melbourne Hotel
Paramount Lodge
Picker's

Pioneer Country Club
ReisReit Hotel
Roseville Hotel
Sashin's Hotel
Seven Gables
Shangri-La
Shapiro's Farm House
Tamarack Lodge
Tetervin Hotel
Ulster Lake House
Windsor Lake Lodge

Grossinger
Grossinger Hotel

Grooville
Rambling Mountain
Spring Hotel

Hankins
Delaware Valley Inn
Grossman's Spring Glen

Harris
American House
Grossman's Inn
Lakeside Inn
Primrose Mansion
Resnick's
Turey Hotel

High View
Bonnie View
Eagle's Nest
High Acres
Kerwin Lodge
Mountain Side Farm
The Overlook
Sha-Wan-Ga Lodge

Highland Lake
Bertram's Lodge
Fern Cliff Lodge
Green Meadows
Highland Lake House
Highland Lake Inn
Highland Villa

Deer Head Lodge
Lake Shore
Lake View House
Lakewood House
Manor House
Mills House
Pine Grove House
Pinehurst on the Lake
Pine Beach Inn
Pine Hill Lodge
Olympic House
Sand Beach
Singing Pines
Sunset View

Hortonville
Hortonville Hotel
Haeling Hotel

Hurleyville
Applebee Inn (later
    Columbia Hill)
Arcadia Lake
Astor Hotel
Brookhaven
Butler Lodge
Columbia Farms Hotel
Columbia Star House
Forest Inn
Garden House
Golden Hotel
Grand View Hotel
Holiday Hotel
King David Hotel
Kramer's on Luzon Lake
Hotel La Salle
Lake Shore House
Majestic (later
    Dunwoodie)
Midwood Hotel
Morningside Hotel
Peneroyal Hill Farm
    House
Pollack's Grand View
Purvis House
Richmond Hotel
Salon's Lodge

Sunset Hotel
Wayside Inn
Wellworth Hotel

Jeffersonville
Charles Arndt's
Ander Von Bergen
Frank Hess
Franklin House
Lake Jefferson Hotel
Likel's
Mall's
Mansion House
Roy Hess
Sohl's
Smith's Maple Grove
Sunnyside Farm
Wahl's
Welch's
Tonnison's White House

Kauneonga Lake
Arlington
Balcony House
Block's Mansion
Buckner's
Carlton
Columbia Hotel
Finneran's
Flag House
Glenwood
Golden Eagle
Hurd's
Kenmore Hotel
Kensington Hotel
Kenneth Hotel
Kroner's Ramsay House
Kushner's
Lynn's
New Empire Hotel
Panzer House
Rita Hotel
Rosedale Hotel
Sylvan Manor
Tieger Inn
Victory
West Shore Country Club

Woodlawn Villa

Kenoza Lake
Adler's
Alexander's
Apple Grove Cottage
Armbrust's
Chautauqua Cottage
Dell House
DeLap's
Edgemere
Fern Hotel
Gedney House
Goldsmith's
Heidt's
Heschle's
Kenoza Falls Lodge
Kenoza Lake Hotel
Lake View Country Club
Luckey's
Miller's
Moran's
Hotel Oneg
Pine Lake Lodge
Rosner's
Sackman's (later Season's)
Mrs. Schwenger's
Valley View
Waterfall House
Weiss

Kerhonkson
Brookside Inn
Colonial Hotel
Granite Hotel
Hillside Mountain House
Millbrook Lodge
Peg Leg Bates Country
    Club
Pine Grove Hotel
Rubin's Maple View

Kiamesha Lake
Concord Hotel (formerly
    Ideal, Overlook,
    Gluck's)
Columbia

Evan's Kiamesha Hotel
Fairmont
Flaxman's
Hotel Gibber (now
    Yeshiva Vizhitz)
Hotel Gradus
Kiamesha Inn
Kiamesha Lodge and
    Country Club
Kiamesha Overlook
Kiamesha Pine Hotel
Lakeside Inn
Mayfair Hotel
Mapledale
Pine Tree Villa
Rosemont Lodge
Hotel Safran
Savoy Hotel
Solnitzky's High View

Lake Huntington
Alpine Haven
Belmont Hotel
Bischoff's Villa
Crestwood Hotel
Furk's Farm
Green Acres (formerly
    Huntington Lakeside)
Hillside
Hillcrest Cottage
Huntington Lodge
Lake Huntington Lodge
Laurel Cottages
Lorraine
Lotus Hotel
Mansion House
Nutshell Hotel
The Lenox
The Pines
Pine Park
Prospect House
Rialto Hotel
Rose View
Sunny Hills
Viola Hotel
West Shore Hotel
White House Hotel

Liberty
Mrs. Joseph Bailey's
Barkley Hotel
Champlin Hotel
Chestnut Ridge House
Claremont Villa
Clements House
Crary Homestead
Darby House
Ruth De Veras
Elihu Hull Farm Boarding
    House
Evergreen Manor
Excelsior Hotel
Fernwood House
Four Corners Inn
Gorton Overlook House
Grand View Heights
Hall House
Heller House
Hilltop Villa
Jaffe's Evergreen Manor
Lancashire Inn
Lenape Hotel
Lennon House
Liberty House
Liberty View House
Liberty Springs House
The Lodge
Mansion House
The Mecca
Melody Country Club
Mrs. Lena F. Miller's
New Liberty House
Hotel Poellman
Shady Grove
Sunny Crest Inn
The Swannanoa
Terrace Cottage
Washington Inn
Hotel Wawonda
Woodland Manor

Livingston Manor
Amber Lake Farm
Arlington Hotel
Beaver Lake Lodge

Beaverkill Valley Inn
Camp Livingston
Hotel Capitol
Chan-Al (Lanza's Country
    Inn)
Collins Hill Farm
Edgewood Inn
Hillside Inn
Hollywood Country Club
Huber's Shandelee Lake
    Farm
Kenmore Lake Hotel
Lake Rest Hotel
Lake View Rest
The Lorraine
Mansion House
Mayflower Inn
Menges Lakeside
Mountain Crest
Mountain Lake Farms
Murray Hill Farm
Orchard Grove House
Parkston Hotel and
    Country Club
Rainbow Lodge
Sand Lake Hotel
Sea Cliff House
Shandelee Camp
Shandelee High View
    Farm
Shandelee Lake Hotel
Sunrise Hotel
Tempel Inn
Trojan Lake Lodge
Waldemere Hotel (now
    Transcendal Meditation
    Center)
Wayside Rest
White Roe Lake Hotel

Loch Sheldrake
Admiral Hotel
Algiers Country Club
Bell House
Brookside Hotel
Brown's Hotel (formerly
    Black Appel Inn; now

Grandview Palace
    condominiums)
Capitol Hotel
Delmar Hotel (formerly
    Cozy Nook Farm, Jacob
    Inn; later New
    Directions)
Ehrenreich Hotel
Evans Hotel (now
    Vacation Village housing
    development)
Ganz Hotel (formerly
    Hungarian Star House)
Goldberg's
Gold's Lakeside
Jewel Country Club
Karmel Hotel (now Stage
    Door Manor Theater
    Camp)
Laufer's River View
Hotel LeRoy (now
    Sullivan County
    Community College)
Lakeview Hotel
Loch Sheldrake Inn
Loch Sheldrake Lake
    Hotel
Loch Sheldrake Rest
Midwood Hotel
Monterey Hotel
Moonglow Inn
Newman's Villa
New Edgewood Hotel
New Roxy Hotel (later
    Green Acres, now New
    Hope)
Normandie Hotel
Overlook Hotel
Park Manor Hotel
Pine Grove Hotel
Pine View Country
    Club
Rapkin's Hilldale
Riverview Lodge
Sadowsky's Mountain Cliff
    Hotel
Schlesinger's

Shady Nook Country Club
Sunny Lake Lodge
Victoria Mansion
Wadler's Hotel
Warnock House
West End Country Club

Long Eddy
Armstrong Hotel (Later
   Maple Grove)

Mamakating Station
Beaver Lake Preserve
Mrs. George Helm's
Maple Dairy Farm
Mrs. Russell Lord's

Masten Lake
Mamakating Park Inn
Mount Prosper Manor

Mongaup Valley
Greisberg's
Riverdale
Polaris Lodge
Sapir's
Morris Shapiro's
Sunnyside
Red Rock Farm
   Springs
Wolf Spring Farm

Monticello
Anderson Hotel
Arcade Hotel
Blackman's Inn
Block's
Blossom View
Capitol
Carlton Hotel
Chernick's
Clover Hill Hotel
Colin's Maple Grove
Colonial Park Hotel
Cooper's Corners
Delano Hotel (formerly
   Rose Glow)

Donde House
Esther Manor (formerly
   Beauty Maple House)
Eusner's
Frank Leslie Hotel
Goldblatt's
Goldenberg's Pleasant
   View House
Hamilton Farms
Harmony Country Club
   (later Kutscher's Sports
   Academy)
Hungarian House
Imperial Hotel
Joyland Hotel
Kahaner's Inn
Kotney Manor
Kutsher's Country
   Club
Lander's Brookside
LaTourette Hotel
Little Hungarian Hotel
Locust Inn
Maple Shade Hotel
Maplewood Inn
Maple Grove
Melberg's
Monticello Inn (once
   Mansion House)
Monticello Overlook
Norman House
Palatine Hotel
Park View Hotel
Patterson Farm
Pine Lodge Hotel
Pine Tree Villa
Riverdale
Rockwell Hotel
Rosery
Royalton
Saxon Hotel
Skliar's Hotel
Slatkin's
Spring Lake Hotel
Star Mountain Hotel
Sunnyside
The Swan

Victoria Hotel (formerly
   Curley)
Washington Farm
Western View
Willow Lane
Wolf's Corner Hotel
Yasgur's

Mountaindale
Chester Hill House
Cold Spring House
Evergreen Hotel
Grand Central Hotel
Green Kretchma
High Cliff House
Hilltop Lodge
Linden Lawn Hotel
Little Falls Hotel
Kirshman House
Mountain Peak Lodge
Nasso Hotel
New Prospect Hotel
Paramount Hotel
Perlin's Star House
Royal Mountain Hotel
Rubinstein's Hotel
Sam Slobodow's Hotel
Wilsonia Hotel

Napanoch
Benenson's
Breskin Hotel
Hoffman Hotel
Napanoch Country Club
Pines
Shanley's Hotel
Sutta Hotel

Narrowsburg
Century Hotel
Hillside Inn
Oakland Hotel
Peggy's Runaway Lodge
River View Farm
Silver Lake Farm
The Rustic
Zehner's

Neversink
Crystal Falls Farm House
  (Archie Dean)
L. Kortright's
Kee's Resort Hotel
Klein's Hotel
Misner Homestead
Mountain Brook Farm
  House
Neversink Inn
New Age Health Spa
Tillson House

North Branch
Antler's Hotel
Chateau Laurier
Frank's Woodlawn House
Maple Hotel
Maud's Summer Ray
Sinclair Hotel (later
  Bauernfeind Hotel)

Oakland Valley
Case's
Crandel House
Engelberg's
Hanford C. Burns
Grand View House
Griffin Farmhouse
Galligan Homestead
Oakland Heights House
Oakland House
Pine Grove House
Riverside House
Rose Cottage
Sunshine House

Parksville
Aden Heights
Aden Mountain House
Ambassador Hotel
Avigail
Belmont House
Breezy Hill House
Brookdale Hotel
Camp Riverside
Charam Hill House

Conklin Hill House
Earlington Hotel
Edgewood House
Fiddle House
Flamenbaum Hotel
Fleisher's Hotel
Fox Mountain House
Glory Hotel
Golden House
Grand Hotel
High View Mountain
  Hotel
Highland House
Hillcrest View House
High View Hotel
Ideal Summer Resort
Kaufman House
Klass Hotel
Klein's Hillside
Lake Plaza Hotel
Lash Hotel
Lincoln Hotel
Malachowsky's Hotel
Maple View House
Merker's Tip Top
Mountain Pleasure Farm
Mountain View Farm
  House
New Brighton Hotel (now
  Hebrew Academy for
  Special Children)
New Mountain House
Overlook Hotel
Paramount House
Park Inn
Park Villa Hotel
Parksville Mansion
Peltz's Lincoln Hotel
Perl House
Pine View House
Prospect Inn
Ridge Mountail Hotel
Rose Hill House
Shady Grove House
Spring Grove
Spring Lake Hotel
Sunnybrook House

Sunnyland Hotel
Sunrise Hotel
Tanzville Hotel
Wallach Farm House
Weinreb Hotel
Westin Hotel
Young's Gap (now Logos)

Rock Hill
Lakewood House

Roscoe
Antim Lodge
Campbell Inn
New Alpine Hotel
Rockland House

Sackett Lake
Belmore Hotel
Congress Hotel
Lake Shore Chateau
Laurels Country Club
Novelty House
Sackett Lake Lodge

Spring Glen
Homowack Lodge
Maple Cottage
Mt. View Hotel
Rieger's Hotel
Shostack's Cottages

Summitville
Mountain View Hotel
Sokoloff's Hotel
White Rose Hotel

Swan Lake
Commodore Hotel
Cromwell
Fieldston
Goldwasser's
The Halcyon
Harden's
High Mountain House
Kramer's Hotel
Lana Hotel

Langer's
Lennon's Farm House
National Hotel and
    Country Club
Pine View Hotel
Paul's Hotel (now Daytop
    Village)
President Hotel
Prospect Hotel
Relis and Relis (Locust
    Grove)
Rockland Lodge
Rotterman's
Schinderman's
Shagrin's
Sherwood's
Stevensville Lake Hotel
    (later the Imperial)
Swan Lake Hotel
Swan Lake Inn and
    Country Club
Swan Lake Mansion
Vacationland
Wasserlauf's
Wellworth Hotel
The Wilshar
Woda's Hotel
Young's House

Swiss Hill
Forest Glen

Tennanah Lake
High View Mountain
    House
Holp's Lodge
Lupo's
Wolff's Tennanah Lake
    Hotel

Thompsonville
S. Mankowitz's
Uretzky's

Ulster Heights
Brookland Hotel
Brustein's Hotel

Central Hotel
Excelsior Lodge
Fogel's Hotel
Lakeside Crest Hotel
Mountain Lake Hotel
New Alpine Hotel
Rainbow Hotel
Rosedale Hotel
Shore's Forest House
Sunrise Manor
Western View Hotel
Woodbine Hotel
Woodleigh Hotel

Walker Valley
Jeronimo's

Wawarsing
Jefferson Hotel

White Lake
Brown's Hotel Royal (later
    Bradstan)
Camp White Lake
    (adult)
Fur Workers' Resort (later
    White Lake Lodge, then
    Camp Hi-Li)
Heilshorn
Hellman's
Lake Shore Chateau
Laurel
Lenox
Mansion House
Pines (later Ranch
    House)
Pontiac Hotel
Prospect House
Racine's
Shanghai Lodge
Sunny Glade
L. F. Taylor
The Waldheim
White Lake Hotel
White Lake Lodge
White Lake Mansion
White Lake Maples

White Sulphur Springs
Barsalee Country Club
Beck's Villa
Happiness House
Hotel Leona
Lesser Lodge
Pinehurst Manor
Tel Aviv Hotel
White Sulphur Springs
    Hotel
Willi Farm House

Woodbourne
Aladdin Hotel (formerly
    Levbourne)
Armstrong Hotel
Belvedere (later Haywire
    Ranch)
Chateau Reaux
Chester's Zunbarg (now
    Chateau Vim)
Chestnut Grove House
Friedman's Lake Hotel
Highview Hotel
Maple Crest
Maple Hill Hotel
Maple Lawn Hotel
Royal Inn
Salhara Hotel
South Wind
Sunset Villa
Woodbourne House
Woodbourne Sky House
Zukor's Lodge

Woodridge
Avon Lodge (formerly
    House of Joy)
Alamac Country Club
Allentoff Hotel
Apple Grove
Apollo Hotel
Berger's Hotel
Biltmore Hotel and
    Country Club
Blinder's Village View
    House

Centerville House
Claremont House
Friedman House
Glory Hotel (once
    Hannover Stock Farms)
Gerson's
Golub's
Highland Farm House
Hotel Israel (formerly
    Rabinowitz, Lindy)
Hummel's (later
    Kantrowitz House)
Kleinberg's
Lake House
Hotel Lindy
New Palace
Olympic Hotel
O'Neill's
Panoramic Health Farm
Pine Tree Country Club
Rosemond Hotel
Roseville Hotel
Shein's (formerly Fairview
    Farm House)
Silver Lake House

Slater House
Stratton Farm House
Sunny Acres Dude Ranch
Sunny Oaks Hotel
Vegetarian Hotel
Village Park House
Waldorf Hotel and
    Country Club
Weinger's
Hotel Weingerson
Welcome Inn

Wurtsboro
Bill's Vegetarian Manor
Blue Paradise
Dorrance House
Gunter House
White House Lodge

Youngsville
Blum's Hotel
Breezy Hill Cottage
Crystal Springs Hotel
    (later Camp Chic-A-Lac)
Frey's

Hotel Clair
Greene's
Kaiser's
Kramer's Union House
Kraussman's
Maple View Manor
Martin Cottage
Miller's
Mount Sunset Farm
    House
Mountain View Cottage
Muller's Breezy Hill
    Cottage
Pammer House
Rasmussen's
Ritterhausen's
Solomon's Sunnyside Inn
Spring Lake Hotel
Youngsville Inn
Youngsville Villa

Yulan
Highland Hotel and
    Cottages
Maple Crest

Notes

Chapter 1

P.   5   On Elat Chayim: Robert Eisenberg. 1995. *Boychiks in the Hood: Travels in the Hasidic Underground*. New York: Harper Collins, pp. 183–88.

P. 17   On removing tables and moving cars: Esterita Blumberg. 1996. *Remember the Catskills: Tales by a Recovering Hotelkeeper*. Fleischmanns, NY: Purple Mountain Press, p. 98.

Chapter 2

P. 23   On boundaries of the Catskills: Arthur G. Adams. 1990. *The Catskills: An Illustrated Historical Guide with Gazetteer*. New York: Fordham University Press, pp. 1–3.

P. 24   On Sholem colony: Oscar Israelowitz. 1992. *Oscar Israelowitz's Catskills Guide*. New York, Israelowitz Publishing, p. 17.

P. 25   On the early hotels and parks of the northern Catskills: Alf Evers. 1972. *The Catskills: From Wilderness to Woodstock*. Garden City, NY: Doubleday, pp. 538–551; Alf Evers. 1995. *In Catskill Country: Collected Essays on Mountain History, Life, and Lore*. Woodstock, NY: Overlook Press; Herbert Tobin. 1974. *A Social History of Jewish Life in the Catskill Mountains, 1865–1975*. Senior Honors Thesis, Brandeis University, Waltham, Mass., pp.18–21.

P. 26   On Thomashevsky: Stefan Kanfer. 1989. *A Summer World: The Attempt to Build a Jewish Eden in the Catskills, From the Early Days of the Ghetto to the Rise and Decline of the Borscht Belt*. New York: Farrar, Straus, Giroux, pp. 60–68.

P. 26   On Simon Epstein: Herbert Tobin. 1979. "New York's Jews and the Catskills Mountains." Pp. 161–75 in Ronald A. Brauner, ed., *Jewish Civilization: Essays and Studies,* vol. 1. Philadelphia: Reconstructionist Rabbinical College.

P. 26   On Jews in Tannersville: Alf Evers. 1972. *The Catskills: From Wilderness to Woodstock.* Garden City, NY: Doubleday, p. 661, 687–89; Abraham D. Lavender and Clarence B. Steinberg. 1995. *Jewish Farmers of the Catskills: A Century of Survival.* Gainesville, FL: University Press of Florida, p. 35.

P. 27   On John Gerson: David Gold. 1981. "Jewish Agriculture in the Catskills." *Agricultural History* 55:31–49.

P. 27   On discrimination: Evers, *The Catskills,* p. 678.

P. 27   Material in Jewish press: Andrew R. Heinze. 1990. *Adapting to Abundance: Jewish Immigrants, Mass Consumption, and the Search for Modern Identity.* New York, Columbia University Press, pp. 125–26, 150.

P. 27   On sales by gentiles to Jews: Lavender and Steinberg, *Jewish Farmers,* pp. 30–31.

P. 28   On sanitariums and recuperation: Tobin, "New York's Jews," p. 165; Kanfer, *Summer World,* pp. 52–54, 80.

P. 28   On divorced woman and boarding house rest: Gold, "Jewish Agriculture," pp. 31–49.

P. 31   On animals at hotels: Lavender and Steinberg, *Jewish Farmers,* p. 112; Myrna Katz Frommer and Harvey Frommer. 1991. *It Happened in the Catskills: An Oral History in the Words of Busboys, Bellhops, Guests, Proprietors, Comedians, Agents, and Others Who Lived It.* New York: Harcourt Brace Jovanovich, pp. 5–8, 104.

P. 31   On Baron de Hirsch: Tobin, *Social History,* pp. 46–51; Lavender and Steinberg, *Jewish Farmers,* pp. xi, 17, 23.

P. 32   Quote on extent of Jewish farming: Lavender and Steinberg, *Jewish Farmers,* pp. 37–38.

P. 32   On growth of Jewish population and acceptance, and on coops: Tobin, *Social History,* p. 46–51; Lavender and Steinberg, *Jewish Farmers,* pp. 42, 46, 59–60 71–72, 110–111, 117; Blumberg, *Remember the Catskills,* pp. 33–39, 57.

P. 34   On *tzedakkah* (charity): Herbert Tobin, 1979. "New York's Jews," pp. 169–170; Tobin, *Social History,* p. 25.

P. 34   On lure of farming: Lavender and Steinberg, *Jewish Farmers,* pp. 59, 85–86.

P. 34   On number of farms and farm income: Lavender and Steinberg, *Jewish Farmers,* pp. 128, 149, 160, 164–65, 191.

P. 36   On installing utility poles: Lavender and Steinberg, *Jewish Farmers,* p. 40

P. 36   Quote from Jewish Colonization Association: Tobin, *Social History,* p. 54.

P. 38   Wallenrod quote on origins of hotel: Reuben Wallenrod, 1957. *Dusk in the Catskills.* New York: Reconstructionist Press, pp. 43–44.

P. 38   Wallenrod quote on familiarity of old hotel: Wallenrod, *Dusk in the Catskills,* p. 120.

P. 39   Wallenrod quotes on Holocaust: Wallenrod, *Dusk in the Catskills,* pp. 256, 151.

P. 41   On 1950s expansion: Kanfer, *Summer World,* p. 23; Blumberg, *Remember the Catskills,* p. 228.

P. 42   Hotel Association census: Gregg Birnbaum and John Emerson. 1991. "The Last Resorts: Part 1." *Middletown Times Herald Record,* September 15, 1991.

P. 43   On Miami Beach hotels: Deborah Dash Moore. 1994. *To the Golden Cities: Pursuing the American Jewish Dream in Miami and L.A.* New York: Free Press, pp. 32–34; Blumberg *Remember the Catskills,* p. 170; Joel Pomerantz. 1970. *Jennie and the Story of Grossinger's.* New York: Grosset and Dunlop, pp. 227–56.

Chapter 3

P. 46   On polio epidemic and selling farm goods: Lavender and Steinberg, *Jewish Farmers,* pp. 87–88.

P. 46   All quotes are from Eugene Calden's unpublished essay, "Kuchalein."

P. 51   Quotes on rents and charges for bungalows: Irwin Richman. 1997. *Borscht Belt Bungalows: Memories of Catskill Summers.* Philadelphia: Temple University Press, all pages from draft manuscript, pp. 38, 47–66.

P. 52   Quotes on post–World War II boom and housing shortage: Richman, *Borscht Belt Bungalows,* pp. 31–48.

P. 55   On Neversink River dam and its effect on bungalow colonies: Richman, *Borscht Belt Bungalows,* pp. 182–84.

P. 56   On social class composition of bungalow colonies: Richman, *Borscht Belt Bungalows,* pp. 101–2.

P. 57   On cooperative system and entertainment in bungalow colonies: Richman, *Borscht Belt Bungalows,* pp. 177–78, 195–98.

P. 59   On revival of kuchalayns: Tobin, *Social History,* pp. 111, 127.

P. 60   On changes in costs, and quote on age composition of bungalow colonies: Richman, *Borscht Belt Bungalows,* pp. 93–94, 245, 248.

Chapter 4

P. 62   On origins of the Flagler Hotel: John Conway. 1996. *Retrospect: An Anecdotal History of Sullivan County, New York.* Fleischmanns, NY: Purple Mountain Press, pp. 23–24.

P. 63   On Chester's: Anne Chester. 1974. "The People I Lived Off Of." Transcription of speech given at The New School, May 1974, p. 1.

P. 64   Mac Robbins quote: Birnbaum and Emerson, "The Last Resorts: Part 1."

P. 65   On basketball league: Frommer and Frommer, *It Happened in the Catskills,* pp. 210–20.

P. 66   On mission architecture: Maurie Sacks lecture, "Synagogues of the Catskills." Presented at the Second Annual History of the Catskills conference. Sunny Oaks Hotel, Woodridge, New York. August 31, 1996.

P. 70   Blumberg quote: Blumberg, *Remember the Catskills,* p. 77.

P. 70   Quote on being slick to survive: Joey Adams. 1966. *The Borscht Belt.* New York: Bobbs Merrill, p. 171.

P. 71   Quote on resort economics: Eileen Pollack. 1998. *Paradise, New York.* Philadelphia: Temple University Press, p. 169.

P. 71   On condolence letters: Pollack, *Paradise,* 124.

P. 71   Elmer Rosenberg on hotel rates: Blumberg, *Remember the Catskills,* p. 104.

P. 73   Jacobs quote on casino: Harvey Jacobs. 1975. *Summer on a Mountain of Spices.* New York: Harper & Row, p. 32.

P. 73   Chester quote: Chester, "The People I Lived Off Of," p. 2.

P. 78   Quote on blintzes: Pollack, *Paradise,* pp. 130–31.

P. 83   Pollack quotes on owners' children: Pollack, *Paradise.* Quote on parents' bed, pp. 173–74. Other quotes appear in draft and have been deleted from the published version.

P. 89   On kickbacks for horseback riding and town outings: Frommer and Frommer, *It Happened in the Catskills,* p. 27; Gregg Birnbaum and John Scibelli. 1991. "The Last Resorts: Part 2." *Middletown Times Herald Record,* September 16, 1991.

P. 91   On Green Acres and politics: Blumberg, *Remember the Catskills,* pp. 68, 167, 171.

P. 91   On Yiddish papers and leftist entertainers: Lavender and Steinberg, *Jewish Farmers,* p. 185.

Chapter 5

P. 110   On Skliar's and the Harmony: Blumberg, *Remember the Catskills,* p. 101.

P. 110   Chester quote: Chester, "The People I Lived Off Of," pp. 6–7.

P. 111   Quotes by Joey Adams: Adams, *The Borscht Belt,* pp. 3, 7, 57.

P. 113   On Paul's Hotel and Broadway shows: Adams, *The Borscht Belt,* pp. 86, 104–23.

P. 119   On end of entertainment staffs: Adams, *The Borscht Belt,* p. 179.

P. 119   On basketball scandal: Kanfer, *Summer World,* pp. 209–19.

P. 119   On NBA and moonlighting: Conway, *Retrospect,* pp. 124–25.

P. 119   On boxers: Pomerantz, *Jennie and the Story of Grossinger's,* pp. 6, 265; Conway, *Retrospect,* pp. 127–29.

P. 122   Quote from Joey Adams: Adams, *The Borscht Belt,* p. 195.

Chapter 6

P. 138   Quote from Mark Hutter: Mark Hutter. 1970. "Summertime Servants: The 'Shlockhaus' Waiter." Pp. 203–25, in Glenn Jacobs, ed., *The Participant Observer.* New York: George Braziller, p. 214.

P. 145   Quote from Vivian Gornick: Vivian Gornick. 1996. "The Catskills Remembered." Pp. 30–61, in Vivian Gornick, ed., *Approaching Eye Level.* Boston: Beacon Press, 39–40.

P. 150   Quote from Kleinman: Birnbaum and Scibelli, "The Last Resorts: Part 2."

Chapter 7

P. 164   Quote from Tania Grossinger: Tania Grossinger. 1995. "Catskills Homecoming." *New York Daily News,* October 1, 1995.

P. 165   Quote from Sydney Offit: Sydney Offit. 1959. *He Had It Made.* New York: Crown, p. 53.

P. 168   Quote from Vivian Gornick: Gornick, "The Catskills Remembered," p. 45.

P. 180   Reuben Wallenrod quote: Wallenrod, *Dusk in the Catskills,* p. 208.

Chapter 8

P. 182   Heinze on expectations of a vacation: Heinze, *Adapting to Abundance,* pp. 14–15, 116–17, 127–28.

P. 182   Gold on vacations: Michael Gold. 1926. "At a Workers' Vacation Camp." *The Nation* 123(3195):294–95.

P. 186   Adams quote on romance: Adams, *The Borscht Belt,* p. 15.

P. 187 Quote by Kanfer on romance and sex: Kanfer, *Summer World*, p. 143.

P. 189 Wouk quote: Herman Wouk. 1955. *Marjorie Morningstar*. Garden City, NY: Doubleday, p. 164.

P. 191 Grossinger quote: Tania Grossinger. 1975. *Growing Up at Grossinger's*. New York: David McKay, p. 65.

P. 191 Eileen Pollack quote: Pollack, *Paradise*, p. 21.

P. 192 Sarah Sandberg quote: Sarah Sandberg. 1964. *Mama Made Minks*. Garden City, NY: Doubleday, p. 82.

P. 193 Tearoom petition: Frommer and Frommer, *It Happened in the Catskills*, p. 207.

P. 196 Blackmar quote: Betsy Blackmar. 1979. "Going to the Mountains: A Social History." Pp. 71–98, in Alf Evers, Elizabeth Cromley, Betsy Blackmar, and Neil Harris, eds., *Resorts of the Catskills*. New York: St. Martin's Press, p. 96.

P. 197 Pollack quotes: Pollack, *Paradise,* pp. 122, 166.

Chapter 9

P. 218 Joselit on "gestural Judaism": Brown University lecture, November 27, 1995.

P. 218 On *shochet* at Ridge Mountain: Frommer and Frommer, *It Happened in the Catskills,* p. 17.

P. 220 On Grossinger's ritual sale: Pomerantz, *Jennie and the Story of Grossinger's,* pp. 253–55.

P. 220 On writing a check to Grossinger's: Frommer and Frommer, *It Happened in the Catskills,* p. 41.

P. 221 Quotes by Rabbi Margolies and Rabbi Kreitman: Kanfer, *Summer World*, pp. 240.

P. 221 Quote by Rabbi Stone: Pomerantz, *Jennie and the Story of Grossinger's*, p. 253.

P. 222 Joselit on "summer resort Judaism": "Summer Resort Judaism," lecture at Third Annual History of the Catskills conference, August 31, 1997.

P. 224 On Isaac Bashevis Singer: Shalom Goldman, "Isaac Bashevis Singer in the Catskills: A Literary and Personal Turning Point," lecture at Third Annual History of the Catskills conference, August 31, 1997.

P. 227 On Yoga Ranch and on Foundation: Ari L. Goldman. 1992. "'New Age' Enlivens Catskills." *New York Times,* August 14.

P. 228 On Messiah on the Thruway: Ari L. Goldman. 1993. "Thruway Rest Stop Provides Place for Jews to Pray." *New York Times,* July 25.

P. 228 Estimate of Hasidic population: Eisenberg, *Boychicks in the Hood*, p. 193.

P. 228 On connections to Williamsburg: George Kranzler. 1995. *Hasidic Williamsburg: A Contemporary Hasidic Community*. Northvale, NJ: Jason Aronson, p. 50.

P. 229 Quote on not taking a vacation from learning: Joseph Berger. 1993. "New Accents for Old Ritual: Vacationing in the Catskills." *New York Times,* July 12.

P. 230 On Hasidim saving the Catskills: Kranzler, *Hasidic Williamsburg*, p. 50.

Chapter 10

P. 231 Quote from Martin Boris: Martin Boris. 1980. *Woodridge, 1946*. New York: Crown, p. 22.

P. 232 Hotel Association data: Bill Lowry. 1976. "'75 Alive in the Catskills." *Middletown Times Herald Record*, January 31.

P. 232 Intermarriage data: Egon Mayer. 1992. *A Demographic Revolution in American Jewry.* Ann Arbor, University of Michigan Press; Peter Steinfels. 1992. "Debating Intermarriage and Jewish Survival." *New York Times,* October 18; Cohen Center for Modern Jewish Studies. 1990. *Intermarriage and American Jews Today: New Findings and Policy Implications—A Summary Report.* Waltham, MA: Maurice and Marilyn Cohen Center for Modern Jewish Studies, Brandeis University.

P. 233 Divorce rates: Andrew Cherlin and Carin Celebuski. 1982. *Are Jewish Families Different?* New York: American Jewish Committee, p. 6.

P. 233 On Jewish population in Florida and California: Lavender and Steinberg, *Jewish Farmers,* p. 214.

P. 237 Blumberg quote: Blumberg, *Remember the Catskills,* p. 269.

P. 237 On convention business: Tobin, *Social History,* p. 132.

P. 237 On Brazilian soccer players: "Beans and Rice in the Borscht Belt." 1995. *New York Times,* October 21.

P. 238 Local population data: Lavender and Steinberg, *Jewish Farmers,* p. 214.

P. 238 On new food at Grossinger's: Grossinger, "Catskills Homecoming."

P. 238 Quote on Hasidim and vacations: Berger, "New Accents for Old Ritual."

P. 238 On condos at Brown's Hotel: Rich Newman. 1996. "Catskills Resort Conversion." *Middletown Times Herald Record,* August 4.

P. 239 On hotel taxes and bankruptcies: Sandra Frinton. 1996. "Resort Owners Hedge Bets." *Middletown Times Herald Record,* August 25; Joseph Berger. 1997. "Catskills Resort Hotel Files for Bankruptcy Protection." *New York Times,* February 29.

P. 239 Quote from Mark Kutsher: Andrew C. Revkin. 1998. "With Defeat of Gambling, Catskill Winter Turns Gloomier." *New York Times,* January 30.

P. 240 Quotes from Pollack: Pollack, *Paradise,* p. 3.

Chapter 11

P. 256 Pollack quote on keeping alive the hotel: Pollack, *Paradise,* p. 88; on personal quest, p. 158; on being nothing without the Eden, p. 61.

P. 256 Quote from Harvey Jacobs: Jacobs, *Summer on a Mountain of Spices,* p. 330.

P. 263 Kanfer quote: Kanfer, *Summer World,* p. 10.

P. 264 Quotes on "What I learned there," and on naming hotels: Frommer and Frommer, *It Happened in the Catskills,* pp. 112, 96.

P. 265 On "permanent tourists": Moore, *To the Golden Cities,* pp. 1–2, 53, 91–92, 264.

P. 266 Quote on Americanization: Frommer and Frommer, *It Happened in the Catskills,* pp. x–xi.

P. 266 On summer camps: Jenna Weissman Joselit. 1993. "The Jewish Way of Play." Pp. 15–28, in Jenna Weissman with Karen S. Mittelman, eds., *A Worthy Use of Summer: Jewish Summer Camping in America.* Philadelphia: National Museum of American Jewish History.

Bibliography

Adams, Arthur G. 1990. *The Catskills: An Illustrated Historical Guide with Gazetteer.* New York: Fordham University Press.

Adams, Joey, with Henry Tobias. 1966. *The Borscht Belt.* New York: Bobbs-Merrill.

"Beans and Rice in the Borscht Belt" 1995. *New York Times,* October 21.

Benincasa, Janis. 1994. "Ethnic Resorts of the Catskills: A Project, A Process, A Product." *New York Folklore Newsletter* 15(2): 6–7.

Berger, Joseph. 1993. "New Accents for Old Rituals: Vacationing in the Catskills." *New York Times,* July 12.

———. 1997. "Catskills Resort Hotel Files for Bankruptcy Protection." *New York Times,* February 29.

Birnbaum, Gregg, and John Emerson. 1991. "The Last Resorts: Part 1." *Middletown Times Herald Record,* September 15.

Birnbaum, Gregg, and John Scibelli. 1991. "The Last Resorts: Part 2." *Middletown Times Herald Record,* September 16.

Blackmar, Betsy. 1979. "Going to the Mountains: A Social History." Pp. 71–98 in Alf Evers, Elizabeth Cromley, Betsy Blackmar, and Neil Harris, eds., *Resorts of the Catskills.* New York: St. Martin's Press.

Blumberg, Esterita. 1996. *Remember the Catskills: Tales by a Recovering Hotelkeeper.* Fleischmanns, NY: Purple Mountain Press.

Boris, Martin. 1980. *Woodridge, 1946.* New York: Crown.

Brown, Phil. 1996. "Catskill Culture: An Ethnography of Jewish-American Resort Society." *Journal of Contemporary Ethnography* 25: 83–119.

Bumiller, Elisabeth. 1997. "A Too Noble Epitaph." *New York Times,* June 19.

Cahan, Abraham. 1917. *The Rise of David Levinksy* New York: Harper.

Calden, Eugene. No date. "Kuchalein." Unpublished essay maintained at the Catskills Institute Archives.

Cherlin, Andrew, and Carin Celebuski. 1982. *Are Jewish Families Different?* New York: American Jewish Committee.

Chester, Anne. May 1974. "The People I Lived Off Of." Transcription of speech given at The New School, New York, NY.

Cohen Center for Modern Jewish Studies. 1990. *Intermarriage and American Jews Today: New Findings and Policy Implications—A Summary Report.* Waltham, MA: Maurice and Marilyn Cohen Center for Modern Jewish Studies, Brandeis University.

Conway, John. 1996. *Retrospect: An Anecdotal History of Sullivan County, New York.* Fleischmanns, NY: Purple Mountain Press.

Eisenberg, Robert. 1995. *Boychiks in the Hood: Travels in the Hasidic Underground.* New York: Harper Collins.

Evers, Alf. 1972. *The Catskills: From Wilderness to Woodstock.* Garden City, NY: Doubleday.

———. 1995. *In Catskill Country: Collected Essays on Mountain History, Life, and Lore.* Woodstock, NY: Overlook Press.

———. 1995. "Mark Twain as an Onteorian—1890." Pp. 45–51 in *In Catskill Country: Collected Essays on Mountain History, Life, and Lore.* Woodstock, NY: Overlook Press.

Evers, Alf, Elizabeth Cromley, Betsy Blackmar, and Neil Harris, eds. 1979. *Resorts of the Catskills.* New York: St. Martin's Press.

Frinton, Sandra. 1996. "Resort Owners Hedge Bets." *Middletown Times Herald Record,* August 25.

Frommer, Myrna Katz, and Harvey Frommer. 1991. *It Happened in the Catskills: An Oral History in the Words of Busboys, Bellhops, Guests, Proprietors, Comedians, Agents, and Others Who Lived It.* New York: Harcourt, Brace, Jovanovich.

Gay, Ruth. 1996. *Unfinished People: European Jews Encounter America.* New York: Norton.

Gold, David. 1981. "Jewish Agriculture in the Catskills." *Agricultural History* 55: 31–49.

———, ed. 1994. *The River and the Mountains: Readings in Sullivan County History.* South Fallsburg, NY: Marielle Press.

Gold, Michael. 1926. "At a Workers' Vacation Camp." *The Nation* 123 (September 29; no. 3195): 294–95.

Goldin, Davidson. 1995. "The Catskills, on the Ropes, Rally for an Indian Casino." *New York Times,* March 10.

Goldman, Ari L. 1992. "'New Age' Enlivens Catskills." *New York Times,* August 14.

———. 1993. "Thruway Rest Stop Provides Place for Jews to Pray." *New York Times,* July 25.

Goldman, Shalom. 1997. "Isaac Bashevis Singer in the Catskills: A Literary and Personal Turning Point." Lecture at Third Annual History of the Catskills Conference (August 31). Sunny Oaks Hotel, Woodridge, New York.

Gornick, Vivian. 1996. "The Catskills Remembered." Pp. 30–61 in Vivian Gornick, ed., *Approaching Eye Level.* Boston: Beacon Press.

Grossinger, Tania. 1975. *Growing Up at Grossinger's* New York: David McKay.

———. 1995. "Catskills Homecoming." *New York Daily News,* October 1.

Hart, Moss. 1959. *Act One: An Autobiography.* New York: Random House.

Heinze, Andrew R. 1990. *Adapting to Abundance: Jewish Immigrants, Mass Consumption, and the Search for Modern Identity.* New York: Columbia University Press.

Hutter, Mark. 1970. "Summertime Servants: The 'Shlockhaus' Waiter." Pp. 203–225 in Glenn Jacobs, ed., *The Participant Observer.* New York: George Braziller.

Israelowitz, Oscar. 1992. *Oscar Israelowitz's Catskills Guide.* New York: Israelowitz Publishing.

Jacobs, Harvey. 1975. *Summer on a Mountain of Spices.* New York: Harper & Row.

Joselit, Jenna Weissman. 1993. "The Jewish Way of Play." Pp. 15–28 in Jenna Weissman, with Karen S. Mittelman, ed., *A Worthy Use of Summer: Jewish Summer Camping in America.* Philadelphia: National Museum of American Jewish History.

Joselit, Jenna Weissman. 1995. Unrecorded lecture given at Brown University.

———. 1997. "Summer Resort Judaism." Lecture at Third Annual History of the Catskills conference (August 31). Sunny Oaks Hotel, Woodridge, New York.

Kanfer, Stefan. 1989. *A Summer World: The Attempt to Build a Jewish Eden in the Catskills, From the Early Days of the Ghetto to the Rise and Decline of the Borscht Belt.* New York: Farrar, Straus, Giroux.

Kay, Terry. 1994. *Shadow Song.* New York: Pocket Books.

Kranzler, George. 1995. *Hasidic Williamsburg: A Contemporary Hasidic Community.* Northvale, NJ: Jason Aronson.

Kugelmass, Jack. 1996. *The Miracle of Intervale Avenue: The Story of a Jewish Congregation in the South Bronx.* New York: Columbia University Press.

Lavender, Abraham D., and Clarence B. Steinberg. 1995. *Jewish Farmers of the Catskills: A Century of Survival.* Gainesville: University Press of Florida.

Lowry, Bill. 1976. "'75 Alive in the Catskills." *Middletown Times Herald Record.* January 31.

Manners, Ande. 1972. *Poor Cousins.* New York: Coward, McCann, & Geoghegan.

Mayer, Egon. 1992. *A Demographic Revolution in American Jewry.* Ann Arbor: University of Michigan Press.

Moore, Deborah Dash. 1994. *To the Golden Cities: Pursuing the American Jewish Dream in Miami and L.A.* New York: Free Press.

Nemy, Enid. 1994. "Gathering to Meet, Perhaps to Marry." *New York Times,* June 2.

Newman, Rich. 1996. "Catskills Resort Conversion." *Middletown Times Herald Record,* August 4.

Nieves, Evelyn. 1994. "Rockin' the Concord: Electric Borscht Land." *New York Times,* March 15.

Offit, Sydney. 1959. *He Had It Made.* New York: Crown.

Perera, Victor. 1995. *The Cross and the Pear Tree: A Sephardic Journey.* New York: Knopf.

Pollack, Eileen. 1998. *Paradise, New York.* Philadelphia: Temple University Press.

Pomerantz, Joel. 1970. *Jennie and the Story of Grossinger's* New York: Grosset and Dunlop.

Revkin, Andrew C. 1998. "With Defeat of Gambling, Catskill Winter Turns Gloomier." *New York Times,* January 30.

Richman, Irwin. 1997. *Borscht Belt Bungalows: Memories of Catskill Summers.* Philadelphia, Temple University Press.

Rise and Fall of the Borscht Belt, The (documentary). 1988. Directed by Peter Davis. New York: Villon Films. Distributed by Arthur Cantor.

Ritzer, George. 1993. *The McDonaldization of Society.* Newbury Park, CA: Pine Forge Press.

Roth, Philip. 1977. *The Professor of Desire.* New York: Farrar, Straus, Giroux.

Sacks, Maurie. 1996. "Synagogues of Sullivan County." Lecture at Second Annual History of the Catskills Conference. Woodridge, New York.

Sandberg, Sarah. 1964. *Mama Made Minks.* Garden City, NY: Doubleday.

Sorin, Gerald. 1997. *Tradition Transformed: The Jewish Experience in America.* Baltimore, MD: Johns Hopkins University Press.

Steinfels, Peter. 1992. "Debating Intermarriage and Jewish Survival." *New York Times,* October 18.

Sweet Lorraine (film). 1987. Directed by Steve Gomer. New York: Autumn Pictures/Angelika Co.

Tobin, Herbert. 1974. *A Social History of Jewish Life in the Catskill Mountains, 1865–1975.* Senior Honors Thesis, Brandeis University, Waltham, Massachusetts.

———. 1979. "New York's Jews and the Catskills Mountains." Pp. 161–175 in Ronald A. Brauner, ed., *Jewish Civilization: Essays and Studies,* vol. 1. Philadelphia: Reconstructionist Rabbinical College.

Wadler, Joyce. 1985. "The Fine Art of Mountain Tummling." *Esquire* 193(June): 242–49.

Wallenrod, Reuben. 1957. *Dusk in the Catskills.* New York: Reconstructionist Press.

Wouk, Herman. 1955. *Marjorie Morningstar.* Garden City, NY: Doubleday.

Index